HOMICIDE: TRENDS, CAUSES AND PREVENTION

HOMICIDE: TRENDS, CAUSES AND PREVENTION

RANDAL B. TOLIVER
AND
ULRICH R. COYNE
EDITORS

Nova Science Publishers, Inc.
New York

For permission to use material from this book please contact us:
Telephone 631-231-7269; Fax 631-231-8175
Web Site: http://www.novapublishers.com

LIBRARY OF CONGRESS CATALOGING-IN-PUBLICATION DATA
Toliver, Randal B.
Homicide trends, causes and prevention / Randal B. Toliver and Ulrich R. Coyne.
p. cm.
Includes index.
ISBN 978-1-60741-625-8 (hardcover)
1. Homicide. 2. Criminal psychology. I. Coyne, Ulrich R. II. Title.
HV6515.T65 2009
364.152--dc22 2009017795

Published by Nova Science Publishers, Inc. ✈ New York

CONTENTS

PREFACE

Homicide refers to the act of killing another human being. There are many types of homicide, including criminal homicide, when a person purposely, knowingly, recklessly or negligently causes the death of another (i.e., murder and manslaughter), and there is non-criminal homicide in which the law allows homicide by allowing certain defenses to criminal charges (i.e, self-defense). This book examines new developments in this field.

Chapter 1 - When examining the literature on profiling homicide offenders, some criticisms can be formulated. One of these criticisms includes the lack of an explicit theoretical framework, encompassing all the different concepts used to explain offense-offender relationships.

In this chapter, a contextualized approach to homicide offending will be presented, together with a possible method for obtaining and analyzing relevant offense information.

This new model of offense pathways provides an overview of the psychological processes the offender experienced during his or her offense, emphasizes the importance of a contextualized perspective, and is consistent with the view that the homicide offense is a process that develops over time.

Results of a preliminary study on the narratives of 48 homicide offenders, based on this new contextualized model, will be presented. Finally, the implications of using such a contextualized approach, for offender profiling, treatment and interviewing strategies will be discussed.

Chapter 2 - The determination of the manner of death, especially the differentiation between homicide and suicide, has always been a major issue in common forensic activity. This is particularly true about violent deaths by firearms wounds and sharp force wounds. Concerning the determination of manner of death, a lot of studies about large series of fatal firearms wounds have been published in forensic literature (624 cases [1], 288 cases [2], 717 cases [3], 107 cases [4], 132 cases [5], 140 cases [6]). Nevertheless, only a few studies about large series of fatal sharp force wounds and differentiation between homicide and suicide have been performed (120 cases [7], 279 cases [8], 70 cases [9]).

Chapter 3 - There have been around 500 – 600 homicides each year in England and Wales in this decade (Coleman et al 2008). These figures include for 2003 the 172 victims of Dr Harold Shipman, an English general practitioner who killed his elderly patients. Around a third of all homicide victims are female (half killed by their partners). This compares with around 16000 externally caused deaths each year (of these, half are suicides, others misadventure, accidents, etc.). Of note is that in England and Wales between 1996 and 1999, the three highest at risk occupational groups of being homicide victims were security staff (25 victims), medical staff (24 victims) and social workers (14 victims) (Brookman and Maguire 2003).

Chapter 4 - The issue of whether the availability of firearms has an impact on the incidence of murder and suicide has long been debated, often with strong emotions on both sides of the debate. In the past, most of the research on this issue has been carried out on the United States, partly because the differing gun control laws in each of the 50 states provides a "natural experiment" to explore this issue (see Lester, 1984). However, the debate is also contentious in Canada (see Gabor, 2003), and several research studies have been conducted on Canadian data. The aim of the present essay is to review this research in order to see whether any sound conclusions can be drawn from it.

Chapter 5 - The purpose of this paper is to examine accounts of a Serbian soldier who participated in the execution of civilians during the Bosnian genocide. The application of Lonnie Athens' violentization theory (Athens, 2003) and the circumplex theory from family therapy (Olson, 1995, 2000) are used to examine the case study. Following Winton's (2008) and Winton and Unlu's (2008) model, the theories are consistent with the data. Suggestions for further research are addressed.

Chapter 6 - Pattern of homicides in Delhi, India was studied over a two year period from November 1991 to October 1993 and repeated over a two year period from January 2006 to December 2007. Both the studies were carried out in a tertiary care teaching hospital catering to North-east district of Delhi, India. The aim was to assess the pattern of homicides in Delhi and to look for any changes in the homicide pattern in Delhi over a period of time (fifteen years).

Delhi, the capital of India, currently has a population of about fourteen million. The murder crime rate for Delhi in1991 was 5.1 and in 2006 was 2.9.The culpable homicide not amounting to murder crime rate for Delhi in 1991 was 0.65 and in 2006 was 0.45. In the two year period of 1991-1993 homicides comprised 12.8% of the total cases brought for autopsy whereas in the two year period 2006-2007 they comprised 6.3% of the total cases brought for autopsy.

The studies took into account the age and sex of the victims, survival time after the incident, types of fatal injuries and the body organs involved. Males were the predominant victims in 1991-1993 and 2006-2007 (79% and 83.6% respectively). Spot deaths and victims brought dead to the hospital constituted a large number of cases (60.4% in 1991-1993 and 59.6% in 2006-2007). The maximum number of victims were in the age group of 21-30 years constituting 45.5% of the total cases in 1991-1993 and 34.9% of the total cases in 2006-2007. Deaths due to stabbing by sharp edged weapons were the commonest in 1991-1993 comprising 41% of the total cases. Deaths due to firearm injuries constituted 10.4% of cases and those due to blunt force injuries made up 15.7% of the cases. Interestingly in 2006-2007 deaths due to stabbing by sharp edged weapons occurred only in 24% of the cases, whereas death due to firearm injuries and blunt force injuries comprised 24% and 28.4% of the cases respectively. Some of the major motives for the homicides in our study were gain, property disputes, personal vendetta, love affairs/sexual causes and dowry. Reasons for the changing trends in Delhi are discussed in the chapter. Homicide trends in Delhi are also compared to the trends seen in other cities of India.

Chapter 7 - Homicide is an especially tragic and very real source of maternal mortality in the United States. An appreciation for this issue was gathered only after so-called "pregnancy-associated" deaths were reported to the Centers for Disease Control and Prevention (CDC) or following an organized review of deaths which were incidental to pregnancy but not directly pregnancy-related. In addition, increasing the time limit up to one year between the conclusion of pregnancy and death also allowed for this source of mortality to be better recognized. Recent literature has highlighted the significant proportion of injury-related deaths which are violent and intentional, in addition to racial and age discrepancies, along with the fact that pregnancy represents a risk factor in and of itself for a woman to fall victim to a violent death. Perhaps the most important related topic is the issue of intimate partner violence (IPV), because of both the potential downstream association with homicide and the opportunity to screen for domestic/sexual abuse and to intervene on behalf of the mother to reduce the risk of maternal mortality. As opposed to pregnancy-related mortality secondary to embolism or pre-eclampsia, for example, prevention of violent acts against pregnant or recently pregnant women requires a unique approach from the physician and staff, including a thorough understanding of the mother's home life and social circumstances within the context of the stress imposed by pregnancy and the nurturing of a newborn child.

Chapter 8 - The nature of the relationship between marital status and homicide risk has been clouded by the use of aggregated data. Further, precise measures of marital status in individual level research are largely unavailable. The present paper tests a multivariate model of the relationship between marital status and homicide victimization among males. It uses individual level data on 826,178 deaths including 7,112 African American and 6,683 Caucasian American male homicide victims. Bivariate analysis demonstrates that single black men are at 7.65 times and single white men are at 8.57 times greater risk of homicide than their married counterparts. However, the results of a multivariate analysis determined that these risks fall to 1.15 and -0.30 once controls are included for the covariates of marital status. Marriage offers only slight protection for black men and aggravates the odds of homicide for white men. The findings are interpreted in light of a subcultural theory of violence.

Chapter 9 - *Introduction:* Fatal sharp injuries need careful post mortem scene investigation and forensic autopsy. Characterization of manner of death and the cause of death in lethal sharp injuries represent an investment in deterring circumstances. Sharp wound are frequently chosen methods of homicides and of suicides as well, however, the final confirmation of suicide or homicide expects a careful and systematic medico-legal investigation. In this chapter the purpose of our examination was to examine the characteristics of homicidal sharp injuries in a 10 year-long period in capital Budapest. Copies of death certificates relating to homicidal sharp damages were obtained. The results of scene investigations were also presented.

Material and methods: Cases with sharp injuries were collected from 1998 to 2007 using the database of the Department of Forensic and Insurance Medicine at Semmelweis University in Budapest. Autopsy reports were analyzed to determine the proportion of fatal sharp injuries. Gender differences, types and location of injuries, survival period, and blood alcohol concentrations were evaluated in different age groups.

Results: A total of 148 (100 males, 48 females) homicidal cases due to sharp force injuries (cut and/or stab wounds) were investigated. 125 (84%) victims were between the age of 20 and 60 years. Data of the scene investigation, detailed forensic autopsy, anamnestic data have important role in the differentiation of fatal homicidal sharp injuries.

Conclusion: Sharp injuries play an important role in homicidal mortality. Our results underline the importance of the careful medico-legal evaluation and the collaboration between the representatives of several sciences, including forensic medicine in every homicidal case.

Chapter 10 - Homicide is the highest level of aggression found in all cultures worldwide. When preplanning or malice aforethought is not evident adequately, the term 'culpable homicide not amounting to murder' is used in India. As per the Indian Penal Code, culpable homicide does not amount to murder, if the offender commits the act whilst deprived of the power of self-control by grave and sudden provocation by the victim; if the act is committed by the offender in good faith of the right of private defense of person or property; if the act is committed by a public servant acting for the advancement of public justice; if the act is committed without premeditation in the heat of passion upon a sudden quarrel; and if the victim aged eighteen years and above takes the risk of death with his own consent. A seven-year retrospective review of files at the Crime Records Bureau, Mangalore, South Canara in South India was undertaken for cases of culpable homicide not amounting to murder occurring between July 2001 and July 2008. A total of five cases were identified in the coastal district of South Canara in the Southern Indian state of Karnataka. In our region, the rate of culpable homicide not amounting to murder was less than 0.10 per 100,000 population per year during the study period which was low when compared to the rate of murder that ranged from 1.27 to 1.84 per 100,000 population per year during the same period. The victims, three males and two females, were aged between three and sixty years (mean = 39 years) and the offenders, all males, were aged between 25 and 45 years (mean = 31.6 years). In all five cases weapons such as blunt objects ($N = 4$) and firearms ($N = 1$) were involved in battery. There were no sharp weapons involved in any of the cases. The head bore the fatal injury in four cases and the abdomen in one case. The circumstances leading to the act of culpable homicide not amounting to murder are discussed with a concise review of the Indian law on homicide.

In: Homicide: Trends, Causes and Prevention
Editor: Randal B. Toliver and Ulrich R. Coyne

ISBN 978-1-60741-625-8

Chapter 1

PROFILING HOMICIDE OFFENDERS: TOWARDS A NEW OFFENDER PROFILING MODEL

An Crabbé and Hans Vertommen*
Catholic University of Leuven, Belgium

ABSTRACT

When examining the literature on profiling homicide offenders, some criticisms can be formulated. One of these criticisms includes the lack of an explicit theoretical framework, encompassing all the different concepts used to explain offense-offender relationships.

In this chapter, a contextualized approach to homicide offending will be presented, together with a possible method for obtaining and analyzing relevant offense information.

This new model of offense pathways provides an overview of the psychological processes the offender experienced during his or her offense, emphasizes the importance of a contextualized perspective, and is consistent with the view that the homicide offense is a process that develops over time.

Results of a preliminary study on the narratives of 48 homicide offenders, based on this new contextualized model, will be presented. Finally, the implications of using such a contextualized approach, for offender profiling, treatment and interviewing strategies will be discussed.

---

* An Crabbé, aspirant, Department of Psychology, Catholic University of Leuven, Belgium. Hans Vertommen, Department of psychology, Catholic University of Leuven, Belgium. The research reported in this paper was supported by the Funds for Scientific Research – Flanders.

Correspondence concerning this article should be addressed to An Crabbé, Catholic University of Leuven, Faculty of Psychology and Educational Sciences, Centre of Assessment and Psychopathology, Tiensestraat 102, B-3000 Leuven, Belgium. E-mail address: a.crabbe@telenet.be

INTRODUCTION

Profiling Homicide Offenders: Assumptions, Theories And Underlying Concepts

Offender profiling is a technique for "identifying the major personality and behavioral characteristics of an individual based upon an analysis of the crimes he or she has committed" [Douglas, Ressler, Burgess, and Hartman, 1986, p. 405]. This implies that offender profiling does not provide the identity of the offender[1], but that it indicates the *type of person* most likely to have committed the crime. This procedure is said to limit or better direct the investigation by providing investigatively relevant strategies such as narrowing down the pool of suspects, predicting subsequent crime locations, providing interview suggestions and strategies, suggesting strategies in which the public becomes a partner in crime solving, assisting with case linkage etc. [e.g., Ainsworth, 2000; Ault and Reese, 1980; Douglas et al., 1986; Holmes and De Burger, 1988; Holmes and Holmes, 1996; Meyer, 2000; Ressler, Burgess, and Douglas, 1988; Turvey, 1998, 2000, 2003].

When reviewing the literature relating to profiling homicide offenders [e.g., Crabbé, Decoene, & Vertommen, 2008], *two approaches* emerged. The first approach, direct offender profiling, investigates which offense relate to which offender characteristics without imposing or inferring some underlying psychological concept. The second approach, indirect offender profiling, hypothesizes about which offense relate to which offender characteristics based on an underlying psychological concept[2]. Although different direct associations between offense and offender characteristics have been found that might be practically useful [e.g., Crabbé et al., 2008], the direct approach to offender profiling makes this a technology, in which relationships are established, but the reason for them are not understood. According to Canter (1994), for the activity of offender profiling to be scientific some explanation, theory, model or framework needs to exist from which the predictable relationships can be derived. Hence, the challenge is to establish the themes that will help to identify and explain the links between crime-based consistencies and offender characteristics [Canter, 1995].

Central to the scientific approach to offender profiling are the premises of offender *consistency*: intraindividual behavior variation across offenses is smaller than interindividual behavior variation, and offender *specificity* (or homology): the manner in which an offense is committed, corresponds with a particular configuration of background characteristics [e.g., Alison, Bennell, Mokros, and Ormerod, 2002; Canter, 1995, 2000, 2003, 2004; Petee and Jarvis, 2000]. When examining the literature with respect to these premises [see Crabbé et al., 2008], it appeared that the *psychopathology* and the *deviant fantasies* of the offender could explain some offense – offender relationships. Furthermore, since indications for consistent homicide signature behaviors[3] have been found, some support has been provided for the

[1] Although we are aware that not all offenders and victims are masculine, they will be described as being male for practical purposes.

[2] See for instance, Mulkers (2002) for the distinction between direct and indirect approaches to offender profiling and Canter (1995, 2000, 2003, 2004) who refers to relationships between available offense information and offender characteristics (useful in facilitating the police enquiry), as profiling equations. Note that both approaches assume a relationship between offense and offender characteristics.

[3] Signature behaviors are those actions that are not necessary to commit the offense, but that the offender has to do to satisfy psychological and emotional needs; it is the unique manner in which the offender commits his crime(s) [e.g., Douglas & Munn, 1992a, 1992b; Holmes & Holmes, 1996; Meyer, 2000; Turvey, 1998, 2003].

hypothesis that these relationships could also be elucidated by underlying *psychological and emotional needs*. This is in accordance with the theory of Holmes and Holmes (1996) who stated that the crime scene reflects the underlying pathology of the offender's personality, that his signature will remain the same and that his personality will not change. The fact that the *style of interpersonal transaction* and hence the type of aggression used (instrumental or expressive[4]) was able to explain victim – offender relationships, is in agreement with the theory of Canter (1994, 1995, 2000, 2003, 2004) who stated that the crucial distinctions between the dramas that violent men write for themselves are the variations in the role that they assign to their victims. These roles can be classified according to the following typology: as an object (something just to be used and controlled through restraints and threats, often involving alternative gains in the form of other crimes, such as theft; central is the lack of any feeling for the victim), as a vehicle (to carry the offender's own emotional state for instance, anger and frustration) or as a person (some level of pseudo-intimacy with attempts to create some sort of relationship). The offender's *motivation*, on the other hand, was also capable to explain offense – offender relationships, which accords with the theory of some authors [e.g., Ault and Reese, 1980; Douglas and Burgess, 1986; Douglas, Burgess, Burgess, and Ressler, 1992; Douglas et al., 1986; Hazelwood and Napier, 2004; Holmes and De Burger, 1988; Ressler et al., 1988] that knowledge of the perpetrator's motivation could provide vital information about the offender. Furthermore, offense location choices seemed to be guided by a recognizable rationality, providing support for the view that *cognitive processes* guide offense behaviors [e.g., Burgess, Hartman, Ressler, Douglas, and McCormack, 1986; Douglas et al., 1986; Holmes and De Burger, 1988]. Finally, some indications have also been provided that the degree of organization, the predatory-fury-perversion-rape[5], and the sadistic-anger (*behavioral) themes* could explain offender – offense relationships in sexual homicide cases.

In contrast with these concrete concepts[6], some authors assigned a special role for the offender's *emotions* [e.g., Ault and Reese, 1980] and *personality* [e.g., Ault and Reese, 1980; Douglas and Burgess, 1986; Douglas et al., 1986; Hazelwood and Douglas, 1980; Holmes and De Burger, 1988; Holmes and Holmes, 1996; Ressler, Burgess, Douglas, Hartman, and D'Agostino, 1986; Ressler et al., 1988] in explaining offense – offender relationships. Empirical evidence for these underlying concepts however, has been less straightforward. In this connection, Homant and Kennedy (1998) pointed out that there does not seem to be any particular personality theory that guides the FBI trained profilers. The authors argue that when profilers refer to the personality of the offender, they are speaking both about the interpersonal style and the underlying motives of the offender. When defining personality in

[4] In instrumental aggression is the victim a target secondary to the offender's instrumental motivations or ulterior criminal actions for instance, money or sex; the victim is used as an object through which to obtain the desired objective. In expressive aggression is the victim a person onto whom the aggression is impulsive; it is an emotional attack with the aim of harming the victim. See for instance, Bushman and Anderson (2001); Canter (2000, 2003); Cornell et al. (1996); Salfati (2000); Salfati and Bateman (2005).

[5] See Kocsis, Cooksey and Irwin (2002). The predatory cluster includes very violent crime scene characteristics, suggesting an element of deliberateness and cruelty in behavior. The fury cluster also contains very violent behaviors, but lacks calculation and deliberation, perhaps coupled with a motive of revenge or anger. The perversion cluster indicates an antisocial perversion theme without the calculation of the predatory cluster. Finally, the rape cluster includes crime scene actions suggestive of less violent intent, where the offender and the victim tended to be acquainted and where brutality was not strongly evident, almost as if death had not been intended.

[6] An exception is the concept of offender signature, which is hardly operationalized and remains very vague [see for instance, Crabbé et al., 2008].

this way, some evidence for the personality as underlying concept has been found (see supra). Furthermore, some investigations indicating themes in offense behaviors (for instance, organized-disorganized; angry-sadistic) did provide significant differences in the emotions the offenders experienced during their offenses. Thus, although no direct evidence has been found for the role of the offender's personality or experienced emotions, we consider these as promising underlying concepts between offense and offender characteristics that should be included in future research.

Criticisms on the Current Offender Profiling Approach

The review on homicide offenders [see Crabbé et al., 2008] provided some support for the consistency and specificity hypotheses, but also drew attention to a number of criticisms against the current (indirect) approach to offender profiling.

First of all, although different constructs emerged as underling concepts between offense and offender characteristics (see supra), there appears to be a lack of an explicit *theoretical framework* encompassing all the different concepts, explaining these relationships.

Secondly, there exists some *conceptual confusion* in the established underlying concepts. When considering the different motivational typologies for instance [see Crabbé et al., 2008], it appeared that these often include more than just the motivation or intention of the offender like type of relationship with the victim (for instance, domestic motivation), external circumstances (for instance, felony and dispute homicides), or the state of mind of the offender (for instance, psychotic homicides). Furthermore, the behavioral themes in sexual offenders, as mentioned above, are also fuzzy, containing elements of deliberateness (for instance, predatory versus fury cluster), degree of violence (for instance, predatory and fury versus rape cluster), motivations (for instance, rape versus fury cluster), and indications of underlying pathology (for instance, perversion cluster).

Additionally, offender profiling relies on a *naïve trait perspective* which attributes behavior to underlying, relatively context-free dispositional constructs (traits) within the offender that are not directly observable, but can be inferred from the crime scene [e.g., Alison et al., 2002; Homant and Kennedy, 1998]. The organized-disorganized distinction, for instance, all place offenders on an underlying trait (degree of organization) and infer some offense and offender characteristics based on the position of the offender on this underlying trait. Review of the consistency of organized-disorganized behaviors across offenses, however, appeared to be limited or nonexistent [see Crabbé et al., 2008]. We argue that a static approach to offender profiling neglects the role of the situation in which the offender finds himself and take the point of view that the behavior of the offender should be explained both in terms of his underlying psychological processes and the situation in which the homicide occurs.

Furthermore, most research in the field of homicide profiling has paid little attention to the homicide offense as a *process that develops over time* [for an overview of exceptions, see Crabbé et al., 2008]. Most investigators take the homicide event as the central focus of their research, without considering the different elements that play a role in the different stages of the offence process and how these elements influence each other in and over these different stages.

Finally, most investigations on homicide perpetrators have neglected *the point of view of the offender*, but focused on behavioral manifestations at the crime scene (except for the organized – disorganized distinction, which was based on interviews with the respective offenders). We argue that including the narrative of the offender could increase the richness of the offense description, its comprehensibility and could add some depth to the profiles rendered by offender profilers in practice.

A New Offender Profiling Model

As mentioned in Crabbé et al. (2008), these criticisms can be accounted for if one: 1) approaches offender profiling from a contextualized perspective in which situational factors are associated with the homicidal act, 2) recognizes the homicide offense as a process that develops over time, in which different elements influence each other in and over the different stages of the offense process, and 3) includes the underlying psychological processes the offender experienced at the time of the execution of his offense. We take the point of view that homicidal behavior is the product of the evolving interaction between personal and situational characteristics. This implies that if one wants to investigate homicide offenses, one needs to look at the offense as a process that develops over time and needs to consider both the personal as well as the situational characteristics of the specific homicidal act.

This focus on behavior as the result of an unfolding interaction between personal and situational characteristics has some linkage to (cognitive) behavioral theories, which provide promising underlying psychological processes between situational characteristics and behavioral outcomes [see for instance, Mischel, 1999; Mischel and Shoda, 1995; Shoda and Leetiernan, 2002]. Other resemblances with this contextualized perspective can be found in the theories and practice of behavioral therapy models [e.g., Hayes, 1990; Hermans, Eelen, and Orlemans, 2007; Ishaq, 1996; Nelson and Hayes, 1981] in which behavior is regarded as the result of individual learning experiences and contextual factors. Furthermore, in behavioral assessment used in behavioral therapy, the importance of behavior as a process developing over time is stressed by stating that (problematic) behavior is integrated into a chain of antecedent and consequent situations and behaviors, whereby the process of looking at behavior at this concrete, descriptive level, is called a topographic analysis [e.g., Cone, 1997; Ferster, 1965; Hermans et al., 2007; see also the behavioral interview as described in Spiegler and Guevremont, 1998].

Looking at criminal behavior in this way (contextualized approach and the significance of investigating behavior as it develops over time), is what Ward and Hudson [1998a, see also Cassar, Ward, and Thakker, 2003; Hudson, Ward, and McCormack, 1999] have denoted as level III theories. Ward and Hudson have formulated a metatheoretical framework that differentiates between different levels of theory, such as comprehensive or multifactorial (level I), middle or single-factor (level II), and micro-level theories (level III). At level I are the multifactorial etiological frameworks attempting to provide a comprehensive and integrated explanation of offense behaviors, that is, theories attempting to explain a phenomenon in terms of the various mechanisms that lead to its occurrence. One such level I theory in homicide offenders is provided by Ressler et al. (1998) who explained sexual homicide by five different phases namely an ineffective social environment, formative events, critical personality traits, actions towards others and self and a feedback filter. Level II theories, on the other hand, focus on specific factors or single issues thought to be particularly important in the generation of crimes (for instance, the role of violent fantasy in sexual homicides). Finally there are level III theories or microtheories [see for instance, Cassar et al., 2003; Polaschek, Hudson, Ward, and Siegert, 2001; Ward and Hudson, 1998b; Ward, Hudson, and Keenan, 1998] which attempt to provide a description of the offense process as it unfolds over time and specify the cognitive, behavioral, motivational, affective and contextual factors associated with the "problem behavior" process. They include an explicit temporal factor and focus on proximal causes, or the how of offending. These microtheories should be articulating what the "higher" theories are trying to explain. They are not explanatory but descriptive, provide the touchstone for all other theoretical frameworks and serve to identify possible clinical phenomena that subsequent theory sets out to explain. In the following, such a descriptive level III theory will be denoted as an offense scenario, the method to construct this scenario will be called the offense scenario procedure, while the individual path followed by an individual offender, will be described as an offense chain or pathway. Such an offense scenario in general homicide offenders has been provided by Cassar et al. and by Demarest (2001) and Vanhumbeeck (2004) in spousal homicide.

In the following paragraphs, we will describe the process of obtaining an offense scenario in more detail. Since we need to consider both the "person" and "situation" component when trying to understand homicidal behavior, we need to have a detailed description of what happened in terms of behaviors, feelings, motivations, situational characteristics... before, during and after the homicidal act. Although different methods could be used to obtain this rich, descriptive information, we point to a procedure used in behavioral analysis, namely the topographic analysis [e.g., Cone, 1997; Ferster, 1965; Hermans et al., 2007; see also the behavioral interview as described in Spiegler and Guevremont, 1998]. In a topographical analysis, concrete behavior is described at a very concrete level: where, when, with whom did the behavior occur, what were the accompanying thoughts, what were the consequences...? The client is asked to remember the situation as lively as possible and to describe this as detailed as possible. This method is sometimes referred to as the "video-method" since a specific episode is reviewed in much detail. The behavioral analyst holds the remote control in his hands and can rewind, zoom in, pause etc. We argue that this interesting method to obtain rich descriptive information could also be used with offenders instead of clients.

Once individual offense descriptions have been provided by a number of offenders, the information needs to be compared and joined into a coherent scheme: the offense scenario. This offense scenario includes the similarities and differences between the individual offense pathways (for instance, those who planned the homicidal act versus those who reacted impulsively on a given situation). One such possible method to order all the qualitative information under a common denominator is grounded theory methodology [e.g., Strauss and Corbin, 1998; see also Cassar et al., 2003; Hudson et al., 1999; Polaschek et al., 2001]. Grounded theory is a set of procedures that seek to inductively derive a theory or model about a particular phenomenon starting from an initial set of qualitative descriptions or transcripts. The value of this methodology lies in its ability not only to generate theory, but also to ground that theory in data. Grounded theory is a nonmathematical process of interpretation, carried out for the purpose of discovering concepts and relationships in raw data and then organizing these into a theoretical explanatory scheme [Strauss and Corbin, 1998]. The procedure starts with a detailed line-by-line analysis to generate initial categories with their properties and dimensions and to suggest relationships among categories, which is a combination of open (identifying concepts and their properties and dimensions) and axial coding (relating categories to their subcategories). If the provisional categories are unable to cope with existing categories, then new categories are formulated and the procedure continues. Once the existing categories are sufficient, that is, they do not need to be modified in the face of new data, the model is saturated. One important note to make in this process is that all the relevant variables need to contain a definition so that the meaning of the variables is as clear as possible, avoiding conceptual confusion and leading to a higher interrater-reliability. Furthermore, although existing literature can provide some guidelines in the organization of the information, one does not start with a detailed theory in mind, but if one finds some variables that seem to be related to variables described in literature, one can always turn to the relevant literature to grasp these variables in more detail. Using the more general, well established terms can also decrease conceptual confusion, but one should always make sure that the generated categories are in line with the information provided by the offenders (the theory should match the data and not the other way round).

After having constructed an offense scenario, possible links between elements of the offense scenario on the one side and offense and offender characteristics on the other side can be investigated (see Figure 1).

Take for instance, the role of emotions in the evolving homicide process. After having determined relevant emotion variables, one can make an offender typology in terms of experienced emotions. Once this emotional typology is obtained (for instance, angry versus "empathic" versus panic), one can investigate the link between the different categories of this typology and offense and offender characteristics. Since one can investigate which combinations of specific offense behaviors are associated with every respective emotion category, one can determine which emotion category seems to be the most likely, given the specific crime scene information. Starting from the hypothesized resulting emotion category, one can deduce offender characteristics, based on the previously found associations between this emotion category and offender characteristics.

In conclusion, considering the homicide offense scenario as a collection of underlying concepts between offense and offender characteristics could provide a coherent theoretical framework encompassing the different explanations for the offense – offender relationships as stated earlier. In this way, one can bring offender profiling more in agreement with recent interactive theories, can clarify the underlying processes in offense – offender relationships, and can account for current criticisms on offender profiling. In the following section, the procedure of obtaining the different elements of an offense scenario will be demonstrated on the narratives of 48 homicide offenders.

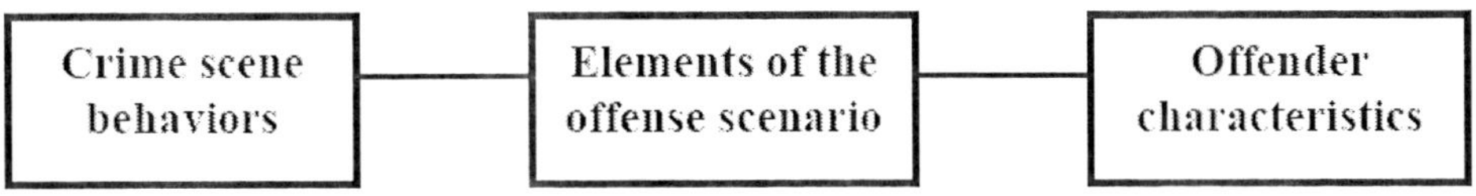

Figure 1. Graphical presentation of the role of the elements of the offense scenario in the practice of offender profiling.

Method

Participants

All participants were convicted for serious violent crimes and all were detained in Belgian prisons at the time of the research[7]. The participants consisted of two groups. The first group included 30 incarcerated offenders (25 men and 5 women). Of this group, 16 offenders were convicted for murder, 2 for attempted murder, 2 for the murder of one's own child, 1 for being an accomplice in a murder case, 4 for manslaughter, 1 for attempted manslaughter, 3 for manslaughter to ease a theft (including murder with robbery cases) and 1 for beatings resulting in death. The second group consisted of 18 male offenders who were judged not be responsible for their criminal acts[8] and were convicted for manslaughter (N=5), attempted manslaughter (N=1), murder (N=10), attempted murder (N=1) or beatings resulting in death (N=1). In the selection of our research sample, no distinction was made between the given verdicts, the only criteria for inclusion in the study being 1) that the offender was already convicted (in order to reduce social desirability and suspicion towards the research), 2) that the offender committed the offense himself, 3) that he agreed to participate, 4) that there were no language barriers between the offender and the researcher and 5) that the mental state of the offender allowed him to participate in the research (for instance, not being psychotic at the time of the study). The reason why we included all homicide or attempted homicide cases regardless of sentence outcome was that we felt that these legal classifications do not reflect psychological patterns of behavior but depend on ad hoc legal procedures.

The mean age of the offenders at the moment of the offense was 29,23 years (range = 18 – 50 years). When discussing their previous criminal history, 33 offenders admitted having a criminal record (these criminal records were varied, including offenses like theft, beatings, drug and sexual offenses, fraud etc.). The mean sentence length for those offenders who received specific sentence lengths was 23,09 (range = 6 – 30 years); as mentioned before, 2 offenders got the death sentence and were later on judged not to be responsible for their subsequent homicidal acts, 16 offenders were immediately judged not to be responsible for their criminal acts and 7 offenders were serving a lifetime sentence. In 23 offenses, the victim was male, in 21 offenses, the victim was female and in 4 offenses, both a female and male victim was wounded. The mean age of the victims in a single homicide was 35,33 (range = 0,3 – 85 years), while the mean age of the victims in those cases involving multiple victims was 35,12 (range = 23 – 74 years). Finally, when considering the relationship between the offender and the victim at the moment of the offense, 12 victims were unknown to the offender. In the cases where the offender and the victim knew each other beforehand, the following relationships were found: the victim was the offender's neighbor (N=5), the victim knew the offender from a pub (N=3), was the offender's partner (N =5), ex-partner (N =2) or rival (N=2). Furthermore, 4 victims were family-in-law, 1 victim was the offender's half-sister, 1 victim was the offender's father and 3 victims were the offender's child. 3 victims know the offender from being in a criminal enterprise, 4 were the offender's friend, and the

[7] Although not all participants were convicted for a homicide offence, they will be denoted as homicide offenders and their offenses will be described as homicide offenses for practical purposes.

[8] Of this group, two offenders initially received the death penalty, but were later on judged not to be responsible for subsequent criminal acts. Hence, they are included in the second group.

remaining 7 victims knew the offender from other occasions (having common acquaintances (N=3), the victim being the offender's social assistant (N=1), having a sexual relationship with the offender (N=1), being the offender's boss (N=1) or being a witness of a crime (N=1)). Note that at this point, this information was only provided by the offenders themselves (except for their sentencing charges, which were checked by using their incarceration files) and needs to be confirmed with their correctional files in subsequent research.

Procedure

All data were collected by the first author. Each potential participant was given a full explanation of the research procedure, the purpose of the research and where to contact the interviewer when necessary. We strongly emphasized that we were interested in their narrative; how they had experienced it and that their participation had no implication for their sentence, chance for parole etc. In a next phase, participants were asked to sign an informed consent. These phases were equal for both offender groups.

The first group of incarcerated offenders, those who were judged to be responsible for their criminal acts, provided a description of their offence process by filling in a semi-structured questionnaire. This questionnaire was divided into three different time blocks (before, during and after the homicidal act) and started with an open question asking for a description of all the elements the offender considered important in explaining the ... time block to an outsider. In this open question (repeated in every time block), we specified that we needed some detail with respect to the situational characteristics, their feelings, behaviors, reactions, thoughts and the behaviors of the victim. After this open-ended question, the different behaviors, thoughts and feelings were further elaborated by explicitly asking the offenders to describe each of these themes chronologically and in much detail. If offenders could not write or were only willing to participate under the condition that they didn't have to write the story themselves, the questions were read to the offender and the answers were noted by the researcher without further questioning them at that time. These written stories were completed by an interview in which the different feelings, behaviors, thoughts and situational characteristics were further explored, which provided us with more detailed information, and the opportunity to clarify or elaborate the narrative. The end result of this procedure was a chronological description of all the situational elements, cognitions, affects and behaviors that played a role in the development of the homicide process, made up by the researcher, together with and in accordance with the respective offender.

The total time of the investigation ranged approximately from two till six hours[9], the time of the research introduction phase ranged approximately between one and two hours, and the time of the interviewing phase ranged approximately between one and four hours (for every investigated crime). The reason why some participants needed more time to explain their narrative, in comparison with other participants, was that some of the crimes were more complex (involving more people, more contextual information on the years/months preceding

[9] In this time estimation, the phase of the filling in of the questionnaire was not included since some of the participants completed the questionnaire in the presence of the interviewer, while others, who were living in a single cell, preferred to fill the questionnaire in in the privacy of their own cell.

the crime in for instance, spousal homicide or parricide...) and/or that some of the participants felt the need to initially talk about other things with the researcher (for instance, their familial situation, their chances for parole etc.) in order to establish a confidential relationship. Participants were given the time they needed to feel comfortable, to explain their narrative as they had experienced it, with all the contextual information they felt necessary to be included in the narrative, and were given the opportunity of a break whenever they wanted it[10].

The second group, those who were judged not to be responsible for their violent acts, provided a description by filling in a structured questionnaire dealing with the same topics as the semi-structured questionnaire of the first group, but formulated in a more specific, detailed manner (for instance, instead of asking about the experienced emotions during the crime, we asked to what degree they were feeling angry during the commission of the violent act[11]). This questionnaire was based on a preliminary analysis of the narratives of the first group, which resulted in a number of themes that appeared to be relevant for a possible homicide offense scenario[12]. The reason why we changed the format of the questionnaire was that we thought that 1) this would reduce the total time of the investigation since we were able to ask more direct information about the committed violent act, 2) this would make the procedure more structured, in the sense that all the participants had to answer all the questions, and 3) this would make the procedure more quantitative, in the sense that participants had to indicate the degree to which a certain element of the offense scenario was present at the time of their offense (in the former procedure, participants provided information about the presence or absence of a specific element of the offense scenario, which differentiates less than information provided on a 6- point scale). In order to make sure that the information provided by the offender was clear and specific, each general question (for instance, *to which degree did you experience problems before the start of the crime? For instance, material problems, money problems, psychological problems, a gambling problem, being homeless, an alcohol or drug problem...*) was followed by the following subquestion: *"if you have answered 4, 5 or 6 on the question, indicate which example (which examples) was (were) applicable to your situation. If your specific situation is not provided in the example list, describe your specific situation(s) on the following line"*. However, when elaborating the information of the structured questionnaire, it became clear that both the participants and the interviewer needed to have a global chronological picture of the homicidal act before being able to discuss specific details about it. Therefore, and in order to have equal data for both groups, the researcher conducted an interview with the participants to obtain a chronological description of their offenses before elaborating the specific questions of the structured questionnaire. This procedure led to the same end product for both groups: an overview of all the situational elements, affects, behaviors and cognitions that played a role in their offense as it unfolded over time, made up by the researcher, together with and in accordance with the respective offenders. The time of the interviews ranged from

---

[10] Surprisingly, few offenders asked for a break during the interview phase of the study. There was, on the other hand, a considerable time interval between the filling in of the questionnaires and the interview since the interview needed to be prepared by the researcher.

[11] Participants had the following answer possibilities: not or very few – few – rather few – rather much – much – very much or always. Under these possiblities, a line was drawn with the numbers 1 to 6 in increasing order.

[12] Relevant in the sense that some offenders had the same experience whereas others had another experience in reference to the specified theme. For instance, it appeared that a distinction between offenders could be made on the fact of whether or not they were angry at the victim at the time of the offense.

2 till 12 hours (for the same reason as mentioned above) and again, participants were given the opportunity for a break whenever needed or requested.

These final descriptions of the offenses as they unfolded over time were analyzed by using Strauss and Corbin's grounded theory procedure (1998, see supra), and is similar to the procedure used by Cassar et al., (2003). The offense narratives of both groups were joined and a random selection of a sample of 15 interviews was made. In order to get some indication about possible categories, each of the three different time blocks of these interview transcripts were broken into meaningful units (small blocks of text containing single words or sentences) and were arranged according to one of the following themes: situational characteristics (including behaviors of the victim, an accomplice or another person), behaviors, feelings and cognitions. Next, meaningful categories were coded into provisional categories on the basis of semantic similarities with other units (for instance, angry, mad, frustrated by... were all considered as being negative feelings towards a person). Descriptive names were developed for each category that best captured the common content of the category at the lowest possible level of abstraction. Each meaningful unit was assigned to one or more categories (multiple coding) and if a concept didn't fit the existing categories, a new category was created, together with a corresponding definition. As this procedure continued, categories were changed and united into more abstract categories, enabling the sorting of large data in fewer categories. At the same time, it appeared that the a priori partition of the offense process into the three time blocks did not capture all the possible phases of the homicide process and a distinction was made between different possible phases of the offense, together with a description of how these phases could be recognized.

In a following stage, the obtained categories and time blocks were tested for their adequacy on an additional sample of 16 narratives (also randomly chosen). Individual categories were again expanded and connected in order to accommodate more data and new categories were created when necessary to allow these new data to be incorporated into the existing categories and time phases. During this process and when comparing the different phases of each of the 31 homicidal incidents, it appeared that our time blocks should be changed in order to grasp all the possible differences and resemblances between the different offenders.

In a final stage, this model, containing information about possible time phases and categories, was checked on the rest of the narratives (N=17) and was considered to be saturated and well-defined. The result is a description of all the elements contained in the global homicide offense scenario (in terms of possible time phases, behaviors, emotions, cognitions and situational characteristics). At this moment, interrater-reliability of the data is being investigated by asking independent colleagues to code a sample of these offenses according to the obtained elements and time phases. In the following section, each of these elements of the global offense scenario will be discussed[13].

[13] Additional information on how to score each of these variables, together with the different codebooks containing definitions and examples, can be obtained from the first author.

Preliminary Results of Homicide Offenders' Narratives

Time Phases, Situational Characteristics and Behaviors in Homicide Offending

Determination of Time Phases

Since the broad preamble of a homicide offense can be either short (for instance, a concrete dispute in a bar between strangers) or rather extended (for instance, in spousal homicide where the problems started years ago), considerable differences in the total time period, discussed by the various offenders, were found. Furthermore, since some offenses were preceded by a concrete preamble situation that differed from the situation in which the trigger of the homicide occurred[14], whereas other offenses were not preceded by this concrete preamble situation, we needed to include this distinction as well. Finally, another characteristic that appeared necessary to be included in the different time phases was that some offenders were capable of not being apprehended for a long time period, while others were arrested immediately or shortly after their crimes.

In order to obtain a classification system that includes all possible time phases and is formulated at a concrete level, leaving little room for interpretation, we decided to take the concreteness of the situations and the possible behavioral reactions of the offender into account in defining the different time phases (See Figure 2 for a graphical presentation of possible time phases in homicide offending).

This graphical presentation of the different time phases in homicide offending includes time blocks, indicated by boxes, and moments in time, denoted in Italic. The central focus of the research, the concrete homicidal offending scene, is denoted in grey. Not all time phases are applicable to all narratives (see arrows in Figure 2): the dashed arrows indicate possible starting points in the narratives of the offenders, while the solid arrows indicate time blocks that could possible be omitted[15]. Note that although not every time block is applicable to every narrative[16], the moments in time are applicable to all narratives since every participant has a beginning and an end to his narrative and since every offender performed violent acts following a concrete situation ("trigger"), in which the victim was wounded ("victim down").

When determining the time phases that are applicable to a concrete narrative, we advice to take the following guidelines into account:

1. Search for that concrete behavior (of the victim and/or another person) or situation, that evoked the first violent reaction/intention of the offender towards the victim. This is the *trigger* of the offense. For instance, a concrete insult of the victim towards the offender, which made the offender hit the victim.

---

[14] For instance, the intention of robbing someone (= concrete preamble situation) that turned out badly (= situation in which the trigger of the homicide occurred).

[15] Some offenders, for instance, omitted the context of their crime since they did not know the victim before the crime and since the crime was committed out of the blue, following a concrete argument (hence the dashed arrow from "begin" to the "situation preceding concrete trigger"). Others omitted the preamble of the violent act (since this was not applicable to their narrative, see solid arrow from "context" to the "situation preceding concrete trigger") or the time phases after the crime (since they were apprehended immediately at the crime scene, see solid arrow from "victim down" to "end") etc.

[16] The only time block that is always present in the narratives of the offenders is the time block of the interaction between the offender and the victim.

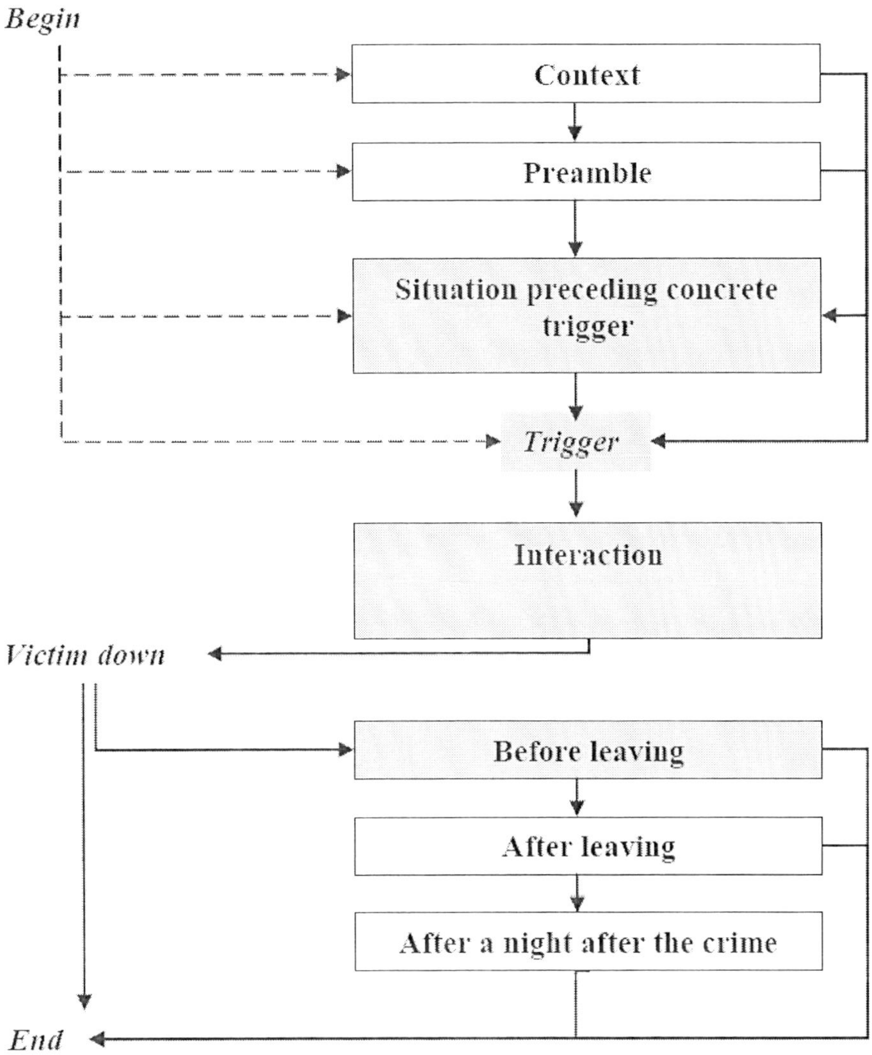

Figure 2. Graphical presentation of possible time phases in homicide offending.

2. Determine whether the situation in which this trigger occured came out of the blue and was immediately followed by a violent reaction of the offender, or was first handled by the offender in another, non-violent way. This is the time block of the *situation that preceded the concrete trigger*. For instance, the beginning of the dispute, in which the victim finally made the insulting remark.
3. Determine whether this situation preceding the concrete trigger was preceded by another concrete situation, that differed from the situation in which the trigger occured. This is the time block of the *preamble* of the offense. For instance, a concrete dispute with a close friend that preceded the dispute with the victim.
4. Determine the time block that provides information about the life of the offender before the crime (years, months, weeks... before the preamble/situation in which the trigger occured). This is the time block of the *context* of the offense. For instance, a longstanding problematic relationship with the victim.

5. Determine the moment when the victim fell down, after the last violent act of the offender towards the living victim. This is the moment when the *victim fell down.* For instance, the offender noticed that the victim was not breathing anymore.
6. Determine what happened between the first violent behavior/intention of the offender towards the victim and the moment when the victim fell down. This is the time block of the *interaction* between the offender and the victim. For instance, the offender kept hitting the victim until the latter didn't fight back anymore.
7. Determine what happened at the crime scene after the victim had fallen down. This is the time block *before leaving.* For instance, the offender tried to cover his tracks at the crime scene.
8. Determine what happened between the moment when the offender left the crime scene and the following morning. This is the time block *after leaving* the crime scene. For instance, the offender came home, tried to forget about the offense by consuming alcohol and went to bed.
9. Determine what happened in the period between the first morning after the crime and the apprehension of the offender[17]. This is the time block *after a night* after the offense. For instance, the way in which the offender tried to hide his responsiblitity, the way in which he interacted with other persons after the first morning after the offense.

Situational Themes Not Restricted to a Specific Time Block

Before describing the situational characteristics and offenders' behavioral reactions in each of these time phases, a number of situational characteristics need to be explained, that are not restricted to a specific time block. The first theme describes the *experienced profoundness of the relationship* with the victim (see Figure 3). The first category of this theme includes offenders who did not know their victim in any way (*unknown).* When the victim and the offender *knew* each other before the crime, however, the relationship could be described as *superficial* (the offender knew the victim without having a profound relationship with him, he knew the victim by sight), *profound* (there was a close relationship between the offender and the victim) or as *intimate* (the offender and the victim had a close relationship and had (former) sexual contacts with each other).

Another relevant theme is the way in which the offender *established contact* with the victim at the moment of the offense (see Figure 4). The contact between the offender and the victim could be *usual,* in the sense that it dependeds on the relationship between the offender and the victim (for instance, the victim being the offender's child or living in the same house as the offender). Another possibility is that this contact was made *by chance* (the contact between the offender and victim was not "usual", and nor the offender nor the victim sought the presence of the other person). In a number of cases, the *victim* initiated contact with the offender (for instance, a neighbor who came knocking on the door), while the final category includes *offenders* who sought contact with the victim, either with or without *negative intention* towards the victim. If the offender contacted the victim with a negative intention, he could have done this by conning the victim (providing another reason for the contact than the real one), by using immediate violence towards the victim ("blitz" approach), by surprising

[17] The offender's narrative ends at the moment when he was being questioned or apprehended by law enforcement agencies, when he turned himself in or resumed his usual life.

the victim (for instance, the offender waited for the victim in the victim's apartment) or by another way ("rest", for instance, using violence after having argued with the victim).

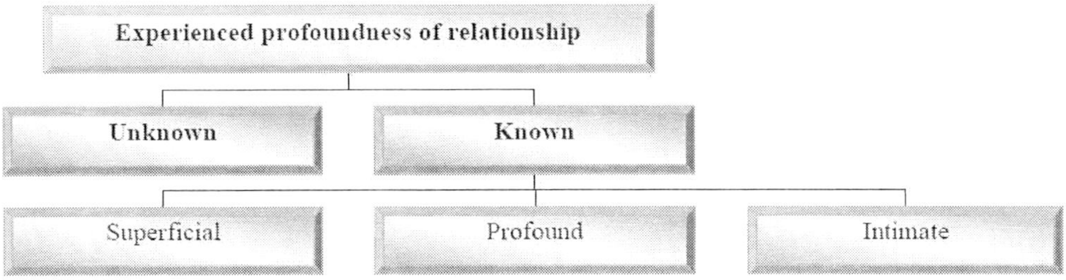

Figure 3. Graphical presentation of possible levels of experienced profoundness of the relationship with the victim.

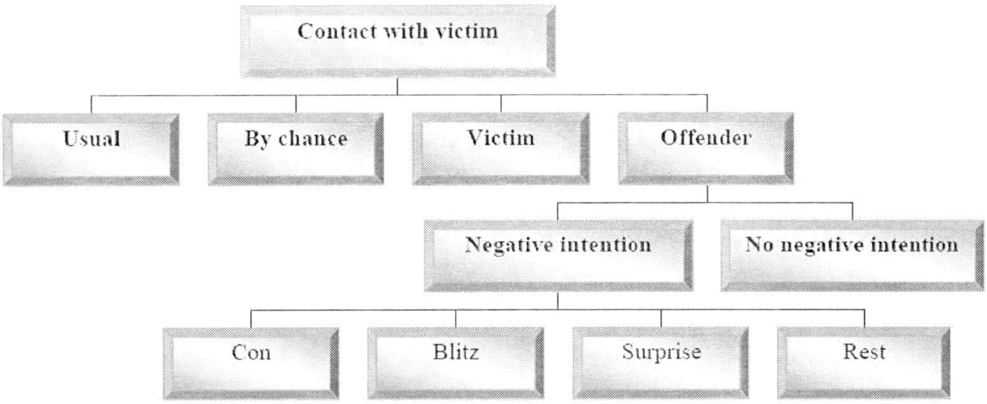

Figure 4. Graphical presentation of possible ways in which the offender and the victim established contact.

The third general situational theme illustrates whether offenders were *under influence* of some mind altering substance at the moment of the offense (see Figure 5). When offenders were under the influence of some drug, one can differentiate according to the type of drug used. *Psychoanaleptica* are those substances that have a stimulating effect (for instance, cocaine, XTC, etc.), while *psycholeptica* are substances with a more relaxing effect (for instance, heroine, codeine etc.; hence the subcategory "alcohol"). *Psychodysleptica,* on the other hand, are substances which alter the perception of the user (for instance, LSD, PCP etc.; hence the inclusion of the subcategory "marihuana"). All other substances can be classified under *rest* (for instance, smart drugs, glue etc.).

The final themes describe both how the offender ultimately *got apprehended* by law enforcement agencies (the offender could have been *betrayed* by someone, could have *turned himself in* or could have been apprehended due to the *judicial investigation*) and whether he acted alone or with a *co-offender*. In the following paragraphs, the different situational characteristics and the behavioral reactions of the offenders will be discussed, for each time phase separately.

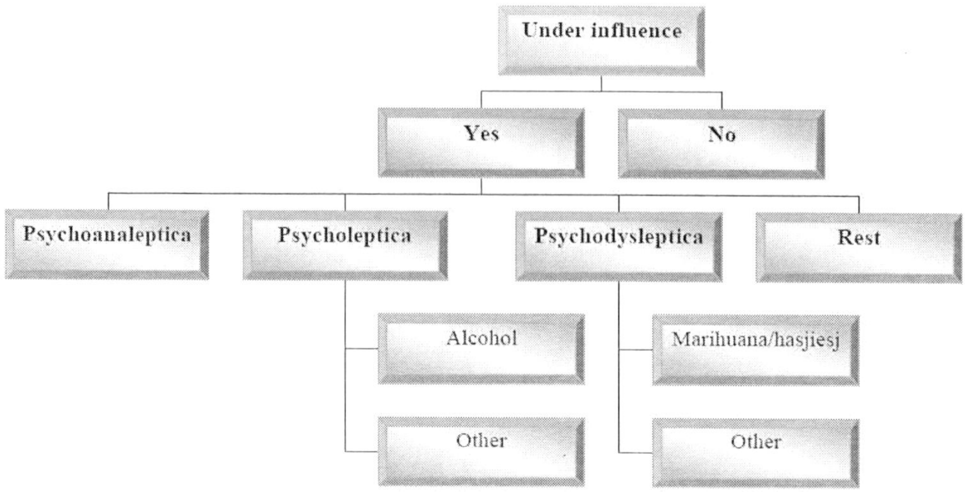

Figure 5. Graphical presentation of possible drugs that could have influenced the offender's behavior.

The Context of the Violent Act, Including the Far Preamble

This time block begins with the description of the broad situation that was going on for an extended period (years, months or weeks) before the crime, and that can be considered as the "usual" (whether or not problematic) life of the offender before committing the violent act. It also includes the far preamble of the violent act namely whether the offender had longstanding problems with the victim or whether the situation that led to the violent act was going on for a longer time period like money problems in a murder with robbery case. For instance: *"I had a lot of problems in my life: I had an alcohol addiction and I had just been released from prison. After a while, I met my wife and we got married. I thought everything would work out and in the beginning, we were very happy. After our first child was born, however, we ended up with a lot of debts since we did not know how to save money and since my wife only wanted the best (the most expensive) for our child. I didn't receive any support from my partner or my mother-in-law (the later victim) in solving this problem; on the contrary, they started blaming me for everything that went wrong. I couldn't do a thing and started drinking more and more to forget about my problems. This didn't work however, and I started thinking about leaving my wife and son."*

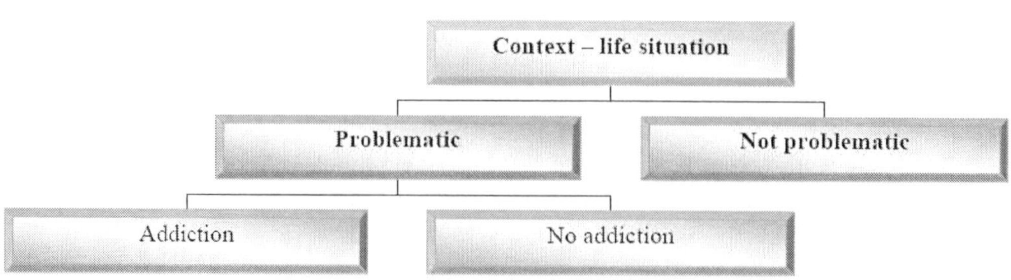

Figure 6. Graphical presentation of possible life situations in the context of the offense time block.

When looking at the *situational elements* in this time block, it appears that two themes play a role in all narratives namely the life situation of the offender and the potential occurrence of additional problems on top of this (problematic) life situation. The first theme describes the *life situation of the offender,* before the beginning of the situation(s) that led to the violent behavioral reaction (see Figure 6).

The first category, *problematic*, includes offenders who experienced a problematic life situation[18], before the beginning of the fatal situation(s).

These offenders experienced longstanding problems that could have had their origin in interpersonal problems or that could have increased due to a lack of social support, but where the emphasis lies on intrapersonal problems, not on actual interpersonal conflicts. This variable is subdivided into those offenders who had problems relating to *addiction* (for instance, an alcoholproblem, a drugproblem, a gambling problem etc.) and those offenders who had problems, *not* related to *addiction* (for instance, being in a criminal organization, having psychological problems, money problems, being illegal in a country etc.). The second category includes offenders who did not experience any of these problems (*not problematic*, for instance, the offender was happy with his life, had no problems, until ... (= beginning of the situation(s) that led to the violent behavioral reaction)).

The second theme describes *potential additional problems*, on top of the (problematic) life situation of the offender (see Figure 7). The first category, *additional problems,* includes offenders who, at a certain moment, experienced additional problems[19] on top of the potential problematic life situation. This category is further divided according to the type of additional problems that appeared in the life of the offender. *Interpersonal problems* are problems were the emphasis lies on interpersonal conflicts, whereas *intrapersonal problems* are problems where the emphasis lies on personal difficulties. Examples of interpersonal problems are for instance, someone wanting to harm the offender, having an argument or relational problems with someone, receiving an unwanted request etc. Examples of intrapersonal problems include for instance, financial problems, an alcoholproblem etc. Offenders who did not experience any of these additional problems, on the other hand, are coded in the category *no additional problems*[20].

If offenders experienced additional problems, two additional subthemes need to be considered, namely the nature and impact of these additional problems. When describing the *nature* of the additional problem, three possibilities exist. The first possibility describes an additional problem that can be nominated at a concrete, specific level and that appeared suddenly in the life of the offender (*specific* for instance, the offender was deceived by someone, got a concrete argument with someone with whom he had a good relationship, the offender got some sleep deprivation etc.).

[18] This variable needs to be coded if the offender had an objective problematic lifestyle, even if this was not experienced by the offender as being problematic (for instance, an alcoholproblem).

[19] These additional problems still played a role at the moment when the situation(s) that ultimately led to a violent behavioral reaction, started. Note that this variable describes the subjective experience of the offender; whether he experienced the situation as being problematic or not.

[20] Note that when the offender had an alcoholaddiction for many years, this is coded under "problematic lifestyle", while offenders, who mentioned that they only started drinking because of something that happened at a certain moment in time, are coded as having "additional problems".

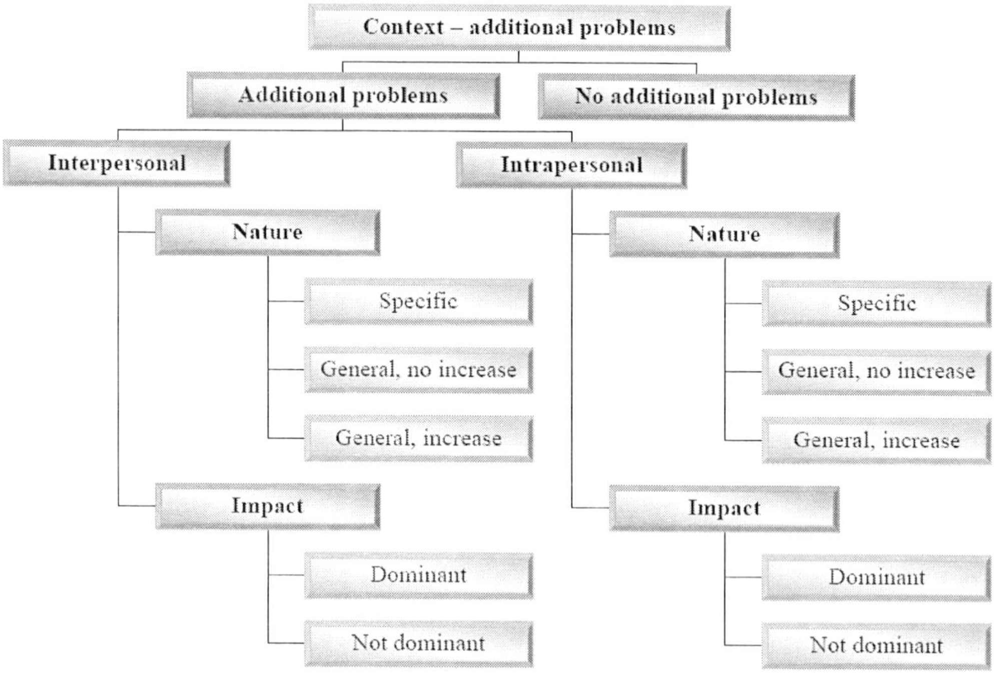

Figure 7. Graphical presentation of possible additional problems in the context of the offense time block.

The second possibility describes problems that are formulated at a general level, that didn't escalate over time and that frequently have to do with longstanding inter- or intrapersonal problems (*general, no increase* for instance, the offender had relational or intimate problems, regarded the victim as a burden, was treated negatively by one's environment, the offender got depressed etc.[21]). The final category depicts additional problems that are formulated at a general level and that became worse over time (*general, increase*). The increase of the problem could be due to an escalation of the problem, to the fact that the offender's possibilities to react to the situation became limited or due to another additional intra- or interpersonal problem, on top of the first additional problem. Examples of the last category include for instance, a relational split-up after having had relational problems, the continuation of a negative situation, after the offender having tried to make the situation better, relational problems that increased due to additional financial problems, and the offender wanting to commit suicide due to a long standing depression. The *impact* of these additional problems can be *dominant*, in the sense that they occupied the life and thoughts of the offender (they took a central place in the life of the offender, limited his possibilities in his daily life, determined his life etc.) or not (*not dominant*, for instance, an unwanted request that did not occupy the offender for a long while, a relational split up that did not dominate the offender's life etc.).

When offenders are classified as having additional interpersonal problems (on top of the potential problematic life style), three additional subthemes have to be considered namely

[21] Note that these examples are formulated at a more general level (for instance, relational problems or depression), in contrast with the examples from the specific category (for instance, an argument about something concrete or not being able to sleep for a while).

whether the offender experienced some alliances, the persons involved in the interpersonal problems and the type of behaviors exhibited towards the offender. The first subtheme, whether the offender experienced *alliances* distinguishes offenders who were standing alone in their "battle" against other people (*offender versus*) from offenders who were experiencing an alliance with or who were standing up for someone else (*offender and third person versus*). The experience of being in an alliance with someone can be due to the fact that the victim did not (only) treat the offender in a negative way, but (also) someone with whom the offender had a close relationship (for instance, the victim harassed the offender's new girlfriend) or can be due to the fact that someone with whom the offender had a close relationship treated the victim in a negative way or stood up for the offender in his interpersonal problems with the victim (for instance, the partner of the offender proposed to teach the victim a lesson or a friend of the offender stood up for the offender in his argument with the victim). The second and third subtheme describe the *persons involved* (not his alliances) in the interpersonal problems of the offender and the behaviors these persons executed towards the offender (see Figure 8). Offenders could have experienced problems with the *victim* (the person who ultimately got wounded by the offender), with their *environment* (those people who were part of the offender's social network for instance, family (in-law), parents, brothers and sisters, partner, the nursing staff of the hospital if the offender resided in a psychiatric institution etc.) and/or with a *third person* (someone who played a role in the narrative of the offender but did not belong to his environment for instance, someone with whom the offender wanted to start a relationship, someone the offender knew from a pub, a friend, a rival etc.). When describing the *behaviors these persons executed towards the offender*, a number of possibilities appear. First of all, it's possible that the person involved did not perform any negative behavior towards the person of the offender, but that this person mistreated someone with whom the offender had a close relationship (*no negative behavior*; for instance, someone raped the offender's child or someone stole money from the offender's mother). The second possibility, *negative impact*, includes those behaviors that were not directed towards the person of the offender, but that caused some negative impact in the offender's life (for instance, an unwanted request from someone, a child victim that was regarded as being a burden to the offender, the offender's partner became depressed etc.)[22]. The last possibility describes negative behaviors directed towards the person of the offender like for instance, sexual harassment, emotional blackmail, threatening the offender etc. (*negative behavior*).

Offenders *reacted* in a number of ways to these situational themes (see Figure 9). First of all, it's possible that the offender did not provide any indication on how he reacted to the situation(s) of the context of the offense (*unknown*), which is mostly the case if an offender did not experience interpersonal problems. If the behavior of the offender in this time block is *known*, it can be classified according to one of the following possibilities.

[22] Although we recognize that a rape of the offender's child has a negative impact on the life of the offender, we maintained the distinction between "no negative behavior" and "negative impact" because 1) in the "no negative behavior" category, the offender is not a person involved in the situation and because 2) "negative impact" does not include actual negative behaviors, which is the case for the "no negative behavior" category.

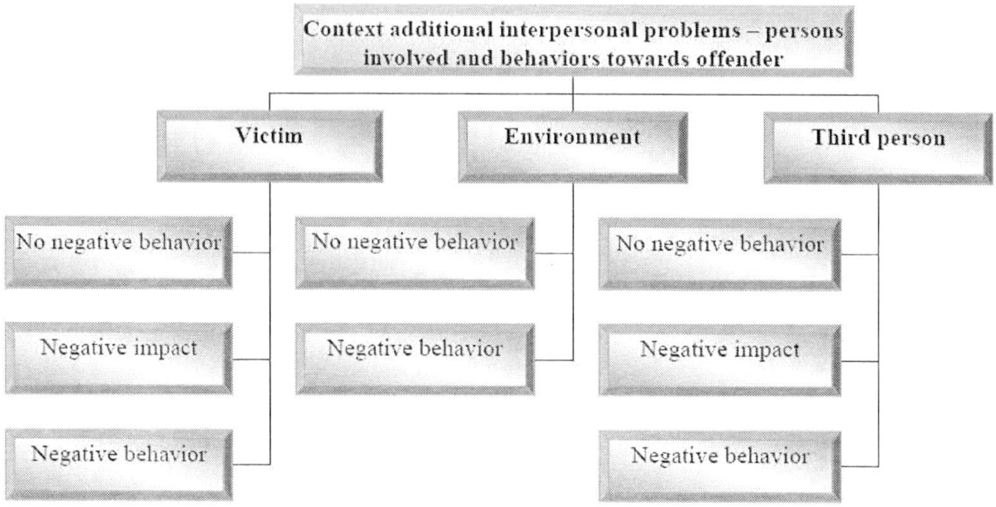

Figure 8. Graphical presentation of possible persons involved and executed behaviors towards the offender in the context of the offense time block.

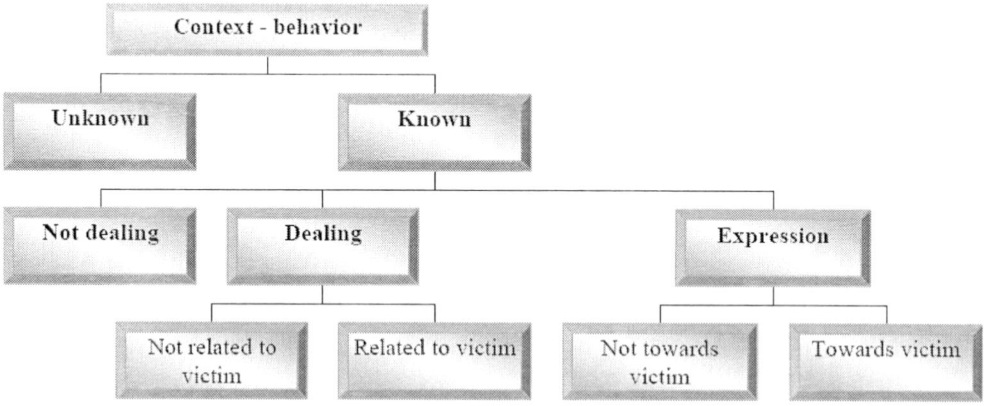

Figure 9. Graphical presentation of possible behavioral reactions to the context of the offense time block.

The first possibility, *not dealing*, includes offenders who did not handle the situation(s) of the context and who did not express their negative emotions in any way. These offenders reacted to the situation(s) by avoiding their problems or by performing behaviors that were not aimed at changing, ameliorating or ending the context or at expressing one's own negative emotional state. Examples of this category include for instance, alcohol consumption, ruminating, avoiding a situation or not acting on it, obtaining information without doing something with this information etc. Another possible behavioral reaction includes those behaviors that deal with the situation(s) of the context of the offense, without expressing negative emotions (*dealing*). These offenders reacted to the context by behaviors aimed at changing, ameliorating or ending the situation(s), independently of whether they succeeded in their attempts or not. This category has two subcategories, depending on whether the offender dealt with a problematic situation *involving the later victim or not*. Examples of this category include for instance, fleeing from a negative person, trying to help someone, trying to solve an argument, searching for work when having money problems, refusing to do something unwanted etc. The final possibility indicates those behaviors that are expressions of the offender's negative emotional state (*expression).* This category has two subcategories as well, depending on whether the offender expressed his negative emotions *towards the later victim or not.* Examples of this category are for instance, arguing, physical or verbal aggression, the commitment of criminal acts, threatening someone etc.

The Preamble of the Violent Act

This time block describes a concrete[23] situation in the life of the offender that preceded and differed from the situation in which the violent behavior or intention towards the victim occurred. The content of this time block is different from the content of the time block in which the concrete trigger occurred, in the sense that they include different actors[24] or include the same actors but with a different definition of the situation[25]. Although the situation described is very concrete, the possible behavioral reactions to this situation can be different and be extended over a longer time period. Generally, this time phase is indicated by words like: at a certain point in time, but then, all of a sudden… For instance: *"At a given moment, I received a letter from the bank, indicating that I had to pay 3000 euros before the end of the month, otherwise, they would confiscate my house. I didn't know how to pay this amount and started drinking even more. I asked my wife if she could ask her mother to help us, but my mother- in-law refused to help us, even though she had enough money. I became angry at my mother in law, why wouldn't she help us? That's why, after a while, I decided to break into the house of my parents-in-law in order to obtain the money".*

The theme, relevant in describing the *situational characteristics* of this time block, is whether the offender experienced a *problematic situation or not* (see Figure 10). Offenders are coded under *not problematic* if they did not describe any problematic situation. This is mostly the case when the offender acted in such a way that he caused negative consequences for another person, without his behavior being a reaction to an interpersonal or intrapersonal problem (for instance, the offender raped the victim without prior negative behavior from the victim towards the offender). The second possibility, *problematic*, includes those situations that were experienced as being problematic from the point of view of the offender. This category is subdivided according to whether this problem is *intrapersonal* and/or *interpersonal.*

When offenders were experiencing interpersonal problems in the time block of the preamble of the offense, a number of additional themes have to be coded namely the occurrence of *alliances* (cf. supra), the *persons involved* in the interpersonal problems (see Figure 11) and the type of behaviors executed towards the offender (see Figure 12). When

[23] A concrete situation indicates that one has to be able to answer concrete questions about the situation for instance, "was the offender under influence of drugs at that moment or not"? If one is not able to answer such concrete questions, this means that the situation has to be included in the broad context of the crime. Applied on the example (see infra): since one can answer the question "was the offener under influence of drugs at the moment when he received the letter from the bank?", this situation is coded in the time block of the preamble of the offense.

[24] For instance, a dispute with a close friend (preamble) versus a dispute with the victim which ultimately led to a violent reaction of the offender (situation in which the trigger of the offense occurred).

[25] For instance, the offender wanted to rob the victim because he had received an ultimatum to pay his debts (preamble; the content of the situation is the intention to rob the victim) versus the victim resisted during the robbery and the offender shot the victim after having argued with the victim (situation in which the trigger of the offense occurred; the content of the situation is the intention to regain control over the situation).

looking at Figure 11, the former distinction between interpersonal problems, involving the *victim* and/or a *third person*, remains[26]. This time however, the category is further differentiated when offenders were having problems both with the victim and a third person. The first possible subdivision, *independently*, denotes offenders who were having problems both with a third person and the victim independently, without the generalization of one interpersonal problem with one person to another. The second category, *victim → third person*, on the other hand, indicates problems that started with the victim, but were generalized to a third person. For instance, the victim raped the child of the offender and due to this, the offender got relational problems with his wife (third person). The final possibility, *third person → victim*, includes problems that had their origin in the interaction between the offender and a third person, but were generalized to the relationship with the victim. For instance, a third person caused some relational problems between the offender and the victim.

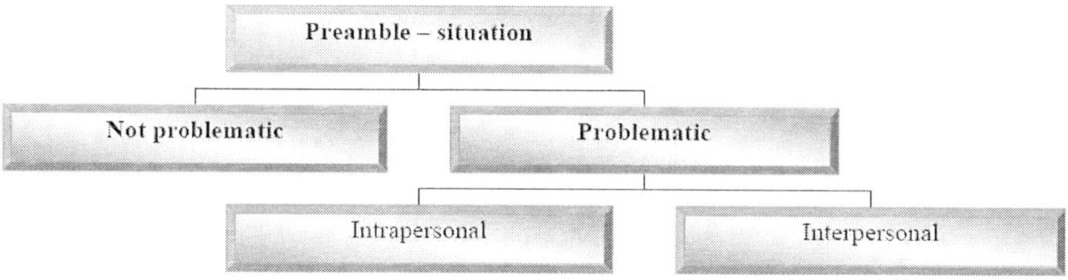

Figure 10. Graphical presentation of possible situations in the preamble of the offense time block.

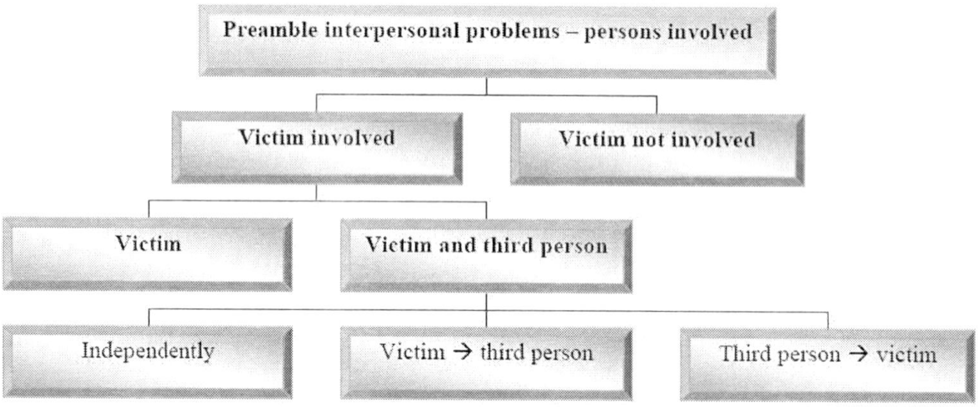

Figure 11. Graphical presentation of possible persons involved in the interpersonal problems of the offender in the preamble of the offense time block.

The description of the *type of behaviors* executed towards the offender (see Figure 12), also includes the distinction between *no negative behavior*, *negative impact* and negative behaviors, as mentioned above. This time, however, the last category is further differentiated depending on whether this behavior is manifested verbally or not.

Verbal negative behavior includes those verbal behaviors that are negative and directed towards the person of the offender. This category is subdivided into those messages indicating

[26] The persons who were coded under "environment" in the context of the offense time block, are from now on

that the person is going to cause some "*problems*" for the offender (for instance, someone informed the offender that he would tell his wife about his affaire) or those messages demonstrating some mistreatment of, or disrespect towards the *"person"* of the offender (for instance, someone told the offender that he was not allowed to see his children anymore). In the case of some verbal negative behavior towards the person of the offender, in the form of physical threats, the subcategory "physical" has to be coded (for instance, someone threatened the offender that one of these days, he was going to get harmed if he did not act upon an unwanted request).

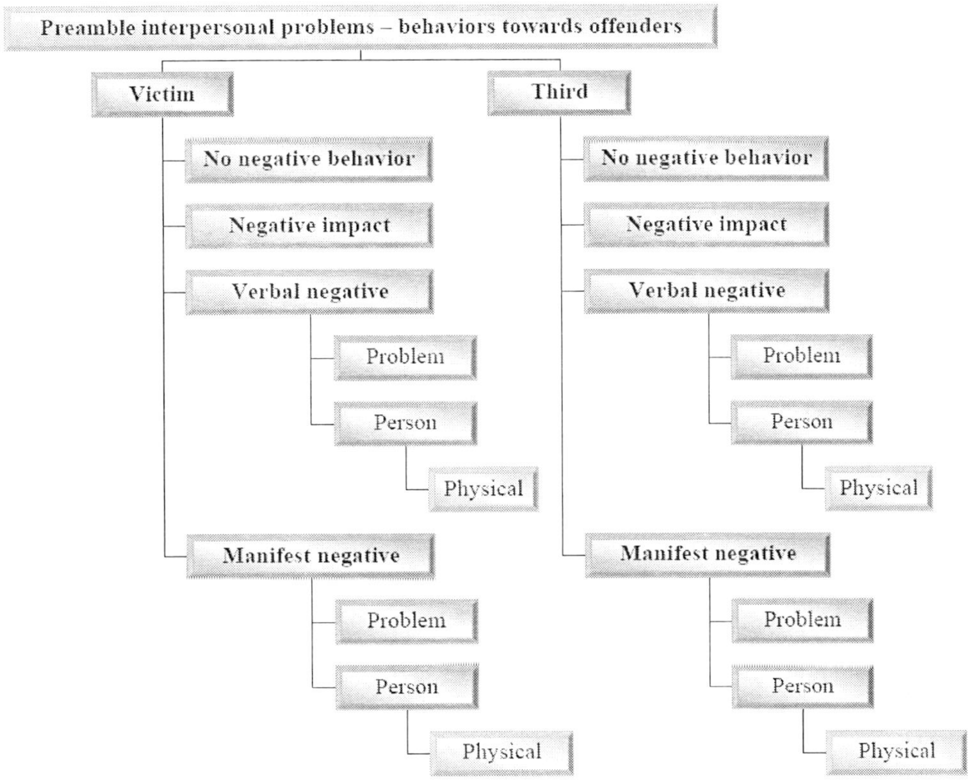

Figure 12. Graphical presentation of possible executed behaviors towards the offender in the preamble of the offense time block.

Manifest negative behaviors, on the other hand, include those negative behaviors that are not verbally and are directed towards the person of the offender. This category is also subdivided depending on whether the person would cause some "*problems*" for the offender (for instance, someone told the offender's wife about his affaire), or mistreated the *"person"* of the offender in any way (for instance, not allowing the offender to see his children anymore). When someone harmed or intended to harm the offender physically, "physical" has to be coded (for instance, hitting the offender).

The offender could have *reacted t*o the concrete situation of the preamble of the offense in a number of ways (see Figure 13). Offenders are coded in the category *not negative* when they did not react negatively in any way to the preamble of the offense, when they did not

included in the category "third person".

perform behaviors that have a negative impact on other people. For instance, asking a friend to lend some money, visit someone to make it up, drinking etc. At the other side, offenders are coded who *reacted negatively* on the given situation, either by performing behaviors that have a negative impact on someone else or by beginning to execute a negative intention[27]. This category of "negative behaviors" has two subcategories depending on whether the offender delayed his reaction or not. Offenders are coded under "*behavior*" when they reacted to the situation of the preamble by performing instant behaviors that have a negative impact on someone else. For instance, physical or verbal aggression. The beginning of the execution of a negative *intention* on the other hand, includes less impulsive, delayed behaviors like for instance, the intention of robbing someone, the intention of threatening the victim, the intention of killing someone else than the victim etc. This latter category has two subcategories, depending on whether this negative intention is *prepared* by the offender beforehand or not.

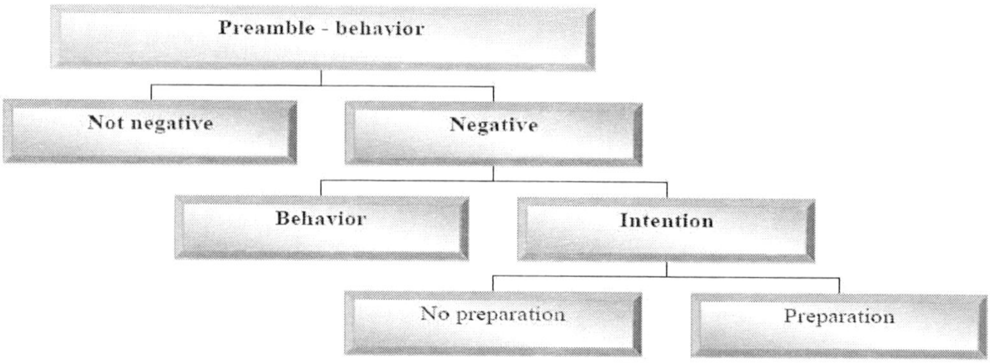

Figure 13. Graphical presentation of possible behavioral reactions to the preamble of the offense time block.

The Situation That Preceded the Trigger of the Offense

This time block starts from the beginning of the concrete[28] situation in which the offender finally reacted by violent behaviors/intentions towards the victim (after having attempted to deal with the situation differently). It describes the beginning of a new, concrete situation that changed the general context (for instance, one day, the partner of the offender decided to leave him), changed the concrete situation of the preamble of the offense (for instance, suddenly the burglary situation has changed into an unexpected encounter with the victim), or is a concrete situation that led to the final escalation of the context of the offense (for instance, at a certain point in time, the victim started to argue with the offender once again about a concrete subject). Although the situation described is very concrete, the possible behavioral reactions to this situation can be different and be extended over a longer time period. The content of this time block is different from the content of the time block of the preamble of the offense (different in the sense that they include different actors or include the same actors but with a different definition of the situation, see supra). Most of the time, this time phase is indicated by words like: at a certain point in time, but then, all of a sudden…

[27] Not the intention to harm the victim, since this is coded as the behavioral reaction of the offender to the concrete trigger of the offense.

[28] See supra.

For instance: *"I was breaking into the house of my mother-in-law, when all of a sudden, she came home unexpectedly. I tried to explain the situation to her, but she started screaming and wouldn't listen to my explanations"*. The *situational theme* most relevant in describing this time block is whether the offender was experiencing some *interpersonal problems*. If the offender was experiencing interpersonal problems, the occurrence of *alliances* (see supra), the *persons involved* in the interpersonal problem (cf. Figure 11) and the *type of behaviors executed* towards the offender (cf. Figure 12) need to be considered as well.

There are only a limited number of ways the offender could have *reacted* to the situation preceding the trigger of the offense (see Figure 14). This classification of possible behaviors also starts from the difference between *negative* and *not negative* behavioral reactions (examples of the latter are for instance, dragging someone away from a fight, not accepting an unwanted proposition, confronting someone without quarreling etc.). The following categories are further differentiations of the *negative behavioral category:* "*quarreling*" with someone, trying to gain "*control*" over the situation (for instance, by using a weapon, by grabbing the victim) and being physically "*aggressive*" towards another person than the victim.

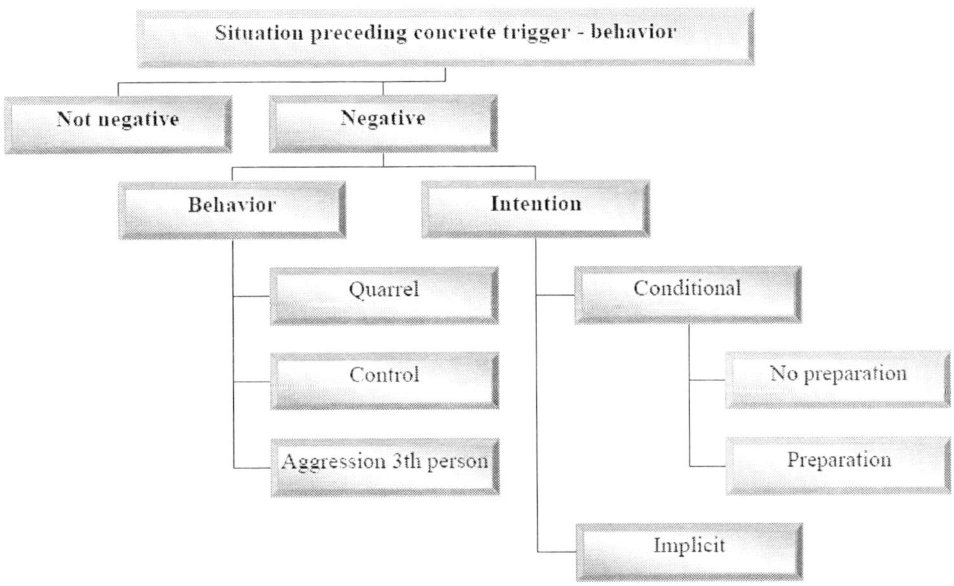

Figure 14. Graphical presentation of possible behavioral reactions to the situation preceding the trigger of the offense.

At the other side, behaviors are coded that imply the conditional or implicit *intention* of harming the victim. This category is also subdivided into subcategories. The first subcategory "*conditional*" represents offenders who got the intention of harming the victim but whose initiation of the violent behavior was dependent on a certain situation or victim behavior (for instance, "I decided only to kill the victim if he wouldn't return my money"). This subcategory is further differentiated by whether or not the offender prepared this conditional negative intention. The second subcategory "*implicit*" indicates a preparation of the violent offense, without conscious knowledge of the offender that this would ultimately lead to the execution of the offense. The offender consciously, or unconsciously, placed himself in a situation were an offense was highly likely to occur (for instance, the offender took a weapon with him without intending to use that weapon towards the victim; the offender accompanied some people who were intending to kill the victim etc.).

The Trigger of the Offense

The trigger of the offense is that (concrete situation or concrete behavior of someone) which led to a violent reaction/intention[29] of the offender towards the victim. It is the event that describes the concrete behavior of someone or the concrete situation when trying to answer the following question: "what specific made the offender use violence or made the offender get the intention to use violence towards the victim?". Most of the time, this time phase is indicated by words like: at a certain point in time, but then, all of a sudden… Note that there is always a trigger in every offense narrative since every offender, included in this study, has used violence towards the victim. For instance: *"All of a sudden, she threatened to phone law enforcement agencies and I panicked. Before I knew what was happening, I found myself hitting my mother-in-law."*

The *situational themes,* relevant in this time block, are identical to those described in the time block of the situation preceding the trigger: whether or not the offender experienced *interpersonal problems*, and if this is the case, the occurrence of *alliances* (cf. supra), the *persons involved* (cf. Figure 11) in the interpersonal problem and the *type of behaviors executed* towards the offender (cf. Figure 12).

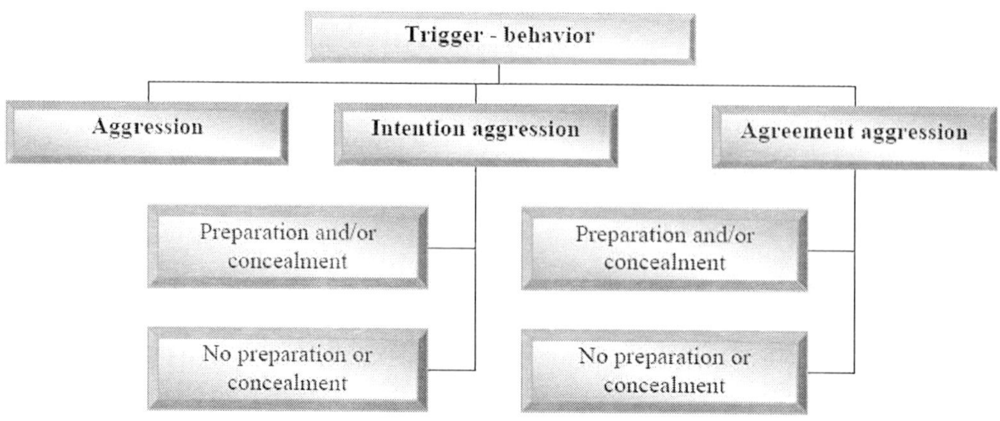

Figure 15. Graphical presentation of possible behavioral reactions to the trigger of the offense time block.

The possible *behavioral reactions* to the trigger of the offense are depicted in Figure 15. The first possible reaction to the trigger of the offense is *aggression* of the offender towards the victim (for instance, hitting, stabbing, strangling the victim etc.). The second possible reaction is the offender's *intention*, while the third possible reaction is the offender's

[29] Note that the focus of this research is extremely violent behavior. Hence, when an offender has killed a victim after having raped her, the killing of the victim is considered to be the violence under investigation, not the violence used in order to rape the victim. The violence used in order to rape the victim is coded in the time block of the preamble of the offense. The first violence that is used towards the victim after the rape, is coded as the behavioral reaction of the offender to the trigger of the offense.

agreement (with a co-offender or the victim himself[30]) to use violence against the victim. The second and third categories are further differentiated by whether this intention/agreement is *prepared or concealed* by the offender[31] before the execution of the offense.

The Interaction between the Victim and the Offender

The time block of the interaction between the victim and the offender provides a description of the reaction of the offender, victim and/or other person, following the violent reaction/intention of the offender on the trigger of the offense. It provides information about the continuation of the same concrete situation, after the offender used violence towards the victim, agreed or got the intention to use violence towards the victim. Note that this time block starts at the moment when the offender has made contact with the victim if the violence towards the victim is planned; when the violence, on the other hand is not planned, this time block starts at the moment when someone (third person and/or victim) reacts to the first violent reaction of the offender. Although the situation described is very concrete, the possible behavioral reactions to this situation can be different and be extended over a longer time period. For instance: *"She fought back and didn't stop screaming. I kept hitting her until the screaming ended".*

The different *situational themes*, relevant in this time block are whether someone performed negative behaviors towards the offender, and if this is the case, the occurrence of alliances (cf. supra), the persons involved, and the executed behaviors towards the offender (see Figure 16). The first relevant question to ask is whether someone performed *negative behaviors towards the offender.* The *no* category has to be coded if the victim or a third person did not act in any way (anymore) or did not behave negatively towards the person of the offender (anymore; for instance, the victim fell to the floor and did not stand up anymore or the victim did not resist when the offender started executing his negative intention). The *yes* category, on the other hand, includes situations in which the victim and/or a third person (re)acted negatively towards the person of the offender. When someone did perform negative behaviors towards the offender in this time block, the occurrence of *alliances*, the *persons* performing the negative behaviors and the *type of negative behaviors executed* have to be coded (both for the role of the victim and/or a third person, see Figure 16).

A *not negative* category is included for the case if someone performed behaviors that were experienced by the offender as being negative, without these behaviors being directed towards the person of the offender (for instance, the victim attacking the offender's co-offender). The *negative* category, on the other hand, includes those behaviors that are directed at the person of the offender and are experienced by the offender as being negative. If the victim is the active person, the category is subdivided according to whether the victim *tried to escape* the presence or aggression of the offender, *reacted emotionally* to the given situation (for instance, screaming, asking for an explanation, appealing to the offender's conscience etc.) or *resisted the offender physically.*

---

[30] Meaning that the victim is the offender's co-offender like for instance, if the offender assisted the victim's suicide or if the offender wanted to help the victim by ending his suffering (euthanasia).

[31] Not concealment towards the victim, since this is coded under "contact with victim", see infra.

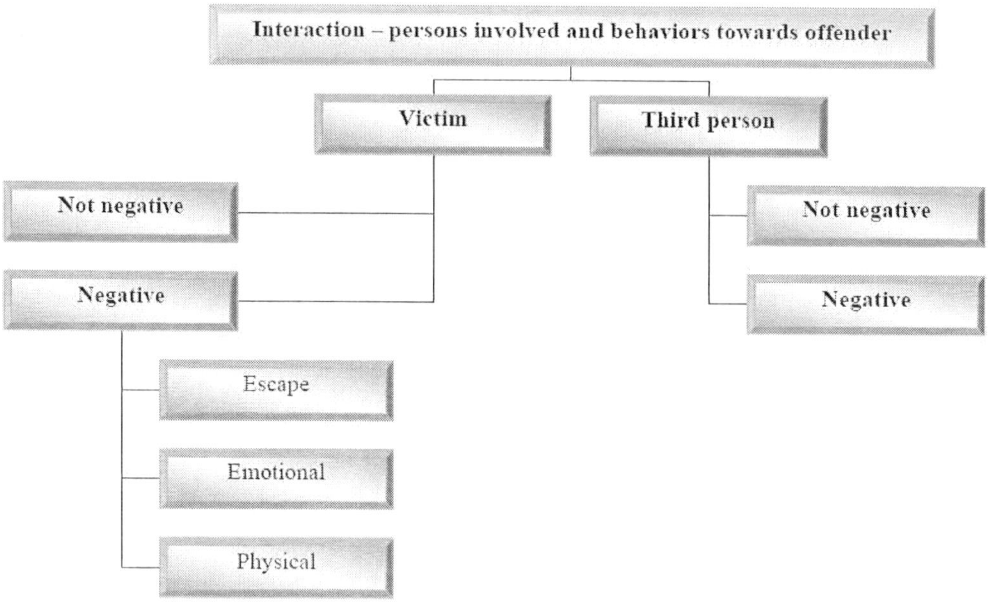

Figure 16. Graphical presentation of possible persons involved and executed behaviors towards the offender in the interaction time block.

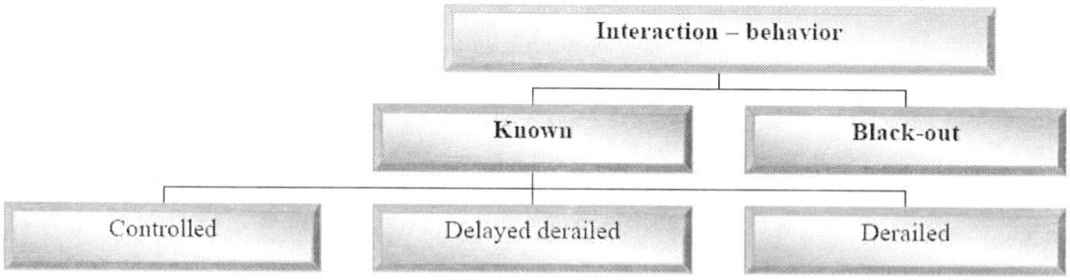

Figure 17. Graphical presentation of possible behavioral reactions in the interaction time block.

There are only a limited number of ways the offender could have *reacted* in this time block (see Figure 17). First of all, since some offenders described a black-out in this time block, a *black-out* category was included. When the behavior of the offender in the interaction time block is *known*, three possible categories are provided. The offender could have reacted *controlled* in the interaction time block, in the sense that he kept processing information from the situation to guide his behavior. Once the violent behavior was initiated or planned, the offender kept control over his behaviors. The offender reacted to behaviors of the victim, of another person, or on the condition of the victim[32]. Offenders who are coded under *delayed derailed* are offenders who initially reacted controlled to the situation, but ultimately lost control over their behaviors (for instance, the offender only initiated planned aggressive behaviors after a co-offender started to harm the victim, but once this aggression was initiated, the offender lost control and couldn't stop stabbing the victim anymore). The final possible behavioral reaction in the violent interaction time block includes offenders who did

[32] Stopped reacting aggressively if the victim was death and the killing was planned or stopped reacting aggressively if the victim was wounded, without a priori intention of killing the victim.

not take any situational information into account in guiding their behaviors. Once the killing was initiated or planned, the offender did not have control over his actions anymore and reacted *derailed.*

After the Crime

The time block *"before leaving"* begins with the description of the concrete situation/concrete behavior of the offender at the crime scene, after the victim had fallen down. This time block stops when the offender left or got apprehended at the crime scene[33]. For instance: *"I didn't know what to do, sat down for a while and decided to cover my traces before leaving the house".*

The situation/behavior of the offender, after having left the crime scene, is described in the time block *"after leaving"* the offense. This time block stops after a night had passed or when the offender got apprehended before the first morning after the offense. Note that in this time block, the offender could still have contact with the victim (for instance, going to hospital) or with the victim's corpse (for instance, transporting the victim's corpse to another place). For instance: *"When I came home, I didn't tell anything to my wife since I was frightened that she would not understand. I drank a whole bottle of vodka and fell asleep".*

The time block *"after one night",* on the other hand, describes the situations/behaviors of the offender, after a night had passed and ends at the moment when the offender was apprehended or questioned by law enforcement agencies, started a new offense pathway (for instance, went out to kill another person) or resumed his usual life. Note that this time block, together with the time block of the context of the offense, are the only two time blocks describing more than one concrete situation, or one concrete moment. For instance: *"The next day, law enforcement agencies informed my wife about the death of her mother and I tried to comfort her, which was not easy since I knew the truth. I asked the police officer whether he knew who did it and was relieved to hear that he did not had a clue. The following days were very difficult for me: I couldn't look my wife in the eyes anymore and started feeling guilty. In the end, law enforcement agencies discovered the truth since a neighbor had seen me at the crime scene at the day of the offense. I was relieved when they came to apprehend me since I could not live like this anymore".*

Since the *situational themes* in the three time blocks after the crime are equal, we will describe them together. The first question that needs to be answered is identical to that in the former time block: did someone perform *negative behaviors* towards the person of the offender? If someone mistreated the offender, the occurrence of *alliances* (cf. supra; this time, however, "alliances" is also coded if offenders received some support in dealing with the offense), the *persons involved and the executed behaviors* towards the offender (see Figure 18) need to be specified. When describing the latter, the same distinction between *negative* and *not negative behaviors* is made; the only difference between these and the former time block is the differentiation of the type of negative behaviors. Both the victim and a third person could have behaved negatively towards the offender because they did not provide enough *support* for the offender (for instance, someone rejected the offender after having left the crime scene), because of the *execution of negative behaviors* towards the offender (for instance, hitting or insulting the offender), or because of behaviors that *revealed* the

[33] The crime scene is the place where the victim got wounded or killed and does not need to be inside a house, it can also be in a car, an open field, the street, a swimming pool...

offender's responsibility in accordance with the offense. The last category is differentiated according to whether the crime is revealed at law enforcement agencies (for instance, betraying the offender) or not (for instance, a witness who fled from the crime scene).

The possible *behavioral reactions* of the offenders in the three time blocks after the crime are, at first, equal (see Figure 19). For those offenders who experienced a black-out before and/or after leaving the crime scene, a *black-out* category is included. When the behaviors of the offender in these time blocks are *known*, two possible categories emerged, depending on whether the offender tried to conceal the offense or not.

Concealing behaviors are those behaviors that are aimed at concealing the offense and/or the identity of the offender like for instance, trying to cover one's tracks, trying to get rid of the victim's body, making sure that the crime scene is not (immediately) visible for outsiders, making sure that one is not noticed at the crime scene or when leaving the crime scene, lying to someone to conceal the offense etc.

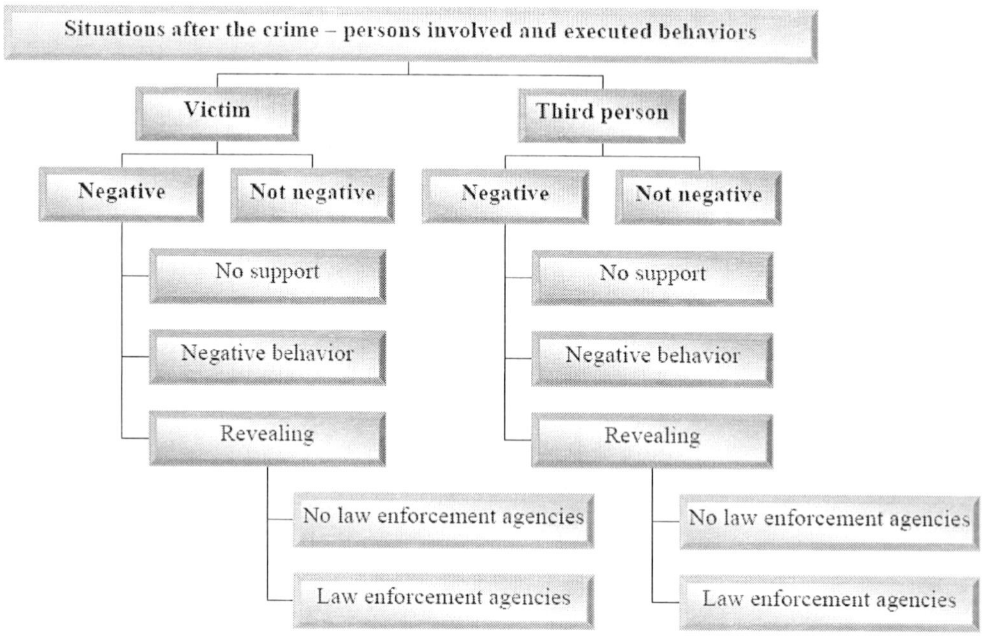

Figure 18. Graphical presentation of possible persons involved and executed behaviors towards the offender after the crime had occurred.

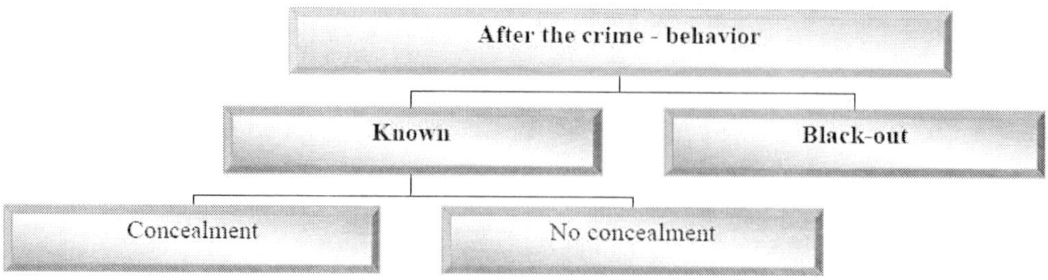

Figure 19. Graphical presentation of possible behavioral reactions in the three time blocks after the crime.

Another distinction that appeared relevant in the time blocks "before" and "after leaving" is whether or not the offender performed additional behaviors (on top of the possible concealment of the crime; see Figure 20).

Some offenders performed *additional behaviors,* not aimed at concealing the crime, which had positive and/or negative implications for the *offender* himself, the *victim* and/or a *third person*. Positive behaviors are those behaviors that have positive consequences for someone while negative behaviors are those behaviors that result in negative consequences. In the case of the offender doing something for himself, positive behaviors include for instance, obtaining something material like money at the crime scene/after having left the crime scene and/or obtaining something not material like for instance, information, support, alcohol etc. Negative additional behaviors that have an impact on the offender include for instance, turning oneself in. Positive behaviors directed at the victim include those behaviors that indicate some sort of empathy towards the victim like for instance, covering the victim's corpse with a blanket (not to conceal the offense) or taking the victim to a hospital.

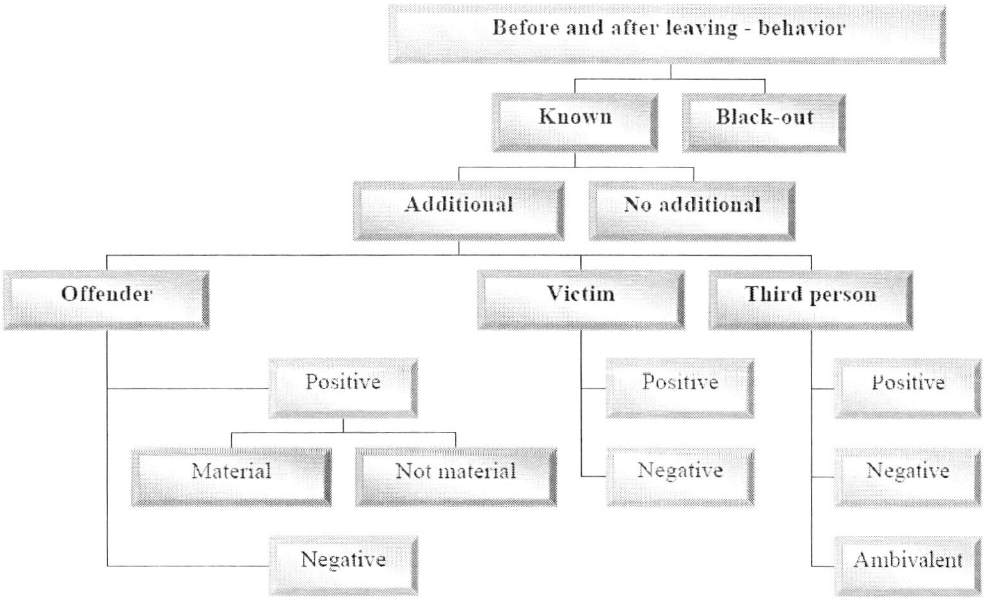

Figure 20. Graphical presentation of possible behavioral reactions in the time blocks before and after leaving the crime scene.

Negative additional behaviors directed at the victim include for instance, taking money from the victim. The same distinction could also be made between positive and negative behaviors directed at a third person. If the offender, however, treated the same third person both positively and negatively, the "ambivalent" category has to be coded.

Aside from the question whether the offender tried to conceal his crime after a night had passed (see Figure 19), another question appeared relevant in this time block namely to what degree the offender remained mentally occupied with the offense (see Figure 21). The offender could have remained *occupied* with the offense, in the sense that the offender kept thinking about the offense. This category could further be differentiated by whether the offender remained occupied with the *implications* of the offense for himself (for instance, thinking about not wanting to go to prison, seeking the presence of a partner to be intimate one last time before being apprehended etc.) or remained occupied with the *severity* of having committed such an aggravated assault (for instance, turning oneself in, trying to cope with the offense, constant reliving the offense, not being able to sleep, eat or work etc.). The final differentiation in this category includes whether or not the offender had the *chance not to be occupied* with the offense anymore. That is to say, offenders who were arrested shortly after the first morning after the crime did not have the possibility to close up the offense mentally, whereas offenders who were capable of not being apprehended for a longer time period, did have the opportunity to close up the offense mentally. The second possible behavioral reaction indicates offenders who closed the offense for themselves, who resumed their lives without thinking back at the crime (*closing*). The life before and after the offense did not differ for these offenders, expressed by behaviors like for instance, selecting another victim, resuming one's life as if nothing had happened, going out to celebrate something, etc. The final category includes offenders who secluded oneself from the world, who tried not to think about the crime by *altering their mental state* in order not to be occupied with the crime anymore (for instance, drug consumption, alcohol consumption, sleeping, black-out...). Characteristic of this category is that the offender was apparently not occupied with the offense anymore, but this was due to the fact that the offender was experiencing another mental condition than the one before the crime.

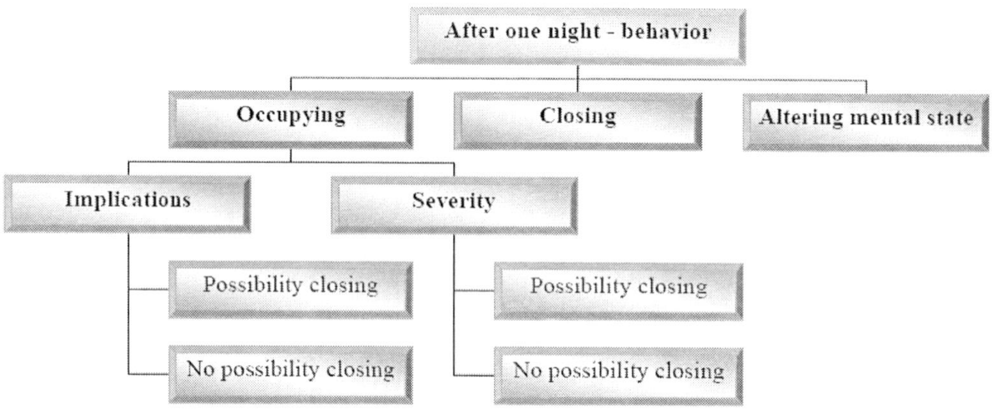

Figure 21. Graphical presentation of possible behavioral reactions after one night after the offense.

Cognitions and Affects in Homicide Offending

Cognitions in Homicide Offending

In these paragraphs, the different cognitions that play a role in the different phases of homicide offending will be discussed. These cognitions cover three broad topics namely the offender's motivations or intentions towards someone else, the certainty with which the offender performed some of his behaviors and the way in which he experienced the situation.

The offender could have had multiple *motivations* for himself, and *intentions* towards the victim and/or a third person (see Figure 22)[34]. The offender's motivation[35] or intention in a certain time block could have been negative, positive or ambivalent (if the offender wanted something positive and negative to happen for the same third person). Negative and positive motivations or intentions cover those aspects that have respectively negative and positive consequences for someone. *Negative motivations* of the offender include for instance, wanting to commit suicide, wanting to harm oneself etc. Note that although the offender could have, for instance, wanted to commit suicide to escape a negative situation, implying that suicide had some positive consequences for the offender, the suicide motivation is coded under "negative" motivation since suicide, objectively, is considered to be harmful to the offender. *Positive motivations,* on the other hand, cover four broad themes: wanting to *escape* a negative situation in the present or wanting the negative situation to stop (for instance, wanting to escape a unpleasant relationship), wanting to *avoid* a possible negative situation in the future (for instance, wanting to avoid losing one's daughter), wanting to *regain* something positive from the past that has disappeared or has been gone (for instance, wanting to regain one's freedom that has disappeared due to birth of a child) or wanting to *obtain* something positive (for instance, wanting to maintain a drug addiction, wanting to have sex or money etc.). When an offender wanted something positive for himself, one can specify the global positive themes (escape, avoid, regain and obtain) by describing the concrete motivation of the offender in all time blocks, except for the time block of the context of the offense[36]. When an offender wanted to escape the present negative situation, he could have wanted to escape the global "situation" in which he found himself (for instance, a negative relationship with someone, a stressful life etc.), or he could have wanted to escape a specific "element" in this global situation (for instance, wanting to escape "violence" against the offender, wanting to escape an "emotional" reaction from someone or wanting to escape another element, different from violence or an emotional reaction ("rest")). Offenders wanting to avoid something negative to happen to them in the future, are subdivided according to the specific element they wanted to avoid: going to "prison", a secret "coming out", future "violence", the possibility of losing one's "honor" or something else ("rest"). The category of regaining something covers those offenders who wanted their good life back ("situation") and those offenders wanting to regain a specific "element" from the past (like for instance, regaining "control" over a situation, regaining their "honor", regaining a "relationships" with someone or something else ("rest")). Finally, offenders who wanted to obtain something positive could have wanted to obtain something "material" like money, something "emotional" like support, "sex" or something different from these ("rest").

---

[34] Only "interpersonal" motivations or intentions have to be considered. A non-interpersonal negative intention (for instance, wanting to rob or rape someone), is not coded in this section unless the offender explicitely stated that he wanted to harm that person by robbing or raping him/her.

[35] The variables concerning the offender's motivation are not coded if the motivation is unknown. This could be due to the fact that the offender did not describe any motivation, because he experienced a black-out, acted on "automatic pilot", did not known why he performed certain behaviors or because he acted impulsively, without explicit motivation.

[36] The context of the offense time block covers a large time interval and hence, a multitude of possible specific motivations.

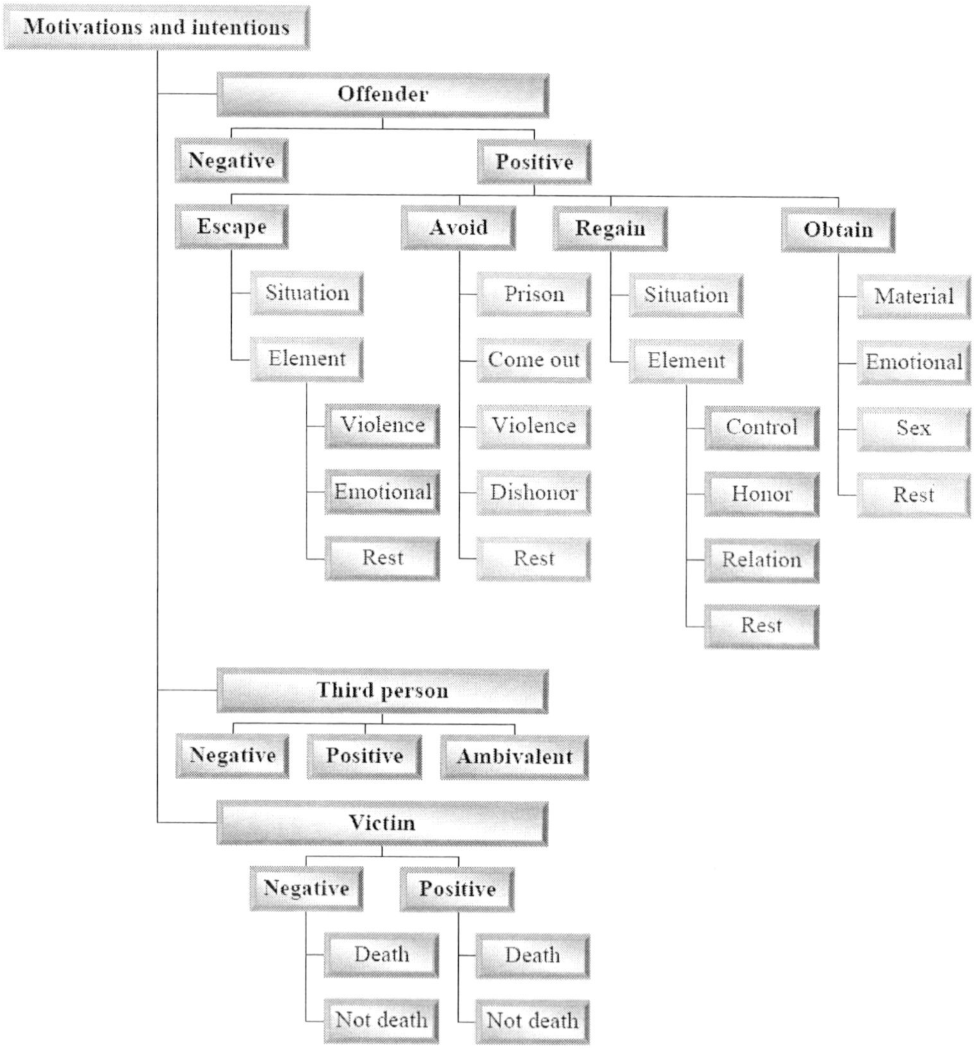

Figure 22. Graphical presentation of possible motivations and intentions in homicide offending.

The *intentions* towards the victim and/or a third person, on the other hand, are also divided according to the consequences the offender wanted his behaviors to have on the victim and/or a third person: positive, negative or *ambivalent.* Wanting something *positive* for the victim and/or a third person includes for instance, wanting to offer a good education to one's child, wanting to keep one's promise, to help someone etc. *Negative intentions* towards the victim and/or a third person, on the other hand, include for instance, wanting to harm the victim and/or a third person, wanting to dominate or intimidate someone etc. Note that in the time blocks of the situation preceding the trigger, the concrete trigger and the interaction between the victim and the offender, a differentiation is made in the negative and positive intentional categories towards the victim, depending on whether the offender wanted the death of the victim or not. When an offender wanted the *death* of the victim, this could be coded under negative (in the case of the offender wanting to kill the victim without considering the victim's thoughts and feelings) or under positive intention (if the offender, for instance, wanted to kill the victim because he wanted to assist the victim's suicide, because he did not wanted the victim to suffer anymore).

The *certainty* with which the offender performed certain behaviors has to be described before and starting from the moment of the execution of the first violent act towards the victim. In the phase before the first violent act (see Figure 23), one needs to indicate whether the offender experienced some *compulsive drive or doubted* to execute a negative intention or a violent act towards the person of the victim. If the offender felt some compulsive drive or doubted to perform some of these behaviors, one can specify which specific behavior the offender doubted to do or felt compelled to do: *act violently* towards the victim (for instance, having planned to kill the victim) or execute a *negative intention*[37] (for instance, robbing someone or threatening the person of the victim). The final question that needs to be answered in this cognitive theme is whether the offender felt compelled to or whether he still doubted to perform this specified behavior. Examples of feeling compelled to are, for instance, a compulsive drive, the thought that one has no other choice than to perform this behavior, the thought that this is the only solution, given the situation, being determined etc. When offenders doubted to perform the specific behavior, one has to indicate whether they were still doubting or whether they made up their mind just before the execution of the violent behavior or intention.

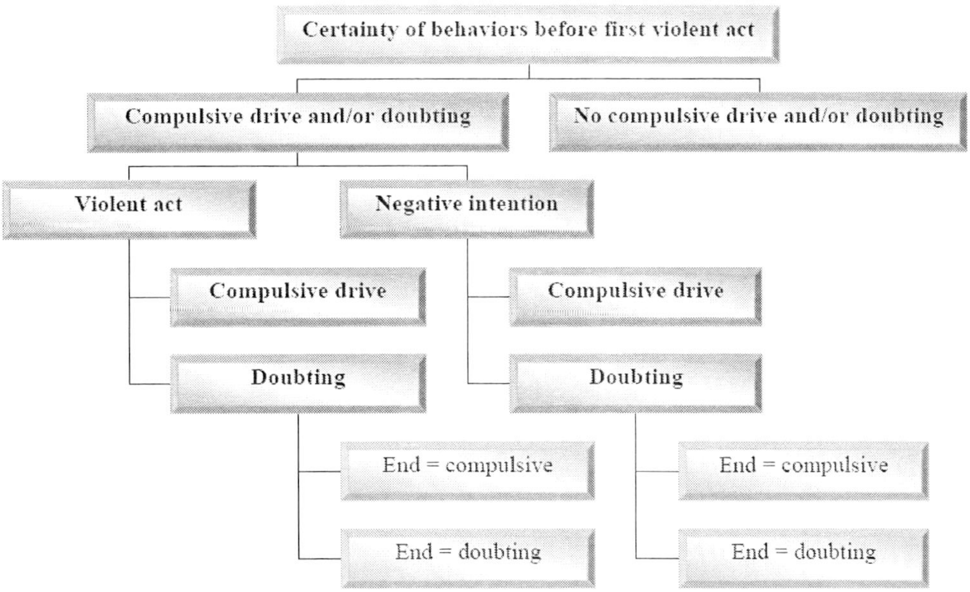

Figure 23. Graphical presentation of certainty of behaviors before the first violent act on the victim.

The certainty with which the offender executed his violent acts towards the person of the victim (see Figure 24) also differentiates between those offenders who felt a *compulsive drive* and those offenders who lacked this feeling of necessity. When offenders felt compelled to harm the victim, one can indicate whether this feeling was already present *at the moment of the first violent act* or whether this feeling only occurred *after the offender had performed his first violent act* towards the victim (for instance, after having hit the victim, the offender

[37] Interpersonal and/or non-interpersonal negative intentions.

thought that there was no way back and that he had to kill the victim in order to avoid going to prison).

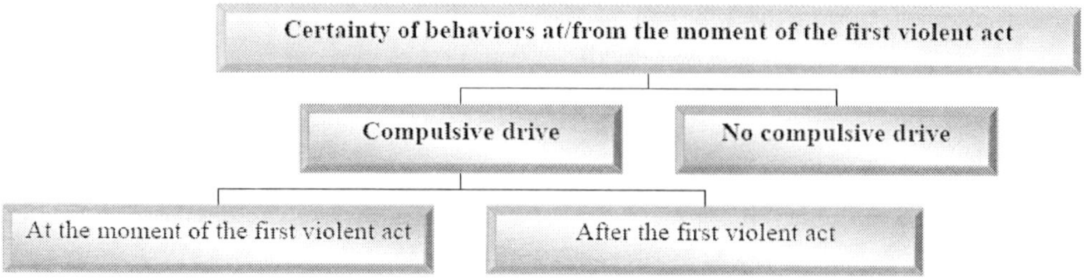

Figure 24. Graphical presentation of certainty of behaviors at/from the moment of the first violent act towards the victim.

The third, and last, theme in describing the possible cognitions of the offender includes the way in which the offender *experienced* the subsequent situations of the homicide process. The first category (see Figure 25) describes whether the offender *knew the accurate condition of the victim* at the moment when he left him. When the offender knew the victim's condition, one can indicate whether the victim was *dead* or not. If the offender did not know the victim's condition or had a wrong idea about the victim's condition (for instance, thinking that the victim was mildly hurt, while the victim, in reality, died shortly after the departure of the offender), one has to indicate whether he thought of the *possibility that the victim would die*. This category has to be coded in the time block "after leaving" the crime scene.

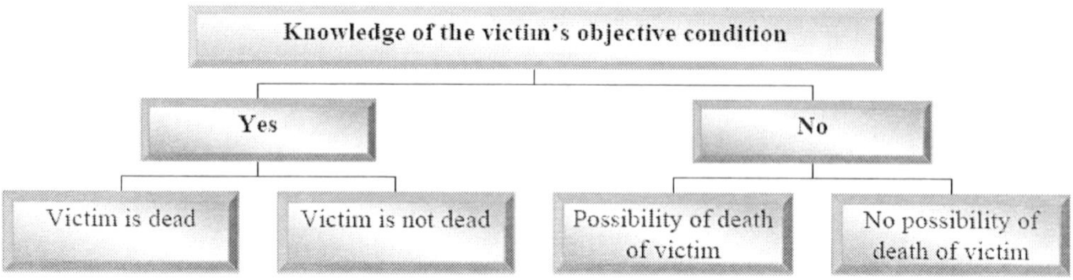

Figure 25. Graphical presentation of knowledge of the objective condition in which the offender left the victim.

The following variables need to be coded in all time blocks, except for the time blocks of the "context" of the offense and "after one night" after the offense since they cover a multitude of situations. These variables indicate whether the situation was *expected by* and/or *clear for* the offender[38], whether he described some *disturbed time experience* (for instance, everything went very fast or a second lasted an eternity) and whether he considered the *victim as being an object or not* (for instance, having experienced the victim as an inanimate object, a doll, etc.). Additionally, the *expected results* of the different situations in the different time blocks need to be indicated, both for what the *offender* expected for himself, as well as what he expected to happen to a *third person*. These expected results can be negative, positive or

[38] A situation could have been unclear if, for instance, someone performed strange behaviors towards the offender, if the offender did not understand what was happening or why someone was behaving in a certain way etc.

ambivalent (in the case of expecting both a positive and negative result for a third person see Figure 26).

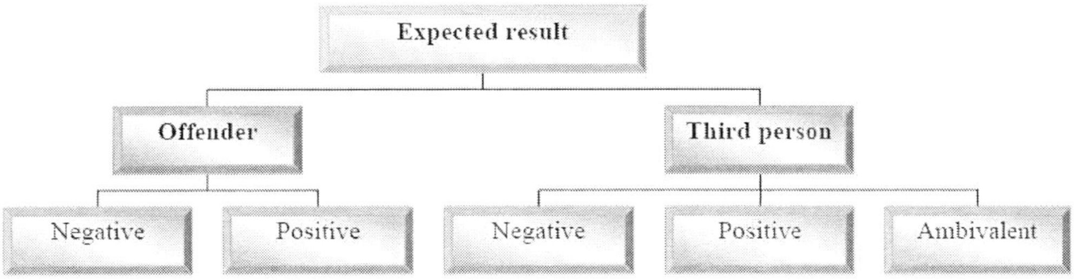

Figure 26. Graphical presentation of possible expected result in the different situations of homicide offending.

The *manner in which the behavior was executed*, on the other hand, only needs to be coded in the time block of the situation preceding the trigger, at the moment of the trigger and in the time block of the interaction between the offender and the victim (see Figure 27).[39] This variable has some resemblances to the degree of planning of the violent act, already covered by the behavioral categories of intention of and agreement with the violent act. The difference between both variables, however, lies in the fact that although an offender could have planned the killing of the victim, the actual execution of the violent act could have been performed in a condition of dissociation or could have been forgotten afterwards (black-out). This variable describes the manner in which the violent behavior is executed, while planning has to do with an a priori mental decision. The execution of the violent act could have been meditated, not meditated or the offender could switch between a meditated and a not meditated state while executing the violent act. When the execution is *meditated* (the behavior is planned, thought off) one needs to consider the difference between those offenders who came to their senses (implying that they did not meditate their violent behavior at a certain point in time) or those who executed the offense in a meditated manner, without ever having lost his senses.

The offenders who did *not meditate* their violent behaviors can be differentiated into those who acted impulsively, those who experienced some dissociative state (for instance, describing the execution of the violent act as being in a dream, as being a robot, as acting on automatic pilot, as having experienced it as an outsider etc.), and those who can not remember the actual violent behaviors (black-out). It's possible that the offender went from one state (for instance, meditated) to another (for instance, not meditated) within a specific time block. In that case, one can indicate the "*mix*" category and can indicate which state followed the other state or, in the case of the offender going through multiple cycles, which was the end state in which the offender executed his violent behaviors.

[39] Note that "mediated" indicates having certain cognitions, while "not meditated" indicates the lack of any cognitions.

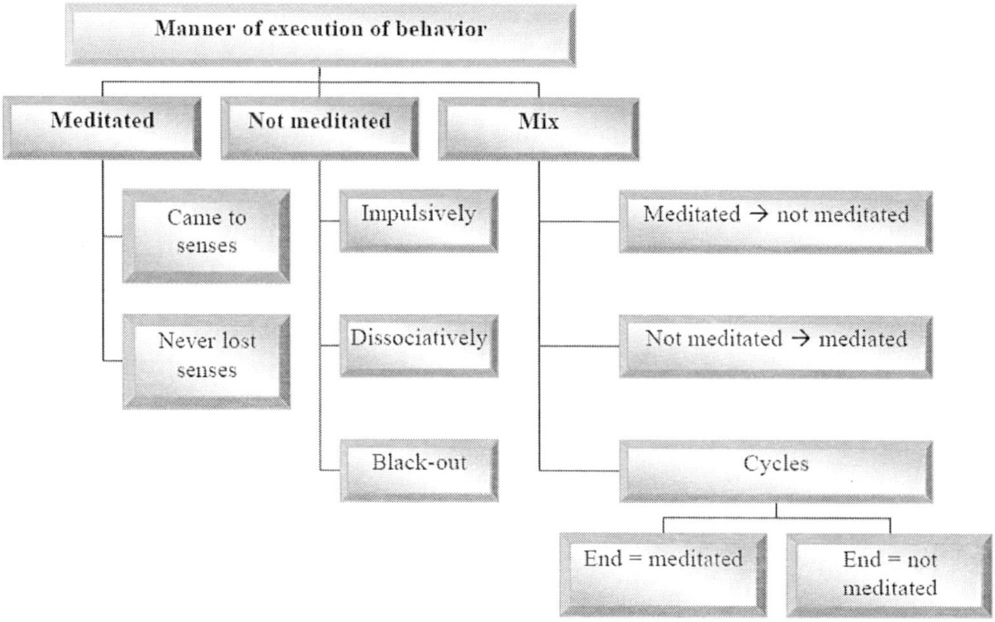

Figure 27. Graphical presentation of possible manners in which the offender could have executed his violent acts.

The final variable describing the way in which the offender experienced the situation, indicates the offender's *evaluation of his violent behaviors* (hence, this variable needs to be coded in the time blocks after the homicidal offending, see Figure 28). The offender could have made *no evaluation*, in the sense that he did not describe any evaluation of his own homicidal behavior (often this is the case when offenders were putting oneself in a condition so that they did not think about the offense anymore) or mentioned that he left the offense behind him, and resumed his usual life. Offenders who made a *positive evaluation* could be differentiated according to whether they made this positive evaluation because the offense had positive consequences for themselves or whether they made a positive evaluation because of the positive consequences for the victim (which is mostly the case when the offender assisted in the victim's suicide).

The offenders who described making a *negative evaluation* when considering their own behavior could also be differentiated according to whether or not they made this evaluation because of the negative consequences for themselves (for instance, going to prison in contrast with those who made a negative evaluation because of moral considerations, considerations of the victim's suffering and/or family, or consideration of the consequences of their behavior for their own family, partner etc.). The latter could also be indicated indirectly by stating that the offender was crying after the homicidal act, that he was feeling guilty, kept reliving the offense etc. The last category includes offenders who were *surprised* about the fact that they acted in a violent way (indicated by statements like "I could not believe I had done that, it was as if the offense had never happened, I tried to repress the thought about the offense since I could not believe it actually happened") or about the manner in which they executed the violent act.

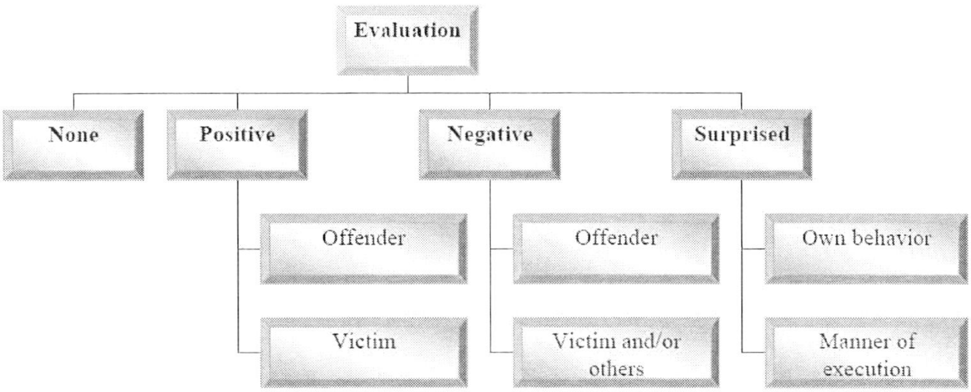

Figure 28. Graphical presentation of offender's possible evaluations of the homicidal act.

Affects in Homicide Offending

The last theme, relevant in describing a homicide offending process, is the offender's affective experience of the situation, covering two broad themes namely his experienced emotions and arousal.

The first theme, the *emotions* the offender experienced, needs to be described both for the *offender*, as well as for the persons at which the emotion is potentially directed (the *victim* and/or a *third person,* see Figure 29). Aside the distinction between *pleasant* and *unpleasant emotions;* how the affect is experienced, the hedonistic value of the emotion [e.g., Barrett and Russell, 1998, 1999; Diener, Smith and Fujita, 1995], this typology also includes the distinction between engaging (or ego-focused) and disengaging (or other-focused) emotions, mentioned in emotion-literature [e.g., Kitayama, Mesquita, and Karawasa, 2006; Markus and Kitayama, 1991]. Disengaging or ego-focused emotions are those emotions that have the internal attributes of the offender as primary referent (his needs, motivations, desires etc.; for instance, feeling angry, pride etc.). Engaging emotions or other-focused emotions, on the other hand, are those emotions that have another person's attributes as primary referent, that are directed at social cohesion. These emotions result from being sensitive to the other, taking the perspective of the other, and attempting to promote interdependency (for instance, love, feeling guilty etc.). When an offender experienced emotions directed at the same third person, that were both pleasant and unpleasant, or that were both engaging and disengaging, one can indicate the "ambivalent" category and can specify this category by indicating which type of emotions the offender experienced. The final distinction in the emotion typology, if the offender experienced an emotion that is directed towards another person, is whether he felt angry towards that person and if the offender experienced an unpleasant emotion that was not directed towards a specific person, whether he was feeling fearful or not.

The second and last variable describes the *arousal* the offender experienced in the different time blocks (see Figure 30). The offender's arousal could have been *high* (for instance, feeling a kick, adrenaline, being very angry, furious, in panic etc.), *low* (for instance, feeling calm, not excited etc.), or the offender could have experienced both high and low levels of arousal in the same time block. If the latter is the case, one can indicate the "*mix*" category and can indicate which state followed the other state, or in the case of the offender going through multiple cycles in which high and low levels of arousal alternated each other in the same time block, which was the end arousal level the offender experienced in that time block.

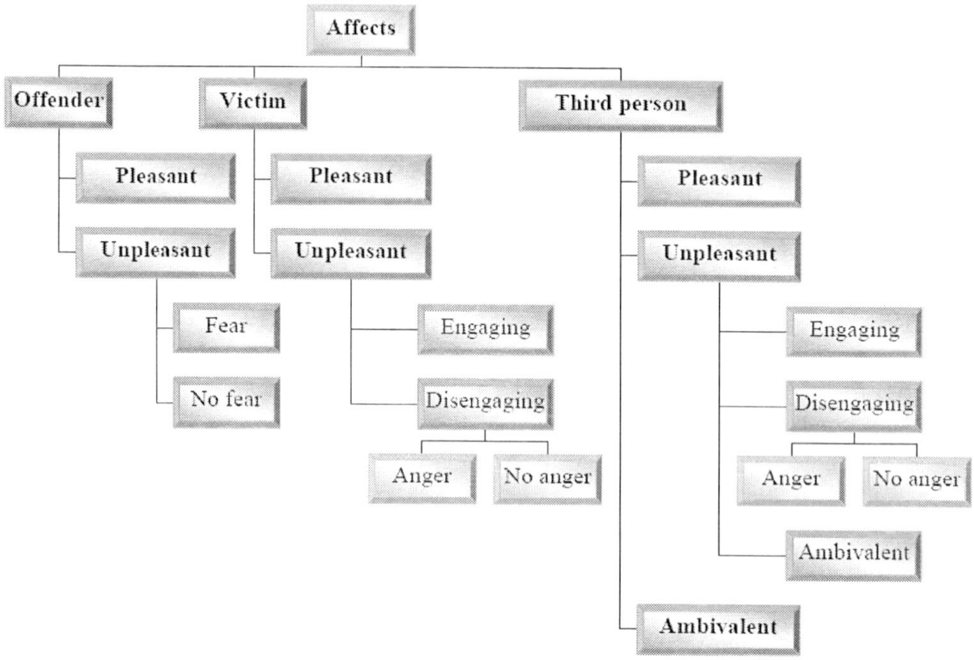

Figure 29. Graphical presentation of possible emotions.

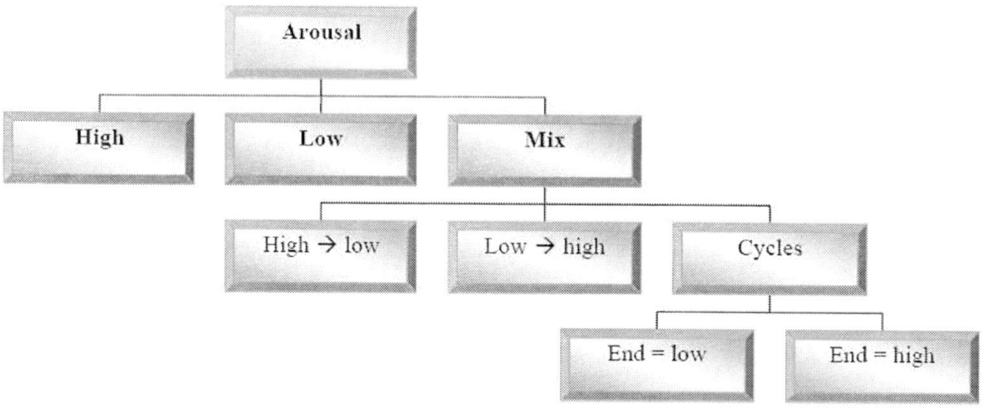

Figure 30. Graphical presentation of experienced levels of arousal.

CONCLUSION

This study provided a preliminary description of both the contextual, behavioral, cognitive and affective concepts, as well as the temporal dimension associated with 48 homicide offenses. When comparing these concepts and time blocks, with those described by Cassar et al. (2003), some differences appear, although both studies used the same data analysis procedure. First of all, the time phases, described by Cassar et al. are less differentiated and consist of only three phases namely the offending history and background, the index offense and post-offense thoughts, feelings, and behaviors. Furthermore, the themes described by Cassar et al. are formulated at a more abstract level and include often compound elements of different domains (for instance, "personal functioning" covered the offenders' internal/emotional and psychological functioning in the days, weeks or months prior to the offense. It included emotional regulation (= behavior), life satisfaction (= affect), relationships with others (= contextual information), self-esteem and belief systems (=cognitions)). Finally, some of the themes, included in the study of Cassar et al., were not always explicitly investigated in our study (for instance, the offender's offending history). This is probably due to the fact that Cassar et al. used a semi-structured interview covering more themes than solely the index offense. The difference with this study is that we asked the offenders to describe all the elements they considered relevant in explaining their offenses to an outsider, without imposing some other topics that needed to be discussed. When offenders did describe a criminal lifestyle, this was coded under "problematic lifestyle, no addiction", but we did not explicitly ask every offender whether he had some previous convictions[40]. Thus, the concepts and time blocks, described in our preliminary study on 48 homicide offenders are more differentiated and are formulated at a more specific level, in comparison with the offense scenario, produced by Cassar et al.

This cohesive model that captures the richness of the original information, however, has some limitations when trying to use these concepts in order to make an offender profile of an unknown homicide offender. Before being able to use these data in practice, a couple of steps needs to be taken namely 1) reducing of the total amount of possible variables; 2) assigning offenders to subtypes in the offense scenario and 3) associating crime scene characteristics with these different subtypes of offenders and associating the latter to offenders' sociodemographic characteristics (see Figure 1).

First of all, since the themes, discussed above, cover a wide range of variables, some procedures have to be developed in order to reduce the total amount of possible variables. This could be achieved 1) by using the most general level of the different themes (for instance, did the offender experience a problematic situation in the preamble of the offense time block?); 2) by introducing some guidelines indicating which element should be considered as being more informative in the offense scenario (introducing a hierarchy in the data) or 3) by performing some data-reduction statistical analysis on the data. Using information at a more general level, however, will inevitably decrease the amount of information provided and hence will lead to less specific predictions. This phenomenon, in which bandwidth is gained at the expense of fidelity has been described by Alison et al. (2002), who stated that examples of offense behaviors at a very general level (for instance, in terms of broad psychological themes underlying offender-victim interactions) may be productive in the sense that one might be able to predict very general information about an offender's background, but that evaluating offense behavior at this aggregate level probably means that profilers will not be able to predict very specific background characteristics. Therefore, we prefer to use the last two methods, depending on the domain under

[40] This information was collected, but only for the description of the sociodemographic characteristics of the participants. Note that the offender's criminal background also has a different function in our model since this is one of the offender characteristics that we will try to predict, based on the offender's position in the offense scenario (see Figure 1).

investigation. In the following paragraphs, the hierarchical rules to reduce the behavioral, situational and cognitive variables will be discussed for each domain separately.

Since the behavioral reactions of an offender in a certain time block can be different and extended over a longer time period, we advice to take the following hierarchy into account when coding the offender's behavior[41]. Given that we are interested in the development of aggressive behavior towards the person of the victim, (more) aggressive reactions and/or behaviors directed towards the victim could be considered as being more relevant in the offense scenario than less or non-aggressive reactions and/or behaviors directed at another person than the victim. Furthermore, behaviors aimed at changing or ameliorating the situation could also be considered as being more relevant than behaviors not aimed at changing or ameliorating the situation. These hierarchical rules provide a chance to differentiate those offenders who reacted, amongst others, negatively on a given situation (potentially in combination with behaviors aimed at changing the situation and/or behaviors not dealing with the situation), from those offenders who, amongst others, dealt with the situation (potentially in combination with behaviors not dealing with the situation but without performing negative or aggressive behaviors), and from those offenders who avoided the situation entirely. Other useful distinctions would be between those offenders who reacted immediately on a given situation and those offenders who were capable of delaying (part of) their negative behavior for a while and between the different manners in which the offender could have reacted to the offense after one night has passed. For the latter, we consider being "occupied" with the offense as standing lower in the hierarchy than being able to "close" the offense mentally and the latter standing lower than putting oneself in such a "condition" that one is not occupied with the offense anymore. This enables us to differentiate those offenders who, amongst others, put oneself in such a condition that they did not think back at the offense anymore, from those offenders who were able to close the offense mentally (after having potentially been occupied with the offense for a while), and from those offenders who remained occupied with the offense the entire time. Since we want to differentiate those offenders who remained occupied with the offense because of personal implications, from those who only remained occupied with the offense because of the severity of the criminal act, we consider "implications" as standing lower in the hierarchy than "severity".

Even in the time blocks describing concrete situations, multiple persons could have performed multiple behaviors towards the offender. In order to reduce the total amount of possible variables, we consider behaviors performed by the victim as being more informative than behaviors performed by another person (that's why the behaviors executed by the victim are often more differentiated than the behaviors executed by a third person). Furthermore, (more) aggressive behaviors directed towards the offender are regarded as being more relevant in the offense scenario than less or non-aggressive behaviors and verbal behaviors directed towards the offender are equally considered to be lower in the hierarchy than manifest behaviors.

Given that offenders could have experienced multiple motivations in a given time block, we decided to apply hierarchical rules, based on the following rationales: not wanting something is considered to be lower in hierarchy than wanting something, which enables us to differentiate those offenders who wanted to obtain something (on top of not wanting the

[41] Information about the application of these hierarchical rules to the different variables, can be obtained from the first author.

present situation) from those offenders whose motivations were restricted to not wanting a certain situation. Furthermore wanting something (additionally) for the future is considered to be higher in the hierarchy than wanting something for the present situation since this would allow differentiating between those offenders who were able to look further than the present situation, and those offenders whose motivations were restricted to the present situation. Since "escape" motivations are restricted to the present situation and do not include the desire to obtain something, they are considered as being lower than wanting to "avoid" a situation, which does not include a desire to obtain something either, but which take the future into consideration. The latter is considered to be lower in hierarchy than "regaining" something since this category also includes a perspective on the future, but at the same time includes the desire to obtain something back, while the latter is considered to be lower, in comparison with wanting to "obtain" something since this includes wanting something that has not been disappeared. When considering the intentions towards the victim, "death" is standing higher in the hierarchical structure than "not death" since the main focus of this research is homicidal behavior. In the rest of this paragraph, the hierarchical rules, for the remaining cognitive components will be discussed. The hierarchical structure, applicable to those offenders who did not meditate their offense (= the manner in which the offense is executed), is based on the different levels of awareness the offender could have experienced, with lower levels of awareness (for instance, impulsively) standing lower in the hierarchical structure than levels indicating full awareness. The evaluation of the offender, on the other hand, differentiates those offenders who made a positive or negative evaluation because of the consequences the offense had for the offender or because of the consequences for the victim and/or other persons.

After having used these hierarchical rules to code the different concepts of the offense scenario, the second step in making an offender profile of an unknown perpetrator is the assignment of each perpetrator to subtypes in the offense scenario. Offenders could be assigned to different groups, according to the results of some cluster analysis method. Offenders could be clustered for each domain separately or could be clustered using all the concepts, discussed above. The latter would provide some indication about possible offender subtypes in terms of types of offense pathways. When clustering offenders for each domain separately, this would give us an indication of possible offender subtypes in terms of cognitions, affects, behaviors, and/or situational characteristics and could provide insight into the way each domain varies across the different offense stadia (for instance, offenders who were already feeling angry in the context of the offense versus those offenders who only became mad at the moment of the trigger of the offense).

The third step consists in making associations both between elements, found at the crime scene and the different subtypes, mentioned above, and between the different subtypes and offender (sociodemographic) characteristics (see Figure 1). Take two concrete examples of crime scenes: in one crime scene, the offender has used much more violence than necessary to kill the victim (overkill) and left the body of the victim undisturbed; in the other crime scene, the offender also used much more violence than necessary to kill the victim, but covered the victim's face with a blanked afterwards. If one investigates the relationship between these behaviors at the two crime scenes and, for instance, the obtained emotional offender typology, one could deduce that in the first crime, the offender ventilated his rage towards the victim, whereas in the other crime scene, the overkill was performed because of some kind of attention for the emotions of the victim (the offender didn't want the victim to suffer too much). Based on the derived emotional category and the obtained associations between these emotional categories and offender characteristics, one can deduce information that could possibly be relevant in a homicide investigation. For instance, in homicides were the offender ventilated his rage towards the victim, there is a higher chance of the victim and the offender having some argument while in homicides were the offender takes the amount of suffering of the victim into account, there is a higher chance of the offender and victim knowing each other, without having a foregoing argument.

The value of this study for profiling homicide offenders lies in the fact that this model describes the diversity found within the offending process and hence captures the essential elements of how offenders commit their criminal acts, including situational influences and affective and cognitive components. The model provides a temporal dimension and could depict the interaction between the cognitive, affective, situational and behavioral components of the offense process. In this way, the model accounts for criticisms on recent offender profiling theories, namely both the lack of an explicit theoretical framework, encompassing all the different concepts, described in the literature and the reliance on a naïve trait perspective [see Crabbé et al., 2008]. The criticism that offender profiling has, mostly, neglected the point of view of the offender is accounted for since we started from offenders' narratives while the division of the different narratives into different time blocks accounts for the criticism that most investigations have neglected the offense as a process that develops over time. Finally, since we remained as closely as possible to the initial data, without making categories that are too abstract, and since we provided every category with an appropriate definition and examples, we hope to minimize the problem of conceptual confusion.

This study, however, also has potential implications reaching further than the domain of offender profiling. The identification of contextual and triggering factors should help clinicians to develop specific strategies in order to prevent offenders from committing other aggressive acts when released. After all, offenders who committed their crime because of some interpersonal conflict are different from offenders who committed their crime because of an intrapersonal problem like money problems. The study pointed to the diversity that exists between homicide offenders. This implies that if one wants to treat an offender, one should regard him as a unique individual, needing a therapy tailored to the individual's particular subtype of offense pathways (in terms of situational characteristics, coping mechanisms, and affective and cognitive components). If suggestions have been made to treat sexual offending differently, depending on different offense pathways [e.g., Bickley and Beech, 2002; Hudson et al., 1999; Ward and Hudson, 1998b; Ward et al.,1998], why should aggression therapy than be equal for all aggressors? Aside the clinical domain, this model could also help law enforcement agencies when interviewing a suspect or offender. The model does not only indicate which elements should be included in the offense narrative, but could also indicate different interviewing strategies, depending on the offense pathway the offender followed when committing his violent crime. Suspects from whom is known, for instance, that the victim harassed his child could be interviewed with an empathic attitude, so that the suspect feels understood and is encouraged to tell the whole story. Offenders who are suspected of using violence, on the other hand, because they needed money, should not be criticized because of their motivation, and interviewers could keep in mind that these offenders have a more instrumental nature, in comparison with the former example, indicating that the suspect would, possibly, only confess when enough evidence is gathered against him. However, before being able to use the model to predict appropriate interviewing strategies, associations between the different types of offense pathways and different types of interviewing strategies should be investigated in future research. The reason why it is important to explicitly ask about all the elements of the offense scenario when interviewing homicide suspects or offenders, is because in Belgium, homicide offenders typically appear before the Assize Court, consisting of a jury of citizens. These persons have to judge the offender and, in our opinion, should be aware of all the relevant offense information, including the offender's narrative before making a judgment that has such dramatic implications.

This study has some limitations that should be considered in future research. First of all, the study is limited both to apprehended offenders and to the amount of participants, indicating the possibility that this study does not cover all homicidal situations and hence, could not be generalized to all homicide offenders. The study, however, did include both male and female offenders as well as offenders who were judged not to be responsible for their criminal acts. Furthermore, the narratives of the offenders are retrospective self-reports, sometimes of events occurring years ago. We tried to tackle this problem by conducting an interview in which the different feelings, behaviors, thoughts and situational characteristics were further explored and by including the possibility of indicating that the offender did not provide the information or that he could not provide the information (by using for instance, the "black-out", "impulsive" or "dissociative" variables). Furthermore, most offenders indicated that the homicide offense was something so exceptional in their lives, that they would not forget it that easily. The third limitation of this study is that the interrater-reliability has not yet been investigated[42] and that the model should be checked for cross-validation by coding other, new homicide narratives to see whether they fit the existing model. In this regard, we must note however, that when the model was checked for it's fit with the last 17 offense narratives, the model was considered to be saturated and well-defined. The final limitation is that the information is only provided by the offenders themselves and that the offenders' correctional files were not yet considered to check the reliability of the offenders' narratives.

REFERENCES

Ainsworth, P. B. (2000). Crime analysis and offender profiling. In P. B. Ainsworth (Ed.), *Psychology and crime: Myths and reality* (pp. 102-120). Harlow: Langford.

Alison, L., Bennell, C., Mokros, A., and Ormerod, D. (2002). The personality paradox in offender profiling: A theoretical review of the processes involved in deriving background characteristics from crime scene actions. *Psychology, Public Policy, and Law, 8*(1), 115-135.

Ault, R. L., and Reese, J. T. (1980, March). A psychological assessment of crime: Profiling. *FBI Law Enforcement Bulletin,* 22-25.

Barrett, L. F., and Russell, J. A. (1998). Independence and bipolarity in the structure of current affect. *Journal of Personality and Social Psychology, 74*(4), 967-984.

Barrett, L. F., and Russell, J. A. (1999). The structure of current affect: Controversies and emerging consensus. *Current Directions in Psychological Science, 8*(1), 10-14.

[42] Interrater-reliability of the data is being investigated at the moment.

behavior therapy: Improving the human condition (pp. 235-259). Plenum Press, New York.

Bickley, J. A., and Beech, A. R. (2002). An investigation of the Ward and Hudson pathways model of the sexual offense process with child abusers. *Journal of Interpersonal Violence, 17*(4), 371-393.

Burgess, A. W., Hartman, C. R., Ressler, R. K., Douglas, J. E., and McCormack, A. (1986). Sexual homicide a motivational model. *Journal of Interpersonal Violence, 1*(3), 251-272.

Bushman, B. J., and Anderson, C. A. (2001). Is it time to pull the plug on the hostile versus instrumental aggression dichotomy? *Psychological Review, 108*(1), 273-279.

Canter, D. (1994). *Criminal shadows: Inside the mind of the serial killer.* HarperCollinsPublishers, Hammersmith: London.

Canter, D. (1995). Psychology of offender profiling. In R. Bull and D. Carson (Eds.), *Handbook of psychology in legal contexts* (pp. 343-355). John Wiley and Sons Ltd.

Canter, D. (2000). Offender profiling and criminal differentiation. *Legal and Criminological Psychology, 5,* 23-46.

Canter, D. (2003). Beyond 'offender profiling': The need for an Investigative Psychology. In D. Carson and R. Bull (Eds.), *Handbook of psychology in legal contexts* (2nd ed., pp. 171-205). John Wiley and Sons, Ltd.

Canter, D. (2004). Offender profiling and investigative psychology. *Journal of Investigative Psychology and Offender Profiling, 1,* 1-15.

Cassar, E., Ward, T., and Thakker, J. (2003). A descriptive model of the homicide process. *Behaviour Change, 20*(2), 76-93.

Cone, J. D. (1997). Issues in functional analysis in behavioral assessment. *Behaviour Research and Therapy, 35*(3), 259-275.

Cornell, D. G., Warren, J., Hawk, G., Stafford, E., Oram, G., and Pine, D. (1996). Psychopathy in instrumental and reactive violent offenders. *Journal of Consulting and Clinical Psychology, 64*(4), 783-790.

Crabbé, A., Decoene, S., and Vertommen, H. (2008). Profiling homicide offenders: A review of assumptions and theories. *Aggression and Violent Behavior, 13*, 88-106.

Demarest, L. (2001). *Het ontwikkelen van een descriptieve theorie van het delictscenario van een partnerdoding* [The development of a descriptive theory of the offense scenario of spousal homicide]. Unpublished master's thesis, Catholic University of Leuven, Leuven.

Diener, E., Smith, H., and Fujita, F. (1995). The personality structure of affect. *Journal of Personality and Social Psychology, 69*(1), 130-141.

Douglas, J. E., and Burgess, A. E. (1986, December). Criminal profiling: A viable investigative tool against violent crime. *FBI Law Enforcement Bulletin,* 9-13.

Douglas, J. E., and Munn, C. (1992a). Modus operandi and the signature aspects of violent crime. In J. E. Douglas, A. W. Burgess, A. G. Burgess, and R. K. Ressler (Eds.), *Crime classification manual* (pp. 259-268). Lexington Books.

Douglas, J. E., and Munn, C. (1992b, February). Violent crime scene analysis: Modus operandi, signature and staging. *FBI Law Enforcement Bulletin,* 1-10.

Douglas, J. E., Burgess, A. W., Burgess, A. G., and Ressler, R. K. (Eds.). (1992). *Crime classification manual.* Lexington Books, New York.

Douglas, J. E., Ressler, R. K., Burgess, A. W., and Hartman, C. R. (1986). Criminal profiling from crime scene analysis. *Behavioral Sciences and the Law, 4*(4), 401-421.

Ferster, C. B. (1965). Classification of behavioral pathology. In L. Krasner and L. P. Ullmann (Eds.), *Research in behavior modification* (pp. 6-26). Holt, Rinehart and Winston, Inc.

Hayes, S. N. (1990). Behavioral assessment of adults. In G. Goldstein and M. Hersen (Eds.), *Handbook of psychological assessment* (2nd ed., pp. 423-463). Pergamon Press.

Hazelwood, R. R., and Douglas, J. E. (1980, April). The lust murderer. *FBI Law Enforcement Bulletin,* 18-22.

Hazelwood, R. R., and Napier, M. R. (2004). Crime scene staging and its detection. *International Journal of Offender Therapy and Comparative Criminology, 48*(6), 744-759.

Hermans, D., Eelen, P., and Orlemans, H. (2007). *Inleiding tot de gedragstherapie* [Introduction to behavioral therapy]. Bohn Stafleu Van Loghum, Houten.

Holmes, R. M., and De Burger, J. (1988). *Serial murder.* Sage Publications, Inc.

Holmes, R. M., and Holmes, S. T. (1996). *Profiling violent crimes: An investigative tool* (2nd ed.). Sage Publications, Inc.

Homant, R. J., and Kennedy, D. B. (1998). Psychological aspects of crime scene profiling: Validity research. *Criminal Justice and Behavior, 25*(3), 319-343.

Hudson, S. M., Ward, T., and McCormack, J. C. (1999). Offense pathways in sexual offenders. *Journal of Interpersonal Violence, 14*(8), 779-798.

Ishaq, W. (1996). The social relevance of applied behavior analysis and psychological intervention strategies. In J. R. Cautela and W. Ishaq (Eds.), *Contemporary issues in* Kitayama, S., Mesquita, B., and Karasawa, M. (2006). Cultural affordances and emotional experience: Socially engaging and disengaging emotions in Japan and the United States. *Journal of Personality and Social Psychology, 91*(5), 890-903.

Kocsis, R. N., Cooksey, R. W., and Irwin, H. J. (2002). Psychological profiling of sexual murders: An empirical model. *International Journal of Offender Therapy and Comparative Criminology, 46*(5), 532-554.

Markus, H. R., and Kitayama, S. (1991). Culture and the self: Implications for cognition, emotions, and motivation. *Psychological Review, 98*(2), 224-253.

Meyer, C. B. (2000, January). Introduction to criminal profiling. *Basel University Law Student's Journal,* 1-11.

Mischel, W. (1999). Personality coherence and dispositions in a cognitive-affective personality systems (CAPS) approach. In D. Cervone and Y. Shoda (Eds.), *The coherence of personality: Social-cognitive bases of consistency, variability, and organization* (pp. 37-60). The Guilford Press, New York.

Mischel, W., and Shoda, Y. (1995). A cognitive-affective system theory of personality: Reconceptualizing situations, dispositions, dynamics, and invariance in personality structure. *Psychological Review, 102*(2), 246-268.

Mulkers, J. (2002). *Offender Profiling: Analyse van een forensische techniek* [Offender profiling: Analysis of a forensic technique]. Police, Policy and Techniques.

Nelson, R. O., and Hayes, S. C. (1981). Nature of behavioral assessment. In M. Hersen and A. S. Bellack (Eds.), *Behavioral assessment: A practical handbook* (pp. 3-37). Pergamon Press.

Petee, T. A., and Jarvis, J. (2000). Analyzing violent serial offending. *Homicide Studies, 4*(3), 211-218.

Polaschek, D. L. L., Hudson, S. M., Ward, T., and Siegert, R. J. (2001). Rapists' offence processes: A preliminary descriptive model. *Journal of Interpersonal Violence, 16*(6), 523-544.

Ressler, R. K., Burgess, A. W., and Douglas, J. E. (1988). *Sexual homicides patterns and motives.* Lexington Books: New York.

Ressler, R. K., Burgess, A. W., Douglas, J. E., Hartman, C. R., and D'Agostino, R. B. (1986). Sexual killers and their victims: Identifying patterns through crime scene analysis. *Journal of Interpersonal Violence, 1*(3), 288-308.

Salfati, C. G. (2000). The nature of expressiveness and instrumentality in homicide. *Homicide Studies, 4*(3), 265-293.

Salfati, C. G., and Bateman, A. L. (2005). Serial homicide: An investigation of behavioural consistency. *Journal of Investigative Psychology and Offender Profiling, 2*, 121-144.

Shoda, Y., and Leetiernan, S. (2002). What remains invariant? Finding order within a person's thoughts, feelings, and behaviors across situations. In D. Cervone and W. Mischel (Eds.), *Advances in personality science* (pp. 241-270). The Guilford Press, New York.

Spiegler, M. D., and Guevremont, D. C. (1998). *Contemporary behavior therapy* (3rd ed.). Brooks/Cole Publishing Company.

Strauss, A., and Corbin, J. (1998). *Basics of qualitative research: Techniques and procedures for developing grounded theory* (2nd ed.). Sage publications: Thousand Oaks, California.

Turvey, B. (1998, January). Deductive criminal profiling: Comparing applied methodologies between inductive and deductive criminal profiling techniques. *Knowledge Solutions Library.* Retrieved May, 25, 2000 from http://www.corpus-delicti.com/Profiling_law.html.

Turvey, B. (2000, March). The estate of Sam Sheppard v. state of Ohio. Retrieved September, 6, 2002 from http://www.corpus-delicti.com/sheppard.html.

Turvey, B. E. (Ed.). (2003). *Criminal profiling: An introduction to behavioral evidence analysis* (2nd ed.). Academic Press: London.

Vanhumbeeck, T. (2004). *Delictscenario's bij plegers van een passioneel delict, een validering* [Offense scenario's in passionate crime offenders, a validation]. Unpublished master's thesis, Catholic University of Leuven, Leuven, Belgium.

Ward, T., and Hudson, S. M. (1998a). The construction and development of theory in the sexual offending area: A metatheoretical framework. *Sexual Abuse: A Journal of Research and Treatment, 10*(1), 47-63.

Ward, T., and Hudson, S. M. (1998b). A model of the relapse process in sexual offenders. *Journal of Interpersonal Violence, 13*(6), 700-725.

Ward, T., Hudson, S. M., and Keenan, T. (1998). A self-regulation model of the sexual offence process. *Sexual Abuse: A Journal of Research and Treatment, 10*(2), 141-157.

In: Homicide: Trends, Causes and Prevention
Editor: Randal B. Toliver and Ulrich R. Coyne

ISBN 978-1-60741-625-8

Chapter 2

HOMICIDAL AND SUICIDAL SHARP FORCE FATALITIES: A STUDY OVER 20 YEARS

***Christophe Brunel*[1], *Christophe Fermanian*[2], *Michel Durigon*[1] and *Geoffroy Lorin de la Grandmaison*[1]**

[1]Department of Forensic Medicine and Pathology,
Raymond Poincaré Hospital, AP-HP,
104 Boulevard Raymond Poincaré, 92380 Garches, France
[2]Clinical Research Unit, Ambroise Paré Hospital, AP-HP,
9 avenue Charles de Gaulle,
92100 Boulogne, France

1. INTRODUCTION

The determination of the manner of death, especially the differentiation between homicide and suicide, has always been a major issue in common forensic activity. This is particularly true about violent deaths by firearms wounds and sharp force wounds. Concerning the determination of manner of death, a lot of studies about large series of fatal firearms wounds have been published in forensic literature (624 cases [1], 288 cases [2], 717 cases [3], 107 cases [4], 132 cases [5], 140 cases [6]). Nevertheless, only a few studies about large series of fatal sharp force wounds and differentiation between homicide and suicide have been performed (120 cases [7], 279 cases [8], 70 cases [9]).

This discrepancy is explained by the low number of suicide cases in sharp force fatalities (17 suicides out of 120 sharp force deaths for Gill and al. [7], 65 sharp force suicides in a 10-years study for Fukube and al. [10], 105 suicides out of 279 sharp force deaths for Karlsson [8], 17 suicides out of 70 sharp force deaths for Scolan and al. [9], 51 sharp force suicides on a 20-years study for Byard and al. [11], 65 sharp force suicides on a 29-years study for Karger and al. [12]). This hinders to easily statistically compare homicide and suicide groups in a population of sharp force deaths, unlike firearms fatalities in which homicides and suicides are common. Moreover, studies about sharp force suicides are rare and often deal with a few cases. For instance, 4 hara-kiri suicide cases [13], 8 sharp force suicide cases [14], 10 suicidal decapitations [15], 9 sharp force suicide cases [16]. On contrary, studies about firearms homicides are frequent and often deal with larger numbers of cases. For instance, 141 cases for Rodge and al. [17], 35 cases for Inoue and al. [18], 142 cases for Ormstad and al. [19]. Thus it seems to be easier to collect statistically comparable populations (homicide *versus* suicide) to study the manner of death in firearms death than in sharp force deaths.

However, sharp force injuries remain a frequent cause of violent deaths. For instance, with the NVDRS (National Violent Death Reporting System), a study performed in 16 states of the USA out of 15,962 violent deaths during the year 2005 shows that 744 of them (4,7 %) were due to sharp force injuries [20]. Also, during the year 2003, according to French authorities mentioned by Scolan and al. [9], 31 % of all homicides have been perpetrated using sharp objects, and 42 % with firearms.

All these observations have led us to perform a retrospective and comparative study based on autopsy findings of sharp force fatalities to determinate relevant parameters in order to differentiate homicide cases and suicide cases for this type of death.

2. Materials and Methods

2.1. Generality

We have performed a retrospective and comparative study on 118 sharp force fatalities. All collected cases have undergone a forensic autopsy in the Department of Forensic Medicine and Pathology, Raymond Poincaré Hospital, Garches, France.

Out of those 118 cases, 70 homicides and 48 suicides were included. In order to avoid bias, cases of each group were consecutive and selected with regard to inclusion and exclusion criteria. Nevertheless, in sharp force deaths, suicide cases are much rarer than homicide cases. Thus the 70 homicide cases have been collected out of a 8-years period of time (from May 2000 to June 2008) whereas the 48 suicide cases were collected out of a 22-years period of time (from May 1986 to June 2008).

The 118 cases have been selected from 6,421 forensic autopsies performed in the Department of Forensic Medicine and Pathology, Raymond Poincaré Hospital, during the period of time between May 1986 and June 2008.

2.2. Inclusion and Exclusion Criteria

2.2.1. Inclusion Criteria

Only cases for which the manner of death (homicide or suicide) was known after complete forensic investigations were included. Other cases (accident or undetermined cause of death) were excluded.

In this study we only considered deaths strictly imputable to sharp force injuries. A death was considered as strictly imputable to sharp force wounds when fatal sharp force wounds were present and when the death could not be explained by another cause than these wounds. Moreover, the anterior pathological status of the deceased was taken into consideration to attribute the death to the sharp force injuries. For instance, multiple superficial cut wounds resulting on a moderate haemorrhage can explain the death of a person suffering from severe ischemic heart disease, whereas the same wounds can not explain the death of a young and healthy subject.

Complex suicides are widely described in forensic literature [21-27]. These deaths have been included in this study when the sharp force wounds could alone explain the death and when no other mean used could explain the death alone. However a complex suicide was not included in this study when the sharp force wounds alone could not explain the death or when another mean used could explain the death alone (cf. 2.2.2. Exclusion criteria).

Sharp objects mentioned in this study were all manually handled objects that could be used as a dangerous weapon and cause wounds such as stabs, cuts or blunts. Thus not only weapon-type sharp objects were included (such as dagger, sword, sabre, bayonet…), also common use-type sharp objects were included (such as knives, cutters, razor blades, choppers, axes…).

At last we took into consideration homicide-suicide cases (homicide followed by the suicide of the murderer) which are commonly described in forensic literature [28-34]. Such cases were included provided that the homicide and the suicide were imputable to sharp force injuries, even if the objects used for each were different.

2.2.2. Exclusion Criteria

As well as deaths strictly imputable to sharp force injuries were included, fatalities not strictly imputable to this kind of wounds were excluded from this study. For instance, a death could be not directly imputable to sharp force injuries when the victim of a sharp force assault benefited from intensive cares to treat sharp force wounds, and died from complications of intensive cares and not from the evolution of wounds.

Especially for homicides, it was possible to find cases with sharp force injuries that could not explain the death alone, associated with other violent traumatic lesions (such as firearm wounds, strangulation, crushing…) that could explain the death alone. These cases were excluded as well.

Also for suicides, complex suicide cases for which sharp force injuries could not explain the death alone were excluded and complex suicide cases for which the associated traumatic lesions could explain the death alone were excluded.

Cases in which the state of the body could cause difficulties in performing the autopsy or analysing autopsy findings were excluded. This concerns carbonized bodies, putrefied bodies, bodies showing fragmentation and skeletons.

At last, circumstances of a violent death can be accidents, even for sharp force fatalities, as it has been described in forensic literature yet [35]. These cases were excluded from this study. Also cases for which the manner of death remained undetermined after complete forensic investigations were excluded.

2.3. Studied Parameters

For each case included in this study, ten parameters have been analysed.

2.3.1. Demographic Parameters

They are victim's age and gender.

2.3.2. Number of Wounds

For each case the total number of wounds was recorded without distinguishing the anatomical sites of them. Also when several sharp objects had been used, all wounds caused by all objects were counted at the same time. This means that associated traumatic wounds (defence, violence or hesitation) were counted as well, provided that they had been caused by a sharp object. Nevertheless associated traumatic wounds were not counted here when they had not been caused by a sharp object.

2.3.3. Type of Wounds

Three patterns of sharp force wounds are commonly described, that is stab wounds, cut wounds and blunt wounds. These three types of wounds can be simultaneously described on a single body or on a single lesion.

This manner of describing lesions reflects the mechanism used with the sharp object. Actually there are three different ways to cause damages with a sharp object to skin or viscera. For instance a kitchen knife causes stab wounds or cut wounds or both of them; a cutter causes cut wounds; a chopper causes cut wounds or blunt wounds or both of them. Studying types of wounds allows to conceive mechanisms of wounds and can confirm or invalidate the possible use of a sharp object.

This parameter must be clearly isolated from the parameter "type of objects used" (cf. 2.3.7.). Indeed one single mechanism is not specific of one single class of sharp objects, one single class of sharp objects can include objects that can be used with several different mechanisms, one single sharp object can often be used with several different mechanisms. For instance among tools, a screwdriver causes stab wounds, an axe causes cut and blunt wounds, a cutter causes cut wounds.

2.3.4. Anatomical Site of Wounds

Nine anatomical sites were described to classify entrance wounds of sharp objects (cf. figures 1 and 2).

2.3.4.1. Site 1: head (including scalp, face, ears, eyes, nose, mouth).
2.3.4.2. Site 2: anterior part of the neck.
2.3.4.3. Site 3: nape of the neck.
2.3.4.4. Site 4: anterior part of the thorax.
2.3.4.5. Site 5: anterior part of the abdomen.
2.3.4.6. Site 6: back.
2.3.4.7. Site 7: both hands.
2.3.4.8. Site 8: anterior parts of both forearms (including anterior parts of both elbows and both wrists).
2.3.4.9. Site 9: the four limbs, excluding sites 7 and 8.

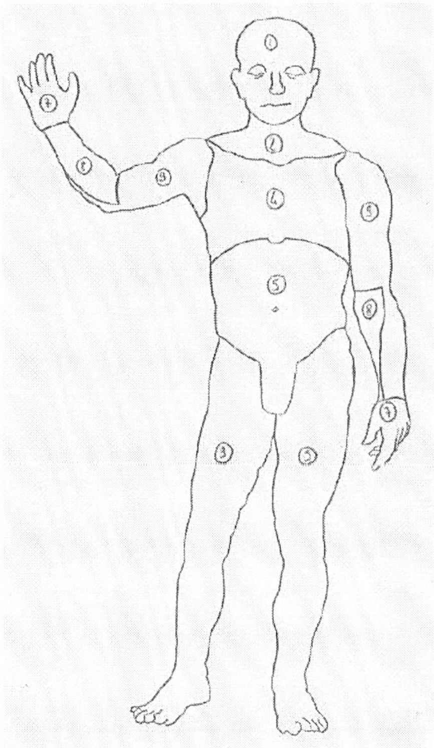

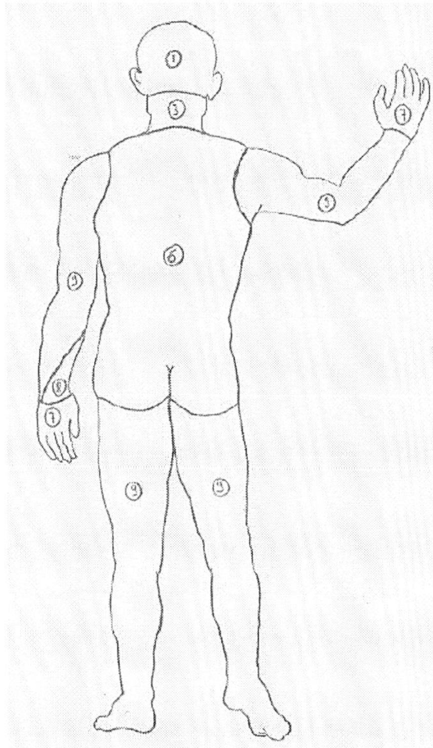

Figures 1. (left) and 2 (right): anatomical sites, numbered as described in the text.

2.3.5. Bone and Cartilage Wounds

The presence or the absence of bone or cartilage wounds associated with skin and viscera wounds was studied. These wounds were considered present when they had been caused by the sharp object, or by an associated mechanism (violence, fall, hesitation, defence). However these lesions were consider absent when they had been caused by a iatrogenic mechanism (for instance rib fractures due to external cardiac massage). Only the pathologist's point of view was used to determine if these wounds were iatrogenic or not.

Bone wounds were mainly ribs and sternum wounds. But every other bone wounds were described the same way (skull, limbs, vertebra…). Moreover, in order to simplify the description of bone wounds, cartilage wounds (rib cartilages for instance) were considered the same value as bone wounds.

2.3.6. Longitudinal Axis of Stab Wounds Located at the Anterior Part of the Trunk

Here we consider the direction of stab wounds in the frontal plane. Thus at the anterior wall of the thorax, a wound was "horizontal" if its longitudinal axis was horizontal or runs parallel with ribs, that is with a up and left direction for wounds located at the left part of the chest, and up and right direction for wounds located at the right part of the chest. A wound was "vertical" if its longitudinal axis was vertical or runs perpendicular with ribs, that is with a up and left direction for wounds located at the right part of the chest, and up and right direction for wounds located at the left part of the chest.

At the anterior wall of the abdomen, a wound was "horizontal" if its longitudinal axis is horizontal or makes an angle lower than 45° with the axial plane. A wound is "vertical" if its longitudinal axis was vertical or makes an angle lower than 45° with the sagittal plane.

2.3.7. Type of Objects Used

In cases where the object used was known, it was classified among both of these categories: the "non-weapon type objects" and the "weapon type objects". Rarely, in a single case, several objects of a single category can be used, or even objects of both categories. Sometimes this parameter is not available, which hindered comparing patterns of wounds and objects used. Attention has to be paid on the fact that this parameter was different from the parameter number 3 described above (cf. 2.3.3. Type of wounds). Indeed a single category can contain objects with different traumatic mechanisms (stab, cut, blunt). For instance, a screwdriver, a chopper, a cutter and a hammer belong to the same category ("non-weapon type objects"), whereas patterns of wounds they make are different (respectively stab wounds, cut and blunt wounds, cut wounds and blunt wounds).

Actually the classification of objects made in this study is theoretical. Its principal aim was to gather objects into separated categories in order to perform statistical analysis.

2.3.7.1. "Non-weapon type objects"

Here we consider all objects of common usage which are misused as sharp force items. In this category can be found kitchen utensils (such as kitchen knife, chopper…), tools (such as saw, hammer, screwdriver, cutter…), and washstand items (such as nail scissors, razor blade…).

2.3.7.2."Weapon type objects"

Here we consider all sharp force objects in the basic sense of the word, that is objects made and used in order to hurt or kill. Patterns of wounds made by this kind of objects have sometimes been studied in forensic literature [36 - 38], whereas this category of objects is less often used than non-weapon type objects [8].

2.3.8. Injury Severity Score (ISS)

To calculate the ISS another score is needed, the Abbreviated Injury Score (AIS).

2.3.8.1. AIS [39]

From early sixties was needed a standardization system about classification of car crash wounds and gravity of car crash wounds. The first version of the AIS was published in 1971. This basic version only treated of lesions due to public highway injuries. Several editions have then improved this first version, among which most the major ones were these of 1976 and 1980. The 1985 version included the classification of penetrating wounds (such as firearm injuries and sharp force injuries), and new descriptions of wounds were developed, especially about thorax, abdomen, vessels and skin injuries. Then the 1990 version brought many improvements, such as a more precise classification of penetrating wounds, a description of paediatric wounds, a greater list of wounds, a numeric code for each wound, a classification of external wounds, a better description of cerebral wounds. The AIS version used in this study is the 1998 edition. The newest version was edited in 2005.

Henceforth the AIS has become a comprehensive and widely used tool for public health research and medical studies about injuries, whatever their origin is. Nevertheless, the successive modifications of the AIS have always respected three major principles. First, the AIS is founded on anatomic lesions and not on physiologic parameters. This means each lesion of a victim has one single gravity AIS, in opposition to physiologic scales in which a lesion can have different gravity scores at different times. Second, AIS values quantify wounds but not consequences of wounds. This means the AIS assesses the specific gravity of a lesion but not incapacities due to this lesion. Third, the AIS is not only founded on the vital risk of each lesion. It also takes into account moderate and minor wounds that do not directly threaten survival. This means it takes into account, for each lesion, the vital risk, but also the diagnosis certainty and the efficiency of the healing, with or without medical therapy.

The numeric code to describe lesions is composed of seven numerals [39]:

- the first numeral identifies the anatomical site:
  1. head
  2. face
  3. neck
  4. thorax
  5. abdomen
  6. spine
  7. upper limbs
  8. lower limbs
  9. external lesions

- the second numeral gives information about the type of anatomical structure:
  1. the whole anatomical site
  2. vessels
  3. nerves
  4. organs (including muscles and ligaments)
  5. bones (including joints)
  6. duration of loss of consciousness (head trauma)

- the third and fourth numerals identify the specific anatomical structure or, concerning external lesions, the type of injuries:
  - whole body:
  - 02. dermabrasion
  - 04. blunt
  - 06. wound
  - 08. wrench
  - 10. amputation
  - 20. burn
  - 30. crushing
  - 40. hand skin removal
  - 50. injury without other data
  - 60. penetrating injury

- 90. non mechanical trauma
- head – duration of loss of consciousness:
- 02. duration of loss of consciousness
- 04. }
- 06. } level of consciousness
- 08. }
- 10. concussion
- spine:
- 02. cervical spine
- 04. thoracic spine
- 06. lumbar spine
- vessels, nerves, organs, bones joints:
- 02 and following

• the fifth and sixth numerals identify the level of a lesion in a single anatomical site and in a single anatomical structure:
  - 02. and following

• the seventh numerals gives the AIS value:
  1. minor gravity
  2. moderate gravity
  3. serious gravity
  4. severe gravity
  5. critical gravity
  6. maximum gravity
  7. no gravity level can be assessed (not enough medical data)

2.3.8.2. ISS [39]

This score is calculated with AIS values of the most severe lesions: it equals the sum of the square AIS of the three most severely injured anatomical sites [39]. Since the 1990 version of the AIS, and notably in the 1998 version which is used in the present study, the ISS is useful to evaluate, not only injuries due to public highway accidents, but also penetrating wounds, among which sharp force injuries. Thus it seemed useful to study the existence of a statistically significant link between the manner of a death due to sharp force injuries (homicide or suicide) and the ISS value showed by victims of such injuries.

To calculate ISS scores of each case included in this study, AIS values concerning "associated lesions" were taken in account, whenever they were present and whenever they concerned one of the three most injured anatomical sites described for the ISS (cf. 2.3.9. associated lesions).

The six anatomical sites used to calculate the ISS with the AIS are the following ones:

1. Head and Neck. Lesions of the head and the neck include cerebral lesions, cervical spine lesions, skull fractures and cervical spine fractures.
2. Face. Lesions of the face include lesions of the mouth, the ears, the eyes, the nose and the bones of the face.

3. Thorax. Lesions of the thorax include lesions of internal thoracic organs, of the diaphragm, of the thorax wall and of the thoracic spine.
4. Abdomen and pelvis. Lesions of the abdomen and of the pelvis include lesions of internal abdominal and pelvic organs, of the abdominal wall, of the lumbar spine and of the sacrum.
5. Limbs. Lesions of limbs include wrenches, fractures, dislocations and amputations, except from lesions of the spine, the skull, the bones of the face and the thoracic wall.
6. External (the whole skin surface). External lesions include wounds, blunts, abrasions and burns, whatever their location on the skin surface.

Anatomical sites used to calculate the ISS differed from anatomical sites used to describe the AIS. For instance, the site "spine" in the AIS is divided in three sites in the ISS: the cervical spine is included in the region "head and neck", the thoracic spine in the region "thorax", and the lumbar spine in the region "abdomen and pelvis".

ISS values vary from 1 to 75, 1 representing the minimal gravity score, 75 representing the maximal gravity score. A score of 75 can be reached by two ways. On one hand three lesions with an AIS of 5 each ($5^2 + 5^2 + 5^2 = 75$), on the other hand one single lesion with an AIS of 6. As soon as a lesion with an AIS of 6 is described, the corresponding ISS is automatically of 75.

The ISS can not be calculated in cases where at least one lesion shows an AIS of 9 (not enough medical data to assess the level of gravity). This shows the necessity to provide to the forensic pathologist complete medical information about each case.

2.3.9. Associated Lesions

First the presence or the absence of associated lesions had to be evaluated. Associated lesions are traumatic lesions that are made contemporary to main lesions which are due to sharp force objects and are responsible for death. These associated lesions, when present, were more or less severe in each case, could have participated or not in the mechanism of death, but never could be directly responsible for death (cf. 2.2.2. exclusion criteria).

These lesions had to be evaluated with the AIS and had to be taken into account to calculate the ISS.

When present, the associated lesions were gathered into four categories: defence wounds, hesitation wounds, violence wounds, and fall wounds. In each case, such lesions were considered present only if the pathologist who had performed the autopsy mentioned them in his medico-legal report.

2.3.9.1. Associated Violence Wounds

Wounds found in this category were most often superficial skin lesions such as abrasions and contusions. More rarely they were severe traumatic lesions, such as bone fractures or intra-cranial haematoma due to strong hits.

In each case these violence wounds were evaluated with the AIS and taken into account to calculate the ISS.

Traumatic associated lesions due to resuscitation cares were not considered as violence associated lesions, even if they were sometimes responsible for severe wounds, such as multiple ribs fractures or sternum fractures for instance.

2.3.9.2. Associated Defence Wounds

They are wounds made by the perpetrator of an assault when the victim tries to protect oneself. Typically, the victim of a sharp force assault tries to protect oneself against the sharp object by opposing upper limbs or by gripping the weapon [40]. In the first case (opposition of upper limbs) were found stab, cut or blunt wounds at the medial part of forearms and hands. In the second case (gripping of the weapon) were found cut wounds located at the anterior part of hands. More rarely other lesions were described, such as, for instance, wounds located at lower limbs when a victim laid down on the ground tried to protect oneself with these limbs.

These lesions rarely modify the ISS value because they are most often superficial wounds.

2.3.9.3. Associated Fall Lesions

They were lesions due to the fall of the victim from his own height on the ground or on any over tough surface. They could often be considered as violence lesions when they were located at the head. At this level, to make the difference between associated violence and fall lesions was described in the medico-legal literature the "hat trim line" [41-43]. According to these studies, wounds located above this line are more often violence wounds and these located below this line are more often fall wounds. Nevertheless this point of view is not widely accepted and the rule of the hat trim line is not widely used because it can be the source of mistakes. Thus only the medico-legal report was used in this study to distinguish fall and violence wounds.

As violence wounds, associated fall wounds could sometimes greatly influence the ISS value, for instance when the victim fell on the head and suffered from intra-cranial haematoma.

2.3.9.4.Associated Hesitation Wounds

They are non lethal superficial lesions. Most frequently they show the same global pattern, are located at the same anatomical sites, and are made by the same sharp object as principal wounds. Actually they represent tries of the object with the same movement used to carry out the main lesions. These associated hesitation wounds are widely described in the forensic literature, especially concerning suicides [7, 10, 11, 13, 14]. However, such lesions have already been described in homicide cases [44].

Hesitation wounds rarely influence the ISS value because they are superficial and located at the same sites as main lesions.

2.4. Statistical Analysis

Two kinds of analysis have been performed: a uni-variate analysis and a multi-variate analysis. These two types of analysis are often used in the forensic literature concerning the same kind of studies [7-9, 45].

2.4.1. Uni-Variate Analysis

Its aim was to study statistical links between the qualitative binary studied variable (homicide *versus* suicide) and each of the ten parameters described above. This link has been studied using logistic regression or, when the variable was unstable in logistic regression, the Fisher exact test.

Thus the following variables have been studied using logistic regression only: "age", "gender", "number of wounds", "bone and cartilage wounds", "longitudinal axis of stab wounds located at the anterior part of the trunk", "ISS", "square root of ISS". In every logistic regression analysis, modalities of the variable were compared with the qualitative binary studied variable "homicide *versus* suicide".

The following variables have been studied using the Fisher exact test only: "type of wounds" and "associated lesions".

The following variables have been studied with both logistic regression and Fisher exact test: "anatomical sites of wounds" and "type of object used".

In every statistical analysis the significance level was 5%.

2.4.2. Multi-Variate Analysis

This statistical analysis followed the uni-variate analysis. The multi-variate analysis allowed to simultaneously compare the qualitative binary studied variable with several co-variables. Th3.e number of co-variables that could be used depended especially on the number of cases included in the study and on the number of missing data for each parameter.

Moreover, for the multi-variate analysis a logistic regression is commonly used, but the Fisher exact test can also be used. Co-variables simultaneously included in the multi-variate analysis are variables significantly linked with the studied variable (homicide *versus* suicide) in the uni-variate analysis. Co-variables finally taken into account for the multi-variate analysis are variables that remain stable after testing this multi-variate model. At last in this study only two co-variables could be simultaneously compared with the studied variable in the multi variate analysis: "ISS" (or "square root of ISS") and "associated lesions".

3. RESULTS

3.1. Population

All the 118 cases of sharp force fatalities included in this study were autopsies performed in the Department of Forensic Medicine and Pathology, Raymond Poincaré Hospital, Garches, France, from May 1986 to June 2008, selected from 6,421 forensic autopsies for this period of time. The table 1 shows the number of medico-legal autopsies, the number of suicides, the number of homicides and the number of sharp force fatalities for each year of this period.

The 70 homicides of this study were recruited out of a period from May 2000 to June 2008, which is 8 years. This represents a mean number of 8.75 sharp force homicides per year, considering exclusion criteria of the study. Nevertheless, the 48 sharp force suicides of this study were recruited out of a period from May 1986 to June 2008, which is 22 years. This represents a mean number of 2.18 sharp force suicides per year, considering exclusion criteria of the study. This means sharp force suicide cases are much rarer than sharp force homicide cases.

Table 1. Number of forensic autopsies, homicide, suicide and sharp force fatalities in the Department of Forensic Medicine and Pathology, Raymond Poincaré Hospital, Garches, France, from May 1986 to June 2008. (NA: non available data)

Period	Forensic autopsies	Suicides	Homicides	Sharp force fatalities
2008 (6 months)	225	48	12	7
2007	482	120	38	12
2006	368	93	27	12
2005	378	100	34	13
2004	268	65	34	12
2003	290	68	36	13
2002	308	63	44	13
2001	278	65	37	18
2000	298	95	35	16
1999	299	63	44	18
1998	274	67	38	10
1997	287	77	30	12
1996	296	74	55	15
1995	281	56	58	12
1994	295	87	58	16
1993	257	57	47	12
1992	308	82	39	15
1991	268	68	43	15
1990	279	68	41	17
1989	266	51	44	20
1988	186	49	39	*NA*
1987	152	34	21	*NA*
1986	78	*NA*	*NA*	*NA*

3.2. Uni-Variate Analysis

3.2.1. Demographic Parameters

Concerning these two parameters (age and gender), all data were available.

First of all, if we consider the whole studied population, the characteristics of age (years) were the following: average = 43.5, standard deviation (SD) = 16.65, median = 43, minimum = 1, maximum = 88. Among these 118 cases, 87 were male and 31 were female, which is a *sex ratio* of 2.81. The figure 3 shows the distribution of the population by age groups.

The characteristics of age (years) of the homicide group (n = 70) were the following: average = 40.2, standard deviation = 16.57, median = 39.5, minimum = 1, maximum = 85. The sex ratio was 2.04 (47 males and 23 females). The distribution of this population by age groups is shown in table 2.

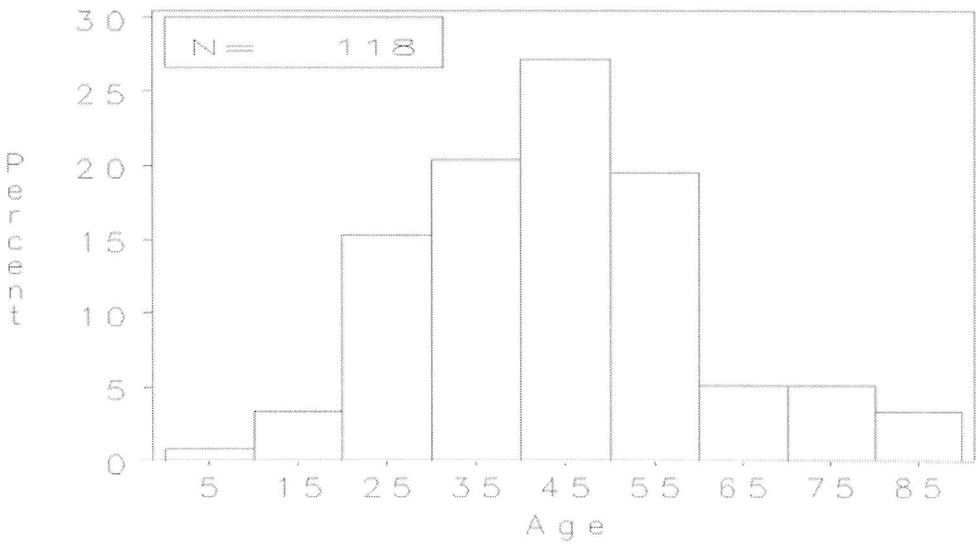

Figure 3: distribution of the population by age groups.

Table 2. Distribution of the homicide population by age groups

Age group (years)	0-9	10-19	20-29	30-39	40-49	50-59	60-69	70-79	80-89	Total
Cases (n)	1	4	13	17	16	11	4	3	1	70

If we consider male victims of homicide (n = 47), their characteristics of age (years) were the following: average = 39.8, standard deviation = 18.4, median = 39, minimum = 1, maximum = 85.

If we consider female victims of homicide (n = 23), their characteristics of age (years) were the following: average = 41, standard deviation = 12, median = 41, minimum = 24, maximum = 69.

The characteristics of age (years) of the suicide group (n = 48) were the following: average = 48.2, standard deviation = 15.59, median = 47, minimum = 20, maximum = 88. The sex ratio was 5 (40 males and 8 females). The distribution of this population by age groups is shown in table 3.

Table 3. Distribution of the suicide population by age groups

Age group (years)	20-29	30-39	40-49	50-59	60-69	70-79	80-89	Total
Cases (n)	5	7	16	12	2	3	3	48

If we consider male cases of suicide (n = 40), their characteristics of age (years) were the following: average = 47.1, standard deviation = 14.65, median = 47.5, minimum = 20, maximum = 82.

If we consider female cases of suicide (n = 8), their characteristics of age (years) were the following: average = 53.8, standard deviation = 18.69, median = 46, minimum = 35, maximum = 88.

All these demographic data are shown in table 4.

Table 4. Demographic parameters of the studied population

	Average age (years)	Median age	SD	Mini. age	Maxi. age	Sex ratio
Whole population	43.5	43	16.65	1	88	2.81
Homicide cases	40.2	39.5	16.57	1	85	2.04
Homicide cases ♂	39.8	39	18.4	1	85	/
Homicide cases ♀	41	41	12	24	69	/
Suicide cases	48.2	47	15.59	20	88	5
Suicide cases ♂	47.1	47.5	14.65	20	82	/
Suicide cases ♀	53.8	46	18.69	35	88	/

Concerning the gender, the uni-variate analysis using logistic regression did not show any statistically significant linkage (P = 0.0535) between this quantitative variable and the manner of death (homicide *versus* suicide). However, even if no statistical linkage was shown, females seemed to be preferentially victims of homicides (Beta = 0.45 +/- 0.23), and males seemed to preferentially commit suicides.

On the contrary, the age was a predictive factor (P = 0.0128) relative to the manner of death (homicide or suicide). The associated regression coefficient being negative (Beta = -0.03 +/- 0.01), there was a lower tendency to be victim of a homicide and a higher tendency to commit suicide when age increased. Nevertheless, the *odds ratio* (OR) kept close to 1 (OR = 0.97 [0.948; 0.994]) reflecting the fact that the age was not a strong predictive factor.

3.2.2. Number of Wounds

For this quantitative variable, data were available in more than 99% of cases. The number of wounds was unknown in one single case. It was a 50 years-old-male who has committed suicide by multiple cut wounds and stab wounds at the anterior part of the neck, the anterior part of forearms, the limbs and the hands. The wounds being very numerous and the most often superficial, their exact total number was not reported.

Concerning the whole studied population, data about the number of wounds were the following: average = 10.3, standard deviation = 16.5, median = 3, minimum = 1, maximum = 122 (see table 5).

Concerning homicide cases, data about the number of wounds were the following: average = 11.5, standard deviation = 14.7, median = 5, minimum = 1, maximum = 65 (see table 5).

Concerning suicide cases, data about the number of wounds were the following: average = 8.6, standard deviation = 18.8, median = 3, minimum = 1, maximum = 122 (see table 5). Moreover only 14 suicides out of the 48 (29.2%) show one single wound.

Table 5. Characteristics of the population for the variable "number of wounds".

	Average	Median	SD	Minimum	Maximum
Whole population	10.3	3	16.5	1	122
Homicide cases	11.5	5	14.7	1	65
Suicide cases	8.6	3	18.8	1	122

The uni-variate analysis using logistic regression showed that the number of wounds was not a predictive factor relative to the manner of death (P = 0.36).

In order to study further the statistical link between the number of wounds and the manner of death (homicide *versus* suicide), two qualitative modalities were defined for this quantitative variable: "a few wounds" (≤ 3) and "a lot of wounds" (> 3), 3 being the median value of the number of wounds for the whole population. However, despite this new distribution, the uni-variate analysis using logistic regression showed that the quantity of wounds ("a few" *versus* "a lot") was not a predictive factor relative to the manner of death (P = 0.28), which confirmed the former results.

3.2.3. Type of Wounds

Concerning this parameter, all data in each of the 118 cases were available. Table 6 shows raw data for this variable.

Table 6. Raw data for the variable "type of wounds" for each manner of death

Type of wound	Stab (+/- other)	Cut (+/- other)	Stab + cut (+/- other)	Blunt (+/- other)
Homicide cases	62 (88.6 %)	33 (47.1 %)	25 (35.7 %)	5 (7.1 %)
Suicide cases	29 (60.4 %)	27 (56.3 %)	8 (16.7 %)	0 (0 %)

The first uni-variate analysis using the Fisher exact test was performed with data shown in table 7. This analysis showed the existence of a statistically significant link (Pr < P: 3.28 E-04) between the type of wounds made by the sharp object and the manner of death.

Table 7. First analysis using the Fisher exact test for the variable "type of wounds"

Type of wound	Stab only	Cut only	Blunt only	Stab + cut	Stab + blunt	Cut + blunt
Homicide	34 (48.6 %)	6 (8.6 %)	1 (1.4 %)	25 (35.7 %)	2 (2.9 %)	2 (2.9 %)
Suicide	21 (43.8 %)	19 (39.6 %)	0 (0 %)	8 (16.7 %)	0 (0 %)	0(0 %)

A second uni-variate analysis using the Fisher exact test was performed with data shown in table 8. Here the three modalities "blunt only", "stab + blunt" and "cut + blunt" were gathered in a single modality "blunt +/- other". Here again the analysis showed the existence of a statistically significant link (Pr < P: 1.08 E-04) between the type of wounds made by the sharp object and the manner of death.

Table 8. Second analysis using the Fisher exact test for the variable "type of wounds"

Type of wound	Stab only	Cut only	Stab + cut	Blunt +/- other
Homicide	34 (48.6 %)	6 (8.6 %)	25 (35.7 %)	5 (7.1 %)
Suicide	21 (43.8 %)	19 (39.6 %)	8 (16.7 %)	0 (0 %)

These results showed that the type of wounds was a predictive factor relative to the manner of death. Thus there was a higher tendency to be victim of a homicide and a lower tendency to commit suicide in cases where wounds were both stabs and cuts. There was a higher tendency to commit suicide and a lower tendency to be victim of a homicide in cases where wounds are only cuts. Moreover the presence of blunts associated with other types of wounds was a predictive factor of homicide.

3.2.4. Anatomical Site Of Wounds

100 % of data were available. Table 9 shows the distribution of wounds among the nine anatomical sites for both groups of the population: the homicide group and the suicide group.

Table 9. Distribution of wounds among the nine anatomical sites for each group

Anatomical site		1	2	3	4	5	6	7	8	9
Homicide	Number of cases	20	32	12	42	20	29	21	4	23
	Percentage (%)	28.6	45.7	17.1	60	28.6	41.4	30	5.7	32.9
Suicide	Number of cases	2	18	0	18	10	0	1	17	3
	Percentage (%)	4.2	37.5	0	37.5	20.8	0	2.1	35.4	6.3

In order to perform the statistical analysis, these nine anatomical sites have been gathered into four anatomical regions:

- the region 1 included "head + nape of the neck + back + limbs + hands"
- the region 2 included "anterior part of the neck + anterior part of the thorax + anterior part of the abdomen"
- the region 3 included "anterior part of forearms"
- the region 4 included "anterior part of the neck + anterior part of the thorax + anterior part of the abdomen + anterior part of forearms", which equals "region 2 + region 3".

A first statistical analysis using the Fisher exact test was performed with data shown in table 10. This analysis showed a global significant difference (Pr < P: 2.68 E-12) concerning the distribution of the anatomical regions of wounds among the two manners of deaths. Thus wounds located at anatomical regions 1 or 1+2 were mainly seen in homicide cases, however wounds located at anatomical regions 2, 3 or 4 were mainly seen in suicide cases.

A second statistical analysis by logistic regression was performed using following modalities of the variables: "anatomical region 4 *versus* anatomical region 1" and "homicide *versus* suicide". This analysis showed that the anatomical region of wounds was a predictive factor relative to the manner of death ($P < 0.0001$).

The associated regression coefficient being negative (Beta = -2 +/- 0.43), there was a higher tendency to be victim of a homicide and a lower tendency to commit suicide when wounds were located at anatomical region 1 ("head + nape of the neck + back + limbs + hands"), and there was a higher tendency to commit suicide and a lower tendency to be victim of a homicide when wounds were located at anatomical region 4 ("anterior part of the neck + anterior part of the thorax + anterior part of the abdomen + anterior part of forearms"). Moreover, the *odds ratio* was equal to 0.05 [0.01; 0.41], reflecting the fact that the anatomical region of wounds was a strong predictive factor relative to the manner of death.

Table 10. Distribution of wounds among the four anatomical regions for each group (Fisher exact test)

Regions	1	2	3	1 + 2	2 + 3 (=4)	1 + 2 + 3
Homicide cases	10 (14.3 %)	21 (30 %)	0 (0 %)	35 (50 %)	0 (0 %)	4 (5.7 %)
Suicide cases	1 (2.1 %)	27 (56.2 %)	10 (20.8 %)	2 (4.2 %)	6 (12.5 %)	2 (4.2 %)

3.2.5. Bone And Cartilage Wounds

For this variable data were missing for one case among the 118 studied cases, which means data were available for more than 99 % of cases.

Table 11 shows raw data for this variable for each of the two groups, homicide and suicide.

Table 11. Distribution of the variable "bone or cartilage wounds" for each group

Bone or cartilage wounds	Presence	Absence	Missing data
Homicide cases	52 (74.3 %)	17 (24.3 %)	1 (1.4 %)
Suicide cases	7 (14.6 %)	41 (85.4 %)	0 (0 %)

This qualitative variable showed two different modalities, "absence of bone or cartilage wounds *versus* presence of bone or cartilage wounds". The uni-variate analysis, using logistic regression with the variable "homicide *versus* suicide", showed that the presence or absence of bone or cartilage wounds was a significant predictive factor relative to the manner of death ($P < 0.0001$). The associated regression coefficient being negative (Beta = -1.44 +/- 0.25), there was a lower tendency to be victim of a homicide and a higher tendency to commit suicide when a bone or cartilage wound was absent.

Likewise, there was a higher tendency to be victim of a homicide and a lower tendency to commit suicide when a bone or cartilage wound was present (data not shown).

The associated *odds ratio* was equal to 0.056 [0.021; 0.147], reflecting the fact that the presence or absence of bone or cartilage wounds was a strong predictive factor relative to the manner of death.

3.2.6. Longitudinal Axis of Stab Wounds Located at the Anterior Part of the Trunk

Each time a sharp force stab wound at the anterior part of the trunk was described in an autopsy report, the longitudinal axis of the wound could be determined, which means 100 % of data were available. However, in 52 cases among the 118 (44.1 %), no stab wound was present at the anterior part of the trunk, and this variable was quoted "no data". In other cases (66 among 118, i.e. 55.9 % of the cases), at least one or several stab wounds were present at the anterior part of the trunk and their longitudinal axis were quoted "horizontal" or "vertical", according to rules described in the "Material and methods" (cf. 2.3.6. Longitudinal axis of stab wounds located at the anterior part of the trunk).

Table 12 shows the distribution of this variable among the two studied groups of the population, homicide cases and suicide cases.

Table 12. Distribution of the variable "longitudinal axis of stab wounds located at the anterior part of the trunk" among the two studied groups of the population

Axis of the wound	Horizontal	Vertical	Both horizontal and vertical	No data
Homicide cases	23 (32.9 %)	38 (54.3 %)	16 (22.9 %)	25 (35.7 %)
Suicide cases	19 (39.6 %)	5 (10.4 %)	3 (6.3 %)	27 (56.3 %)

The uni-variate analysis by logistic regression showed significantly that the longitudinal axis of stab wounds located at the anterior part of the trunk was a strong predictive factor relative to the manner of death ("homicide *versus* suicide"):

- the associated regression coefficient with the modalities "horizontal axis *versus* vertical axis" being negative (Beta = -1.62 +/- 0.42), an horizontal axis of stab wounds located at the anterior part of the trunk was a predictive factor of a suicide (P = 0.0001), this statistical linkage being strong (OR = 0.04 [0.007; 0.217],
- the associated regression coefficient with the modalities "vertical axis *versus* horizontal axis" being positive (Beta = 1.61 +/- 0.6), a vertical axis of stab wounds located at the anterior part of the trunk was a predictive factor of a homicide (P = 0.0066), this statistical linkage being strong (OR = 25.1 [4.6; 137.4],
- the associated regression coefficient with the modalities "both horizontal and vertical axis *versus* horizontal axis" was positive (Beta = 0.88 +/- 0.52), which suggests that the presence of both horizontal and vertical stab wounds at the anterior part of the trunk can be predictive of a homicide, but this statistical linkage did not appear to be statistically significant: P = 0.09.

3.2.7. Type of Objects Used

For this variable, 67.8 % of the data were available, which means they were missing in 38 cases among the 118 studied cases.

Table 13 shows raw data for this qualitative variable in each group of the population. Abbreviations are: NWTO for "non weapon type objects" and WTO for "weapon type objects" (cf. 2.3.7 Type of objects used in materials and methods). In the column "NWTO (kitchen utensil + tool)" were gathered cases where several objects were used, among which at least one kitchen utensil and one tool. In this study, most of kitchen utensils were kitchen knives, tools are always cutters, and washstand items were razor blades except from one case in which the washstand item was nail scissors.

Table 13. Distribution of types of objects used for each group (homicide and suicide)

Object	NWTO (kitchen utensil)	NWTO (tool)	NWTO (washstand item)	NWTO (kitchen utensil + tool)	NWTO (total)	WTO	Unknown
Homicide cases	30 (42.9 %)	6 (8.6 %)	0 (0 %)	2 (2.9 %)	34 (48.6 %)	12 (17.1 %)	24 (34.3 %)
Suicide cases	14 (29.2 %)	14 (29.2 %)	4 (8.3 %)	0 (0 %)	32 (66.7 %)	2 (4.2 %)	14 (29.2 %)

A first statistical analysis using the Fisher exact test was performed with data shown in table 14. This analysis showed a global significant linkage (Pr < P: 2.19 E-04) between the type of the object used and the manner of death.

Table 14. Distribution of types of objects used, first statistical analysis (Fisher exact test)

Object	NWTO (kitchen utensil)	NWTO (tool)	NWTO (washstand item)	NWTO (kitchen utensil + tool)	WTO	Unknown
Homicide cases	28 (40 %)	4 (5.7 %)	0 (0 %)	2 (2.9 %)	12 (17.1 %)	24 (34.3 %)
Suicide cases	14 (29.2 %)	14 (29.2 %)	4 (8.3 %)	0 (0 %)	2 (4.2 %)	14 (29.2 %)

A second statistical analysis using a logistic regression was performed with data shown in table 15, with the modalities "WTO *versus* NWTO" and "homicide *versus* suicide". The type of object was not a predictive factor relative to the manner of death (P = 0.0595). However, P being close to 0.05 and the associated regression coefficient being positive (Beta = 0.99 +/- 0.53), weapon type objects seemed to be mostly used in homicides.

Table 15. Distribution of types of objects used, second statistical analysis (logistic regression)

Object	NWTO	WTO	Unknown
Homicide cases	34 (48.6%)	12 (17.1%)	24 (34.3%)
Suicide cases	32 (66.7 %)	2 (4.2 %)	14 (29.2 %)

The relevant conclusions we can make about this variable were the following:

- kitchen knives seemed to be mostly used in homicides,
- cutters and razor blades seemed to be mostly used in suicides,
- the use of a weapon type object could be predictive of a homicide, but this link was not strictly significant.

3.2.8. Injury Severity Score

For this variable 100 % of data were available.

Concerning the whole population, the characteristics of the ISS were the following: average = 23.7, SD = 13.3, median = 25, range = 1 – 75. The characteristics of the √ISS were the following: average = 4.68, SD = 1.36, median = 5, range = 1 – 8.66.

Concerning the homicide group, the characteristics of the ISS were the following: average = 29.17, SD = 13.27, median = 26, range = 10 – 75. The characteristics of the √ISS were the following: average = 5.28, SD = 1.12, median = 5.1, range = 3.16 – 8.66.

Concerning the suicide group, the characteristics of the ISS were the following: average = 15.73, SD = 8.34, median = 16, range = 1 – 29. The characteristics of the √ISS were the following: average = 3.79, SD = 1.16, median = 4, range = 1 – 5.39.

These raw data for ISS and √ISS are shown in table 16.

Table 16. Numerical characteristics of the variable "ISS" among the studied population

	ISS					√ISS				
	average	median	SD	min	max	average	median	SD	min	max
All cases	23.7	25	13.3	1	75	4.68	5	1.36	1	8.66
Homicide cases	29.17	26	13.27	10	75	5.28	5.1	1.12	3.16	8.66
Suicide cases	15.73	16	8.34	1	29	3.79	4	1.16	1	5.39

The uni-variate analysis, using logistic regression with the variables "ISS value" and "homicide *versus* suicide", showed that the ISS value was a significant predictive factor relative to the manner of death (P < 0.0001). The associated regression coefficient being positive (Beta = 0.16 +/- 0.03), there was a higher tendency to be victim of a homicide and a lower tendency to commit suicide when the ISS value increased. Nevertheless, the *odds ratio* (OR) kept close to 1 (OR = 1.17 [1.1; 1.24]) reflecting the fact that the ISS was not a strong predictive factor relative to the manner of death.

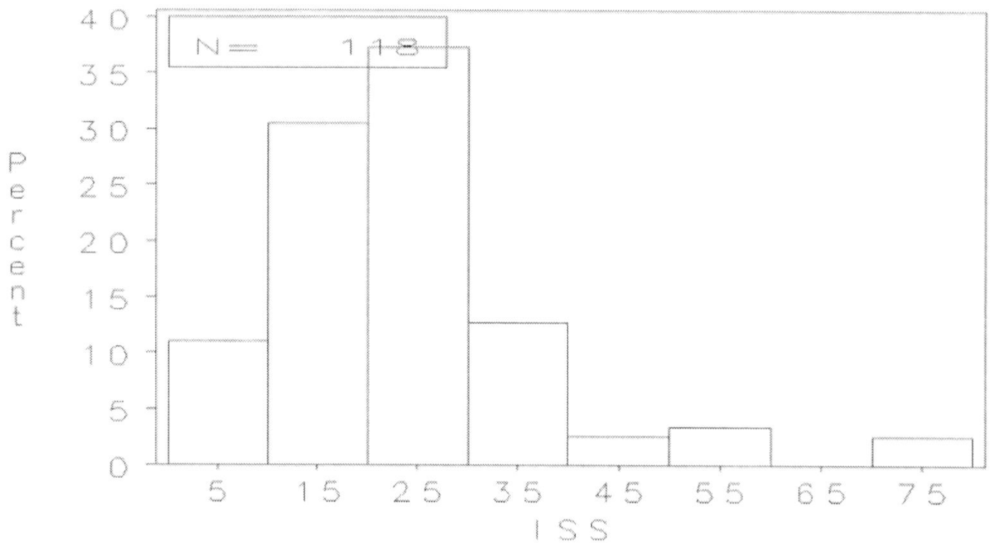

Figure 4. Distribution of the population by ISS values groups.

The uni-variate analysis, using logistic regression with the variables "√ISS value" and "homicide *versus* suicide", showed that the √ISS value was a significant predictive factor relative to the manner of death (P < 0.0001). The associated regression coefficient being positive (Beta = 1.37 +/- 0.27), there was a higher tendency to be victim of a homicide and a lower tendency to commit suicide when the √ISS value increased. Moreover, the *odds ratio* (OR) was equal to 3.94 (OR = 3.94 [2.31; 6.73]) reflecting the fact that the √ISS was a stronger predictive factor relative to the manner of death than the ISS.

3.2.9. Associated Traumatic Lesions

For this data 100 % of data were available.

Table 17 shows the distribution of the modalities of this variable among the two studied groups of the population. We reported one suicide case in which violence associated lesions have been described. This case was a psychotic 41 years-old-man who stabbed himself in the thorax and the abdomen. In addition to this suicidal behaviour he showed a violent delirium. This led the police to use a *Flashball* and a *Taser* to control this person. He finally died of his sharp force injuries, but wounds caused by the *Flashball* and the *Taser* were mentioned in the autopsy medico-legal report as violence associated wounds.

Table 17. Distribution of the modalities of the variable "associated traumatic lesions" among the two groups, homicide and suicide

Associated lesion	Violence	Defence	Fall	Hesitation	Absence
Homicide cases	31 (44.3 %)	28 (40.0 %)	9 (12.9 %)	0 (0 %)	15 (21.4 %)
Suicide cases	1 (2.1 %)	0 (0 %)	6 (12.5 %)	13 (27.1 %)	30 (62.5 %)

A uni-variate analysis using the Fisher exact test was performed with the modalities of the variable gathered as following: "absence", "violence + defence", defence +/- fall", "violence +/- fall", hesitation +/- fall", "fall +/- hesitation". This distribution of the modalities is shown in table 18. This analysis showed a global significant linkage (Pr < P: 1.89 E-15) between the type of associated traumatic lesions and the manner of death.

Table 18. Distribution of the modalities of the variable "associated traumatic lesions" used for the Fisher exact test statistical analysis.

Associated lesions	absence	violence + defence	defence +/- fall	violence +/- fall	hesitation +/-fall	fall +/- hesitation
Homicide cases	15 (21.4 %)	9 (12.9 %)	19 (27.1 %)	23 (32.9 %)	0 (0 %)	4 (5.7 %)
Suicide cases	30 (62.5 %)	0 (0 %)	0 (0 %)	1 (2.1 %)	13 (27.1 %)	6 (12.5 %)

Thus we can conclude that:

- the presence of violence, defence, or both violence and defence associated wounds were mainly seen in homicides,
- the presence of hesitation associated wounds or the absence of associated wounds were mainly seen in suicides,
- the presence of fall wounds was not a predictive factor relative to the manner of death.

3.3. Multi-Variate Analysis

After testing the multi-variate model with the co-variables significantly linked with the reference variable in the uni-variate model, two co-variables remained simultaneously linked with the reference variable:

- the ISS value (or √ISS)
- the associated traumatic lesions.

For the co-variable "associated traumatic lesions", two new groups of modalities have been tested. Table 19 shows the three groups of modalities used: the first group was used in the uni-variate analysis (see Table 18), the two other groups were used in the multi-variate analysis.

Table 19. Three groups of modalities for the co-variable "associated traumatic lesions"

Original modalities	New groups of modalities		
	group 1	group 2	group 3
absence of associated lesion	absence	absence	absence
fall	fall +/- hesitation	fall or hesitation	fall
fall + hesitation	fall +/- hesitation	fall or hesitation	hesitation
defence or defence + fall	defence +/- fall	violence or defence	violence or defence
hesitation or hesitation + fall	hesitation +/- fall	fall or hesitation	hesitation
violence or violence + fall	violence +/- fall	violence or defence	violence or defence
violence + defence	violence + defence	violence or defence	violence or defence

3.3.1. *First Multi-Variate Model*

The first multi-variate model is a logistic regression performed with the co-variables "associated lesions (group 2)" and "ISS". Results are shown in table 20.

Table 20. Results of the first multi-variate model (logistic regression)

co-variables	Beta +/- standard error	Pr > Chi^2	Odds Ratio	$IC_{0,95}$
fall or hesitation *vs.* absence	- 0.27 +/- 0.71	0.71	0.77	[0.19; 3.1]
violence or defence *vs.* absence	4.41 +/- 1.1	< 0.0001	82.6	[9.6; 709]
ISS	0.14 +/- 0.04	0.0011	1.15	[1.06; 1.25]

3.3.2. *Second Multi-Variate Model*

The second multi-variate model is a logistic regression performed with the co-variables "associated lesions (group 2)" and "√ISS". Results are shown in table 21.

Table 21. Results of the second multi-variate model (logistic regression)

co-variables	Beta +/- standard error	Pr > Chi²	Odds Ratio	$IC_{0,95}$
fall or hesitation *vs.* absence	- 0.29 +/- 0.72	0.69	0.75	[0.19; 3.06]
violence or defence *vs.* absence	4.38 +/- 1.1	< 0.0001	79.4	[9.3; 682]
√ISS	1.24 +/- 0.39	0.0013	3.44	[1.62; 7.33]

3.3.3. Third Multi-Variate Model

The third multi-variate model is a Fisher exact test performed with the co-variables "associated lesions (group 3)" and "ISS". Results are shown in table 22.

Table 22. Results of the third multi-variate model (Fisher exact test)

co-variables	exact Beta	P value	exact Odds Ratio	$IC_{0,95}$
fall	1,44	0,25	4,2	[0,5 ; 42,2]
hesitation	- 1,78	0,1	0,17	[0 ; 1,31]
violence or defence	4,29	< 0,0001	72,7	[9,4 ; > 999]
ISS	0,15	< 0,0001	1,17	[1,07 ; 1,3]

3.3.4. Conclusions of the Multi-Variate Analysis

Results of the multi-variate analysis with co-variables "associated traumatic lesions" and "ISS" (or "√ISS") and the studied variable (homicide *versus* suicide) allow us to make these conclusions:

- the presence of violence or defence associated lesions AND a high ISS value were simultaneously predictive of a homicide,
- the absence of associated lesion AND a low ISS value were simultaneously predictive of a suicide.

4. Discussion

4.1. Collection of Data and Bias

In the present study and during the studied period of time, sharp force suicides (2.18 per year) were four times rarer than sharp force homicides (8.75 per year). Thus the two studied groups (homicides and suicides) have been recruited out of periods of 8 years long and 22 years long respectively, in order to establish two groups statistically comparable. The long period of time taken into account in this study (22 years) and the difference of the periods taken into account for each group (8 years *versus* 22 years) could have caused bias in the collection of data. Indeed, significant differences could have occurred in the autopsy protocol or in autopsy reports during these years. Nevertheless, both protocols and reports were unchanged during the period of the study. Moreover, even if several pathologists have performed the autopsies used in this study, they all have used the same type of medico-legal report. These facts allowed us to consider the absence of any bias in the collection of data from the autopsy reports used in this study.

4.2. Not Studied Parameters

Several parameters, which are usually studied in forensic literature, have been ignored in the present study.

The trajectories of sharp force wounds could have been analysed, as trajectories of projectiles are widely analysed about firearm wounds [5]. But these data about sharp force injuries were most often lacking in the autopsy reports, either because the determination of trajectories was impossible (numerous adjacent wounds for instance), or because estimated trajectories were to imprecise. Likewise, the depth of sharp force wounds was ignored, because its determination was too imprecise in most of the cases.

Victim's clothes were also often taken into account in studies about sharp force fatalities [8, 9, 49, 50]. Authors exhibited that clothes taken off or raised up were predictive of a suicide [9]. However this parameter could be hardly analysed by a pathologist because most of the autopsy cases included in the study were presented naked at autopsy.

Likewise, the place of death was often mentioned in forensic literature [8, 9, 12, 17, 19, 48, 51]. Thus bodies were mostly found dead at home, with no significant difference between homicide cases and suicide cases, but sharp force suicides seemed to take place quite often in the bathroom [7, 8]. Here again information about place of death depends from police investigations and not from the autopsy findings, and we could not take it into consideration.

The presence or the absence of a sharp object on the place of death was another relevant item for the diagnosis of the manner of death, but once again this information depends from police investigations and not from the autopsy findings, except in rare cases for which the sharp object was still in place in the body.

In forensic literature, the psychiatric profile of the victim was often analysed, especially in studies about suicides. However, sharp force suicides were very peculiar [7, 8, 10, 12, 19, 46, 48]. Indeed, this way of suicide was particularly violent and the victim frequently suffered from psychiatric diseases such as psychosis [10, 12]. The presence of this kind of disease could also sometimes explain the great violence of sharp force suicides, in which many wounds could be described, located on several anatomical sites, even associated with bone wounds. But the description of the psychiatric profile was part of the police investigation, and not of the autopsy findings.

At last, toxicological data (essentially blood alcohol rate) performed on victims (and/or murderers in homicide cases) were often studied [7, 8, 17, 19, 46]. Authors showed that positive blood alcohol rates were predominantly seen in homicides, and with higher values than in suicides [7, 8]. Nevertheless, toxicological analyses were not always carried out and results of these toxicological analyses were not always known by the pathologist who performed the autopsy. Thus we could not consider the influence of toxicological findings in this study.

4.3. Results

4.3.1. Demographic Parameters

For these variables (age and sex), the population of this study was comparable with populations described in other similar studies in the forensic literature. According to our data, the mean age was 43.5 +/- 16.65 years. It was 42.3 +/- 18.6 years in the population of Scolan et al. [9]. We showed the existence of a significant link between the victim's age and the manner of death: sharp force homicides were statistically younger (mean age = 40.2 +/- 16.57 years) than sharp force suicides (mean age = 48.2 +/- 15.59 years). This result was coherent with most of other published studies [8, 11, 12, 46, 48]. For instance, Scolan et al. reported a mean age of 38.9 years for sharp force homicides and 52.8 years for sharp force suicides. The fact that infants and children do not commit suicide and can be victims of sharp force assaults could be an explanation of this discrepancy.

According to the same study (Scolan et al. [9]), suicide cases were predominantly males. We observed the same result (*sex ratio* M/F = 5 for suicide cases). This male preponderance was confirmed in several other studies showing a *sex ratio* for sharp force suicides above 3 [8, 11, 12, 46]. Concerning sharp force homicides, opinions were divergent. We found in the present study a male preponderance (*sex ratio* M/F = 2.04). Karlsson [8] and Ormstad et al. [19] showed the same kind of results, the former author with a *sex ratio* M/F = 3.2. In return, Scolan et al. [9] and Hunt et al. [47] found a weak female predominance in sharp force homicide victims (50.9 % according to the former author).

4.3.2. Number of Wounds

According to our data, the number of sharp force wounds was not a statistically significant predictive factor relative to the manner of death. This was in opposition to the basic impression that there is a higher tendency to be victim of a homicide when there are a lot of wounds and a higher tendency to commit suicide when there are a few wounds. For instance, within our population was included the case of a 57 years-old-man who committed suicide by 122 sharp force stabs and cuts in thorax, abdomen, forearms and limbs, using a kitchen knife.

Our data were in opposition to these of Scolan et al. [9] who showed the existence of a significant link between the number of wounds and the manner of death. According to this author, a high number of injuries was predictive of a homicide and a low number of injuries was predictive of a suicide. Likewise, Start et al. [46] showed that most of sharp force suicides showed one single wound, however Gill et al. [7] considered that only 24 % of sharp force suicides showed one single wound. Our data were coherent with the latter author as we found only 29.2 % of sharp force suicides showing one single wound.

4.3.3. Type of Wounds

Isolated cut wounds were predictive of a suicide whereas the presence of both stab and cut wounds or blunt wounds was predictive of a homicide. Nevertheless a sharp force injury can be hard to analyse and to classify within categories "stab", "cut" and "blunt". Indeed a thrust hit with a pointed blade sharp object causes a "stab wound", however while the blade goes through the skin, it can also cause an associated "cut wound" aspect. Thus there can be a thin line between an isolated stab wound and a wound associating aspects of both stab wounds and cut wounds.

Gill et al. [7] also considered that isolated cut wounds were predominantly seen in sharp force suicide cases. Nevertheless Scolan et al. [9] showed that the presence of blunt wounds, in association with stab wounds, was not a significant predictive factor relative to the manner of death.

4.3.4. Anatomical Site of Wounds

According to our data, sharp force injuries located only at the site "head + nape of the neck + hands + limbs + back" were predictive of a homicide. Wounds located only at the site "anterior part of the neck + anterior part of the trunk + anterior part of forearms" were predictive of a suicide. At last, wounds located simultaneously at the sites "head + nape of the neck + hands + limbs + back" and "anterior part of the neck + anterior part of the trunk" were predominant in homicides. Indeed, in sharp force suicides, the victim can hardly hit some anatomical sites, for instance the posterior part of the body (back, nape of the neck). Contrary to firearm suicides [1, 2, 5, 6] injuries in the head were very rare in sharp force suicides, probably due to the presence of bones, which require a high energy to be perforated. Hands and limbs injuries (except from anterior part of forearms) were predominantly seen in homicide cases and often corresponded to defence wounds, as these parts of the body are often used to protect oneself against the sharp object. Likewise, the higher frequency of injuries located at the anterior part of forearms in sharp force suicides corresponding to self-inflicted phlebotomies, either these lesions were responsible for death (arteries wounds) or not (veins, muscles and tendons wounds). In return, the presence of lesions located at the anterior part of the body (anterior parts of neck and thorax) were much harder to interpret in term of diagnosis of the manner of death. Indeed, sharp force aggressors try to hit vital structures such as heart or carotid arteries, but suicide victims often suffer from sever psychiatric diseases [10, 12, 19, 46] and also try to hit vital organs in accessible parts of the body due to strong suicidal intentions. This explained the high frequency of injuries located at anterior parts of neck and thorax in both homicide and suicide cases. Abdominal wounds were less frequent among sharp force fatalities because these injuries are less quickly lethal and more accessible to surgical cares than neck or thorax wounds.

Our conclusions about this variable were in accordance with other studies. For instance, Scolan et al. [9] and Ormstad et al. [19] showed that the neck, wrists, the precordial region and the epigastrium were frequently injured in sharp force suicides. Gill et al. [7] and Karlsson [8] reported the absence of lesion located at the face in their series of sharp force suicides. Our data were in agreement with the two latter authors, when Vanezis et al. [52] noticed the presence of such lesions in their series. Neither our data nor Karlsson's [8] included any wound located at the back in sharp force suicides. This author did not describe any lesion of external genital organs whereas our series included one sharp force suicide with several wounds including emasculation wounds. Karger et al. [12] mentioned the case of a 45 years-old-male who cut his penis and died of external haemorrhage.

4.3.5. Bone and Cartilage Wounds

According to our data, the presence or absence of bone or cartilage wounds was a strong significant predictive factor relative to the manner of death: there was a lower tendency to be victim of a homicide and a higher tendency to commit suicide when bone or cartilage wounds were absent, and there was a higher tendency to be victim of a homicide and a lower tendency to commit suicide when bone or cartilage wounds were present. About suicidal sharp force injuries located at the anterior part of the thorax, it was possible to assume that the victims avoided solid anatomical structures like ribs and sternum, which could explain the lower frequency of bone or cartilage wounds in sharp force suicides. In return, in sharp force homicides, the aggressor might not take the presence of these solid structures into consideration, which could explain the higher frequency of bone or cartilage wounds in sharp force homicides, either at the anterior part of the thorax or at the head, neck, back or limbs.

Unfortunately this parameter was not often analysed in forensic literature in term of diagnosis of the manner of death in sharp force fatalities, even if several studies mentioned it. Thus Ormstad et al. [19] found that bone wounds were not exceptional in sharp force suicides, even if they were not frequent. This was in agreement with our series in which 14.6 % of suicide cases showed bone or cartilage wounds. According to Karlsson [8], 7.6 % of sharp force suicides showed ribs or sternum lesions, which represented 35 % of suicide cases showing wounds located at the chest.

4.3.6. Longitudinal Axis of Stab Wounds Located at the Anterior Part of the Trunk

Statistical analysis performed in this study showed that the longitudinal axis of stab wounds located at the anterior part of the trunk was a strong predictive factor relative to the manner of death: a horizontal axis was predictive of a suicide; a vertical axis was predictive of a homicide. Here again it was possible to assume that, in sharp force suicides, the victims handled the sharp object holding the blade in a horizontal plane or more commonly in a plane parallel with ribs in order to avoid them. On the contrary, in cases of homicides, the aggressor might not take this into account.

As bone or cartilage wounds, this parameter was rarely studied in forensic literature. However, since 1910, Stoll (quoted by Karlsson [8]), noticed that, in sharp force suicides, stab chest wounds which hit the heart were commonly horizontal. In 1998, Karlsson [8] confirmed this result, showed it was also true about all stab wounds of the anterior thoracic wall, and added that vertical stab wounds of the chest were predictive of a homicide. At last, Scolan et al. [9] described horizontal stab wounds of the chest more frequent in suicides and vertical stab wounds of the chest more frequent in homicides.

4.3.7. Type of Objects Used

Only a few relevant conclusions were made in the present study. The use of a kitchen knife seemed to be predictive of a homicide, the use of a cutter or a razor blade seemed to be predictive of a suicide, and the use of a weapon type object could be predictive of a homicide, but this link was not strictly significant. Moreover, objects most frequently used in suicides were kitchen utensils and tools, both with the same proportion (29.2 %), which made interpretations harder. Actually it is important to note that this parameter did not strictly belong to autopsy findings. The information was usually given by police officers, when possible. Particularly in homicide cases, the object used was not often found at the place of death.

Difficulties about the data collection might explain why this parameter was not often studied in forensic literature. However Karlsson [8] showed in his series that weapon type objects were more frequent in sharp force homicides, when kitchen knives and razor blades were more frequent in sharp force suicides.

4.3.8. Injury Severity Score

The statistical analysis performed in this study showed that the ISS (or √ISS) was a significant predictive factor relative to the manner of death. There was a higher tendency to be victim of a homicide and a lower tendency to commit suicide when the ISS (or √ISS) increased, and there was a higher tendency to commit suicide and a lower tendency to be victim of a homicide when ISS or √ISS decreased. Moreover the √ISS seemed to be a stronger predictive factor than the ISS. These results meant that wounds caused by murderers to their victims were more severe than those inflicted by victims of suicides to themselves. Indeed, in a context of assault, the possibility for the victim to defend oneself against the aggressor might explain the necessity of making stronger lesions to cause death than in a context of suicide. Moreover, in a context of homicide, emergency cares might be warned quickly, either by witnesses or by the victim itself, whereas in a context of suicide, the emergency cares might not be warned so fast. So there might be a delay in the emergency care in suicide cases in comparison with homicide cases. Lesions in homicide cases had to be particularly severe to cause death in spite of the early intensive cares, whereas in a context of suicide less severe lesions could cause death.

The ISS remained statistically linked with the manner of death in the multi-variate analysis, simultaneously with the associated lesions. This showed the strength of the link between wounds' severity and the manner of death. It also showed that this significant linkage was not due to the statistical effect of associated lesions. Indeed, a high ISS value in homicides could have been biased by the presence of severe associated traumatic lesions not due to sharp objects but taken into account in the determination of the ISS.

In forensic literature, up to now no other study has analysed the statistical relation between severity of injuries and the manner of death in sharp force fatalities. It would be interesting to confirm our data, using either the ISS or other traumatic lesions severity scores. It could also be relevant to determine a level of ISS value to help in distinguishing sharp force homicides and sharp force suicides.

4.3.9. Associated Traumatic Lesions

Our data allowed us to consider that the presence of violence, defence, or both violence and defence associated wounds was predominantly seen in homicide cases, the presence of hesitation associated wounds or the absence of associated wounds was predominantly seen in suicide cases, and the presence of fall wounds was not a predictive factor relative to the manner of death. Moreover the associated traumatic lesions remained linked with the manner of death, simultaneously with the ISS, in the multi-variate analysis: the presence of violence or defence associated lesions AND a high ISS value were simultaneously predictive of a homicide, and the absence of associated lesion AND a low ISS value were simultaneously predictive of a suicide. Concerning this variable, attention had to be paid on both importance and difficulty of the diagnosis of such injuries during the autopsy. For instance the distinction between violence and fall traumatic lesions can be difficult, notably when located at the head, and the rule of the "hat trim line" quoted above (cf. 2.3.9.3. fall associated wounds) may be very often wrong. Likewise, in order to make the diagnosis of violence or defence wounds and prove they are contemporary with the sharp force lesions, a precise dating of associated injuries should be performed. The macroscopic dating is too much indefinite, and a histological examination should always be performed, that can succeed in differentiating wounds separated by several hours.

This variable was widely studied in forensic literature [7 – 11, 19, 46, 51]. Hesitation wounds were commonly described in suicide cases [7, 9 – 11, 19] and defence wounds were typically seen in homicide cases [7, 8]. Our results were in agreement with these results, and we added that the absence of associated lesion was evocative of a suicide. Nevertheless, these data always had to be discussed, as typical hesitation wounds could be found in homicides [44], and typical defence wounds could be found in suicides [51].

Table 23 sums up frequencies of defence wounds in sharp force homicides and hesitation wounds in sharp force suicides found in several studies about sharp force fatalities previously published in the forensic literature. Our data were in agreement with former studies concerning defence wounds in homicide cases. In return, we found a lower frequency of hesitation wounds in suicide cases compared with these authors.

Table 23. Frequencies of defence wounds in sharp force homicides and hesitation wounds in sharp force suicides.

Authors	Frequency of defence lesions in homicide cases	Frequency of hesitation lesions in suicide cases
Vanezis [52]		55 %
Hunt et al. [47]	15 % (single wound) 54 % (multiple wounds)	
Rouse et al. [51]	45 %	75 %
Karlsson [8]	41 %	65 %
Karger et al. [12]		77 %
Byard et al. [11]		45 %
Gill et al. [7]	49 %	65 %
Fukube et al. [10]		57 %
Present study	40 %	27 %

CONCLUSION

The use of sharp weapons is a frequent cause of violent death, especially in countries with a severe legislation on firearms. It should also remain a widely spread mean of violence, seeing that prevention strategies on sharp weapons are hard to implement.

In common medico-legal practice, for instance about sharp force fatalities, it is important and sometimes hard to diagnose the manner of death and to differ homicides and suicides. Table 24 sums up some relevant parameters that can help determining the manner of death in sharp force fatalities according to the results of our study.

Thus, the autopsy remains a major element in the diagnosis of manner of death, and the pathologist must record parameters useful for this diagnosis. However, only the confrontation between police investigations and autopsy findings can succeed in determining precisely the manner of death in sharp force fatalities.

Table 24. Some relevant parameters that can help determining the manner of death in sharp force fatalities

Parameter	Data predictive of a homicide	Data predictive of a suicide
Age	Young victim	Old victim
Type of wounds	Stabs and cuts associated	Cuts isolated
Anatomical sites of wounds	Head and nape of the neck Posterior part of the trunk Hands and limbs	Anterior part of the trunk Anterior part of the neck Anterior part of forearms
Bones and cartilage wounds	Present	Absent
Axis of wounds at the anterior part of trunk	Vertical	Horizontal
Type of object used	Kitchen knife	Razor blade, cutter
Injury Severity Score	High	Low
Associated wounds	Defence or violence	Absence or hesitation

References

[1] Karger B, Billeb E, Koops E, Brinkmann B. Autopsy features relevant for discrimination between suicidal and homicidal gunshot injuries. *Int. J. Legal Med.* 2002 Oct;116(5):273-8.

[2] Druid H. Site of entrance wound and direction of bullet path in firearm fatalities as indicators of homicide versus suicide. *Forensic Sci.* Int. 1997 Aug 4;88(2):147-62.

[3] Solarino B, Nicoletti EM, Di Vella G. Fatal firearm wounds: a retrospective study in Bari (Italy) between 1988 and 2003. *Forensic Sci Int.* 2007 May 24;168(2-3):95-101.

[4] Kohli A, Aggarwal NK. Firearm fatalities in Delhi, India. *Leg. Med.* (Tokyo). 2006 Oct;8(5):264-8.

[5] de la Grandmaison GL, Fermanian C, Aegerter P, Durigon M. Influence of ballistic and autopsy parameters on the manner of death in case of long firearms fatalities. Forensic *Sci. Int.* 2008 May 20;177(2-3):207-13.

[6] Cina SJ, Ward ME, Hopkins MA, Nichols CA. Multifactorial analysis of firearm wounds to the head with attention to anatomic location. *Am. J. Forensic Med. Pathol.* 1999 Jun;20(2):109-15.

[7] Gill JR, Catanese C. Sharp injury fatalities in New York City. *J. Forensic Sci.* 2002 May;47(3):554-7.

[8] Karlsson T. Homicidal and suicidal sharp force fatalities in Stockholm, Sweden. Orientation of entrance wounds in stabs gives information in the classification. *Forensic Sci. Int.* 1998 Apr 22;93(1):21-32.

[9] Scolan V, Telmon N, Blanc A, Allery JP, Charlet D, Rouge D. Homicide-suicide by stabbing study over 10 years in the toulouse region. *Am. J. Forensic Med Pathol.* 2004 Mar;25(1):33-6.

[10] Fukube S, Hayashi T, Ishida Y, Kamon H, Kawaguchi M, Kimura A, Kondo T. Retrospective study on suicidal cases by sharp force injuries. *J. Forensic. Leg. Med.* 2008 Apr;15(3):163-7.

[11] Byard RW, Klitte A, Gilbert JD, James RA. Clinicopathologic features of fatal self-inflicted incised and stab wounds: a 20-year study. *Am. J. Forensic Med Pathol.* 2002 Mar;23(1):15-8.

[12] Karger B, Niemeyer J, Brinkmann B. Suicides by sharp force: typical and atypical features. *Int. J. Legal Med.* 2000;113(5):259-62.

[13] Di Nunno N, Costantinides F, Bernasconi P, Di Nunno C. Suicide by hara-kiri: a series of four cases. *Am. J. Forensic Med. Pathol.* 2001 Mar;22(1):68-72.

[14] Ohshima T, Kondo T. Eight cases of suicide by self-cutting or -stabbing: consideration from medico-legal viewpoints of differentiation between suicide and homicide. *J. Clin. Forensic. Med.* 1997 Sep;4(3):127-32.

[15] Tsokos M, Türk EE, Uchigasaki S, Püschel K. Pathologic features of suicidal complete decapitations. *Forensic. Sci. Int.* 2004 Jan 28;139(2-3):95-102.

[16] Mazzolo GM, Desinan L. Sharp force fatalities: suicide, homicide or accident? A series of 21 cases. *Forensic Sci. Int.* 2005 Jan 17;147 Suppl:S33-5.

[17] Rogde S, Hougen HP, Poulsen K. Homicide by sharp force in two Scandinavian capitals. *Forensic Sci. Int.* 2000 Mar 27;109(2):135-45.

[18] Inoue H, Ikeda N, Ito T, Tsuji A, Kudo K. Homicidal sharp force injuries inflicted by family members or relatives. *Med. Sci. Law.* 2006 Apr;46(2):135-40.

[19] Ormstad K, Karlsson T, Enkler L, Law B, Rajs J. Patterns in sharp force fatalities - a comprehensive forensic medical study. *J. Forensic Sci.* 1986 Apr;31(2):529-42.

[20] Karch DL, Lubell KM, Friday J, Patel N, Williams DD; Centers for Disease Control and Prevention (CDC). Surveillance for violent deaths--National Violent Death Reporting System, 16 states, 2005. *MMWR Surveill Summ.* 2008 Apr 11;57(3):1-45.

[21] Nadjem H, Weinmann W, Pollak S. *Forensic Sci. Int.* Ingestion of pointed objects in a complex suicide. 2007 Aug 24;171(1):e11-4.

[22] Racette S, Sauvageau A. Planned and unplanned complex suicides: a 5-year retrospective study. *J. Forensic. Sci.* 2007 Mar;52(2):449-52.

[23] Palmiere C, Risso E, van Hecke O, La Harpe R. Unplanned complex suicide by self-strangulation associated with multiple sharp force injuries: a case report. *Med. Sci. Law.* 2007 Jul;47(3):269-73.

[24] Racette S, Sauvageau A. Suicide by drowning after two gunshots to the head: a case report. *Med. Sci. Law.* 2008 Apr;48(2):170-2.

[25] Altun G. Planned complex suicide: report of three cases. *Forensic. Sci. Int.* 2006 Mar 10;157(2-3):83-6.

[26] Türk EE, Anders S, Tsokos M. Planned complex suicide. Report of two autopsy cases of suicidal shot injury and subsequent self-immolation. *Forensic Sci. Int.* 2004 Jan 6;139(1):35-8.

[27] Cingolani M, Tsakri D. Planned complex suicide: report of three cases. *Am. J. Forensic Med. Pathol.* 2000 Sep;21(3):255-60.

[28] Maglietta RA, Di Fazio A, Greco MG, Introna F Jr, De Donno A. A singular case of murder-suicide committed with a homemade firearm. *Am. J. Forensic Med. Pathol.* 2005 Mar;26(1):89-91.

[29] Travis AR, Johnson LJ, Milroy CM. Homicide-suicide (dyadic death), homicide, and firearms use in England and Wales. *Am. J. Forensic Med. Pathol.* 2007 Dec;28(4):314-8.

[30] Gupta BD, Gambhir Singh O. A unique trend of murder-suicide in the Jamnagar region of Gujarat, India (a retrospective study of 5 years). *J. Forensic Leg. Med.* 2008 May;15(4):250-5.

[31] Saint-Martin P, Bouyssy M, O'Byrne P. Homicide-suicide in Tours, France (2000-2005) - description of 10 cases and a review of the literature. *J. Forensic Leg Med.* 2008 Feb;15(2):104-9.

[32] Felthous AR, Hempel A. Combined homicide-suicides: a review. *J. Forensic. Sci.* 1995 Sep;40(5):846-57.

[33] Saleva O, Putkonen H, Kiviruusu O, Lönnqvist J. Homicide-suicide - an event hard to prevent and separate from homicide or suicide. *Forensic Sci. Int.* 2007 Mar 2;166(2-3):204-8.

[34] Turillazzi E, D'Errico S, Neri M, Fineschi V. An unusual mechanical asphyxia in a homicide-suicide case by smothering and strangulation. *Am. J. Forensic Med. Pathol.* 2006 Jun;27(2):166-8.

[35] Reuhl J, Bratzke H. Death caused by a chain saw - homicide, suicide or accident? A case report with a literature review (with 11 illustrations). *Forensic Sci. Int.* 1999 Oct 25;105(1):45-59.

[36] Nadjem H, Bohnert M, Pollak S. Appearance of injuries caused by machetes and unusually large knives. *Arch. Kriminol.* 1999 Nov-Dec;204(5-6):163-74.

[37] Grellner W, Buhmann D, Giese A, Gehrke G, Koops E, Püschel K. Fatal and non-fatal injuries caused by crossbows. *Forensic Sci. Int.* 2004 May 28;142(1):17-23.

[38] Ciallella C, Caringi C, Aromatario M. Wounds inflicted by survival-knives. *Forensic Sci. Int.* 2002 Mar 28;126(1):82-7.

[39] AAAM (Association for the Advancement of Automotive Medicine). The Abbreviated Injury Scale, AIS, Version 1998.

[40] Tsokos M, Braun C. Injury pattern on the hand after slipping onto the blade during a knife attack - a contribution to the differential diagnostic classification of sharp force injuries of the upper extremities. *Arch. Kriminol.* 2005 Jan-Feb;215(1-2):1-10.

[41] Kremer C, Racette S, Dionne CA, Sauvageau A. Discrimination of falls and blows in blunt head trauma: systematic study of the hat brim line rule in relation to skull fractures. *J. Forensic. Sci.* 2008 May;53(3):716-9.

[42] Ehrlich E, Maxeiner H. External injury marks (wounds) on the head in different types of blunt trauma in an autopsy series. *Med. Law.* 2002;21(4):773-82.

[43] Maxeiner H, Ehrlich E. Site, number and depth of wounds of the scalp in falls and blows - a contribution to the validity of the so-called hat brim rule. *Arch. Kriminol.* 2000 Mar-Apr;205(3-4):82-91.

[44] Betz P, Tutsch-Bauer E, Eisenmenger W. "Tentative" injuries in a homicide. *Am. J. Forensic Med. Pathol.* 1995 Sep;16(3):246-8.

[45] Karlsson T. Multivariate analysis ('forensiometrics') - a new tool in forensic medicine. Differentiation between sharp force homicide and suicide. *Forensic Sci Int.* 1998 Jun 22;94(3):183-200.

[46] Start RD, Milroy CM, Green MA. Suicide by self-stabbing. *Forensic Sci. Int.* 1992 Sep;56(1):89-94.

[47] Hunt AC, Cowling RJ. Murder by stabbing. *Forensic Sci. Int.* 1991 Dec;52(1):107-12.

[48] Karlsson T, Ormstad K, Rajs J. Patterns in sharp force fatalities - a comprehensive forensic medical study: Part 2. Suicidal sharp force injury in the Stockholm area 1972-1984. *J. Forensic. Sci*. 1988 Mar;33(2):448-61.
[49] Knight B. Some medicolegal aspects of stab wounds. *Leg Med. Annu*. 1977;1976:95-105.
[50] West I. Single suicidal stab wounds-a study of three cases. *Med. Sci. Law*. 1981 Jul;21(3):198-201.
[51] Rouse DA. Patterns of stab wounds: a six year study. *Med. Sci. Law*. 1994 Jan;34(1):67-71.
[52] Vanezis P, West IE. Tentative injuries in self stabbing. *Forensic Sci. Int*. 1983 Jan-Feb;21(1):65-70.

In: Homicide: Trends, Causes and Prevention
Editor: Randal B. Toliver and Ulrich R. Coyne
ISBN 978-1-60741-625-8

Chapter 3

HOMICIDE BY MENTALLY DISORDERED OFFENDERS IN ENGLAND AND WALES

I. H. Treasaden
Three Bridges Medium Secure Unit, West London Mental Health NHS Trust, UK

DEFINITION

Homicide is the killing of another human being. It is not necessarily unlawful.

EPIDEMIOLOGY

There have been around 500 – 600 homicides each year in England and Wales in this decade (Coleman et al 2008). These figures include for 2003 the 172 victims of Dr Harold Shipman, an English general practitioner who killed his elderly patients. Around a third of all homicide victims are female (half killed by their partners). This compares with around 16000 externally caused deaths each year (of these, half are suicides, others misadventure, accidents, etc.). Of note is that in England and Wales between 1996 and 1999, the three highest at risk occupational groups of being homicide victims were security staff (25 victims), medical staff (24 victims) and social workers (14 victims) (Brookman and Maguire 2003).

LEGAL CLASSIFICATION IN ENGLAND AND WALES

In the UK, there are different legal systems for Scotland and Northern Ireland
Homicide may be lawful or unlawful.

Lawful Homicide

Lawful homicide may be:

- Justifiable, e.g. on behalf of the state, such as actions taken by people in the army or the police;
- Excusable, e.g. a pure accident or an honest or reasonable mistake.

Unlawful Homicide

Unlawful homicide is defined in England and Wales as the unlawful killing of any reasonable creature in being and under the Queen's (or King's) Peace. Types of unlawful homicide include:

- murder
- manslaughter
- child destruction
- genocide
- causing death by dangerous driving
- suicide pacts
- infanticide

Clinical Categories of Homicide

Parricide, the killing of near relatives, is disproportionately committed by males in late adolescence (Shon and Targonski, 2003) and includes patricide (killing of one's father), matricide (killing of one's mother), which in the United Kingdom is more common than patricide (Green, 1981) and tends to be committed by those with schizophrenia (Gillies, 1965), perhaps reflecting the psychological difficulty of normally doing so, uxoricide (killing of one's wife) and filicide (the killing of one's child).

Serial killing involves killing individuals over time, spree killing involves killing individuals in different locations during one episode and mass killing involves killing multiple individuals at the same time and same location.

Murder

Murder is an offence at common, as opposed to statute (Parliament passed) law in England and Wales. It is defined as an unlawful killing with *malice aforethought*. Malice aforethought requires either an intention (mens rea) to kill or cause grievous bodily harm. Murder, like any other crime requiring proof of intent, involves proof of a subjective state of mind on the part of the accused. The *actus reus* of murder consists of both of the following:

- an unlawful act;
- the act causes the death of another human being.

Murder results in a mandatory life custodial sentence in England and Wales. On average 11.5 years is served in prison, and then the prisoner is released on life licence. A few murderers do serve life.

Manslaughter

Manslaughter may be categorised into three groups, namely;

- voluntary manslaughter
- involuntary manslaughter
- corporate liability

The third of these will not be considered further here.

Voluntary Manslaughter

There are cases of homicide in which the defendant would be guilty of murder if it were not for the availability of one of the following partial defences:

- Diminished responsibility (Section 2 Homicide Act 1957)

As a reaction against the fact that mentally disordered people who had killed were still being hanged, given the then mandatory death sentence for murder which was abolished in the UK in 1965, despite other defences, such as not guilty by reason of insanity (the McNaughton Rules), a movement was created to bring in a defence of diminished responsibility, i.e. the responsibility of the offender is not totally absent because of mental abnormality but is only partially impaired; therefore, the offender would be found guilty but the sentence modified. This was made law in the *Homicide Act 1957* and applies only to a charge of murder. The murder charge is reduced to manslaughter on the grounds of diminished responsibility.

Under the 1957 Homicide Act (Section 2), as a defence against the charge (only) of murder, the offender may plead that at the time of the offence, he or she had diminished responsibility. The offender has to show that at the time "where a person kills … he shall not be convicted of murder if he was suffering from *such abnormality of mind*, whether arising from a condition of arrested or retarded development of mind or any inherent causes or induced by disease or injury, *as substantially impaired his mental responsibility for his acts".*

'Abnormality of mind' is left to the defendant (or his or her medical advisors) to define and is not synonymous with mental disorder as defined in the Mental Health Act 1983. It has been ruled in the Court of Appeal, in the case of R v Byrne (1960), regarding this defence that 'abnormality of mind' would have affected at the time of the offence the individual's perception, judgement (between right and wrong, between good and bad) and/or the voluntary control of (capacity to control, a legal concept) his or her actions.

> 'Substantially' is also undefined and is left to the jury to decide, although the doctors may give their opinions.
>
> "Substantial does not meant total ... At the other end [it] does not meant minimal or trivial. It is something in between." (R v Lloyd (1996))

The effect of a successful plea of diminished responsibilty is to reduce the charge from murder to manslaughter. The verdict 'unties the judge's hands'. Murder carries a statutory sentence of life imprisonment, but the court is free to make any sentence at all with regard to manslaughter, including a hospital or community rehabilitation (probation) order or, indeed, a life prison sentence, in which case research has shown that such individuals may spend longer in custody than those convicted of murder (Dell 1984). This may reflect concern that while abnormality of mind was identified in these cases of diminished responsibility, no ameliorating treatment is undertaken, for example in hospital, if the individual received a life prison sentence.

In addition to a report supporting the plea of diminished responsibility, the psychiatrist may also, if appropriate, wish to arrange for the appropriate hospital treatment and offer the appropriate Mental Health Act 1983 section (detention) recommendations to the court to help them with their sentencing.

The diminished responsibility defence has been used where a defence of insanity would have no hope of success. Examples include:

- mercy killing
- when the subject kills his or her spouse in a state of reactive depression
- individuals who kill in jealous frenzies
- individuals who are subject to an 'irresistible impulse' to kill (cited more often in the USA)
- subjects who kill and who are 'deranged' by psychopathic disorder

The diminished responsibility defence has largely replaced the insanity defence in England and Wales for those charged with murder.

The most important points in favour of diminished responsibility are that:

- it allows for an overall assessment of the person
- it leads to more flexible sentencing

Against diminished responsibility are the following points:

- There is a problem of balancing the concept of responsibility with 'determinism', e.g. does a greater propensity to lose one's temper imply less responsibility?
- It assumes that a distinction can be made between psychopathy and wickedness in terms of moral or criminal responsibility.

- Does diminished responsibility mean less power to resist temptation? If so, should the irresponsible be punished less than the responsible?
- Does an irresponsible act in a normally responsible person indicate a greater aberration of mind than irresponsible behaviour in the irresponsible?
- If a person is found to have diminished responsibility, then it may mean that the court will return such a person to society faster than a responsible offender.
- Provocation (Section 3 Homicide Act 1957): Provocation is the sudden or temporary loss of control under provocation that might make a normal person kill. Whether this occurred is for the jury to decide, although a psychiatrist's opinion may be requested. More recently, psychiatric evidence about the propensity of individuals with certain vulnerable personalities or conditions, such as learning disability, to be provoked has been accepted as admissible.

Following criticism that this defence is used inappropriately by those who kill after losing their temper and that it is not sufficiently tailored to those who kill out of fear of serious violence e.g. those subject to prolonged domestic violence, the Ministry of Justice (2008) has proposed that this defence should be replaced with a new partial defence for those who kill in response to (a) fear of serious violence and/or (b) have a justified sense of being seriously wronged.

- Killing in pursuance of a suicide pact (which the offender has to prove) (Section 4 Homicide Act 1957): A suicide pact is defined as being a common agreement between two or more persons, having for its object the death of all of them, whether or not each is to take his or her own life.

Involuntary Manslaughter

Involuntary manslaughter refers to cases of homicide without malice aforethought. It can take several forms including:

- an unlawful and dangerous act – 'constructive manslaughter': the *actus reus* consists of an unlawful act that is dangerous and causes death;
- gross negligence: the *actus reus* consists of a breach of a duty of care that the accused owes to the victim, with the result that his beach leads to the victim's death.

Infanticide

Under the Infanticide Acts 1922 and 1938 (Section 1), infanticide is defined as having occurred when a woman by any wilful act caused the death of her child under the age of 12 months, but at the time of the act or omission the balance of her mind was *'disturbed by reason of her not being fully recovered from the effect of giving birth to the child or the effect of lactation consequent upon the birth of the child'*. This is technically an offence rather than a defence.

The grounds for this plea, as an alternative to murder, are less stringent than those for diminished responsibility (i.e. there is no need to prove abnormality of mind); nor does it require proof of a mental disorder, e.g. mental illness. It is the policy of the Director of Public Prosecution and the Crown Prosecution Service to use this plea for such mothers. It does not apply to adopted children or to any child other than the youngest (otherwise a manslaughter plea has to be used), as it is possible to give birth on two occasions within one year.

When this plea was introduced, many such mothers had acute organic confusional puerperal psychoses. Nowadays, infanticide is rather an historical anachronism; only about one in six of such mothers have functional puerperal psychoses, the remainder being not dissimilar from those who batter their children. A conviction for infanticide usually results in a sentence of a community rehabilitation (probation) order, often with a condition of psychiatric treatment (outpatient or inpatient).

Amnesia

Between 40 and 50 per cent of people charged with homicide claim amnesia for the actual act.

Amnesia is not in itself a defence; the underlying condition may be, for example, a post-traumatic state, epileptic fits or acute psychosis. In the 1959 Podola Appeal case in England and Wales (Podola's amnesia was, in fact, not genuine), it was ruled that even if amnesia is genuine, it is no bar to trial.

Amnesia may be feigned by lying or caused by:

- hysterical amnesia (denial)
- failure of memory registration owing to overarousal (comparable to "exam phobia")
- alcohol
- other psychoactive drugs
- head injury

Drugs and Alcohol

It has always been considered in England and Wales that a person is fully responsible for their actions if they knowingly used drugs or alcohol (voluntary intoxication). It is assumed that everyone knows that drunkenness is associated with aggressive and irresponsible behaviour and therefore one is responsible for not becoming drunk. The same rule applies to drug abuse. This would not apply if an individual were 'slipped' drugs or alcohol or if their doctor did not inform them of side-effects and interactions (e.g. with alcohol) of prescribed medication.

Successful defences have been based on:

- being so drunk as to be incapable of forming intent in offences requiring specific intent;

- developing a mental illness, e.g. psychosis, as a result of the ingestion of a drug or alcohol (as in delirium tremens);
- where the use of a drug, which might be quite legitimate, produces a mental state abnormality that could not have been anticipated by the subject, e.g. hypoglycaemia after the use of insulin.

Thus, overall, successful defences following consumption of alcohol or drugs are based on either (i) involuntary intoxication or (ii) if intoxicated voluntarily, lack of specific intent where offences, such as murder, require this.

Criminal Procedure (Insanity and Unfitness to Plead) Act 1991

Two other legal defences in England and Wales that do not apply exclusively to homicide offences arise under this Act.

a) UNFIT TO PLEAD

A mentally disturbed offender may plead that he is unfit to plead (under 'disability' in relation to trial). This refers to the time of trial, not the offence.

The defendant would have to prove, using medical evidence, in a Crown Court Hearing that he was not fit to do at least one of the following (based on the original test used in 1836 in R v Pritchard):

(1) Instruct counsel ("so as to make a proper defence")
(2) Appreciate the significance of pleading
(3) Challenge a juror
(4) Examine a witness
(5) Understand and follow the evidence of Court procedure.

Note that the defendant does <u>not</u> have to be fit to give evidence himself.

If found unfit to plead by a Crown Court Judge, there is provision for a trial of facts. If it is concluded that the individual did commit the offence, this results in discretionary sentencing, including compulsory admission to hospital as directed by the Secretary of State.

Historically the concept originates from dealing with deaf mutes. In medieval times defendants were pressed under weights to give a plea, without which they could not be convicted, executed or their property given to the Exchequer. Hence the term "press for an answer".

b) NOT GUILTY BY REASON OF INSANITY ("SPECIAL VERDICT") (INSANITY DEFENCE) (McNAUGHTON RULES)

The offender is arguing that he is not guilty (not deserving of punishment) by reason of his insanity. It has to be proven to a Crown Court, on the balance of probabilities, that at the time of the offence, the offender laboured under such defect of reason that he met the McNaughton Rules i.e.,

(1) That by reason of such defect from disease of mind, he did not know the nature or quality of his act (this means the physical nature of the act), OR
(2) Not know what he was doing was wrong (forbidden by law).
(3) If an individual was suffering from a delusion, then his actions would be judged by its relationship to the delusion, i.e., if he believed his life to be immediately threatened, then he would be justified in striking out, but not otherwise.

Evidence from 2 or more medical practitioners, one approved under Section 12 of the Mental Health Act 1983, is required before of the verdict Not Guilty by Reason of Insanity can be returned.

Under the Criminal Procedure Act 1991, if found Not Guilty by Reason of Insanity, the judge has freedom to decide on the sentencing and disposal of the defendant, i.e., discretionary sentencing, including detention in hospital.

Historically this defence arises from the case of McNaughton who, in 1843, believing himself to be poisoned by a then Liberal political party, the Whigs, attempted to shoot Sir Robert Peel, missed (or alternatively misidentified Peel) and shot and killed Peel's secretary. Because McNaughton was deluded and insane, he was acquitted but this caused a great deal of argument in the country, which included Queen Victoria ("Insane he may be, but not guilty he is not"), and the Law Lords were asked to issue guidance in response to 5 questions for the courts. Their guidance is known as the McNaughton rules.

Homicide Followed by Suicide

This outcome, which, of course, precludes a criminal trial, occurred in around 7 per cent of such offences between 1966 and 2004 in England and Wales (Large et al, 2008). The rates of homicide followed by suicide have probably been higher in England and Wales in the past, with estimates of up to a half attempting suicide and a third succeeding in the 1960s, at a time when most homicides were domestic (West, 1965) and thus, perhaps, more psychologically difficult to cope with the consequences.

Psychodynamic Aspects

Most individuals who have killed do not regard themselves as typical murderers and many resent the implications of the word "manslaughter". Nevertheless while murderous thoughts can be normal, acting on them is not. Homicide can be seen as preventing something even more psychologically worse for the individual. Following committing a homicide, some individuals, due to psychological defence mechanisms, can appear callously indifferent, idolise the victim or claim amnesia as the act is too painful to think or talk about (Treasaden, 2003).

TRENDS IN HOMICIDE RATES DUE TO MENTAL DISORDER IN ENGLAND AND WALES

Using the legal classifications of homicide I have described, Large et al (2008) have shown that in England and Wales the annual number of homicides due to mental disorder rose from under 50 in 1957 to above 100 in the 1970s but has now returned to the earlier low levels while other homicides have continued to rise. The initial rise in homicide by the mentally disordered was attributed to the same factors responsible for the increase in other homicides e.g. substance misuse and increased availability of weapons, and the subsequent decline to the improved awareness of, services for and treatment of mental disorder.

These findings contradict those of Coid (1983), who argued that the rate of homicide by the mentally ill is related to the prevalence of mental illness, which itself is fairly constant in all countries i.e. in countries with high homicide rates, this is due to high numbers of non-mentally ill offenders, their violence being related to criminal activities, drug dealing and subcultural and economic factors, and, as a conseqeuence, these countries with high homicide rates had a lower proportion of mentally ill homicide offenders.

HOMICIDE, VIOLENCE AND MENTAL ILLNESS

There is thus no evidence of increasing rates of homicide by mentally ill people in England and Wales (as supported by Bennett (1996) and Taylor and Gunn (1999)) in spite of this being the media and the public's perception, which in turn, probably reflects only increasing awareness. Homicides by mentally ill people have a negligible effect on public safety in England and Wales compared with other factors, such as road traffic accidents. In the past, factors associated with violence were said to be the same, regardless of whether the offender was mentally ill, i.e. personality disorder, impulsivity, anger, violent family background and substance abuse. However, since 1992, studies have shown that having a diagnosis of mental illness is associated weakly with violence due to a subgroup with specific types of symptoms such as paranoid (persecutory) delusions (false beliefs) and delusions of passivity (being under external control). It is thus certain symptoms, and not particular psychiatric diagnoses alone, that are associated with violence. Nevertheless, the risk of violence is still better predicted by being a young male than by having a diagnosis of schizophrenia (Swanson et al 1990).

Psychiatrists are better than chance or lay people in predicting violence and better still at assessing situations where there is no risk; however, they tend to underestimate the risk of violence in females (Lidz et al, 1993). Professionals also underestimate the high background base rates of violence in the community in general e.g. up to 40 per cent of males in a London sample had been seriously violent by the age of 32 years (Farrington, 1995). The majority of violence never results in criminal charges. This also applies to inpatients who are violent, where formal charges may often be seen as serving little purpose if the patient is to remain in hospital.

Among individuals with mental illness, affective disorders are under represented in forensic psychiatric facilities. Violence is, however, increased in people with schizophrenia, especially those who have drifted out of treatment, and in young males with acute schizophrenia compared with those with chronic schizophrenia. Violence may arise directly from positive symptoms of mental illness, such as delusions (false beliefs) and hallucinations (e.g. voices). Mental illness, especially schizophrenia, may, however, lead indirectly to violence through associated deterioration in social functioning and personality, so that such individuals become more antisocial and impulsive and develop a lower tolerance to stress. This sometimes leads to disputes in court in England and Wales about the disposal of such individuals with few or no positive psychotic symptoms, who have killed, with such individuals sometimes being given, wrongly, an additional diagnosis of personality disorder to explain their violence. A mentally ill individual may also behave violently for "normal" emotional reasons, such as fear and anger, and then experience accompanying corresponding psychotic symptoms, e.g. hallucinations of aggressive content. Violence, law involvement and imprisonment may themselves precipitate mental illness.

For a mentally ill person, the key issue is whether the individual has a delusion of a content on which he or she might act dangerously, e.g. of persecution or infidelity, but even then not all morbidly jealous individuals, for instance, assault their spouse. Twenty per cent of people presenting to hospital with their first episode of schizophrenia have threatened the lives of others, but among these half have already been ill for a year (Humphreys et al, 1992). Overall, however, it is unusual for a person with schizophrenia to present for the first time with serious violence, including homicide. One established period of higher risk is within a few months of discharge from hospital (Taylor, 1993). People with both schizophrenia and substance abuse have higher rates of violence than those with substance abuse alone, who, in turn, have higher rates than those with schizophrenia alone (Swanson et al, 1990).

Research has generally shown, but not universally (Applebaum et al, 2000), a consistent association between violence and delusions, particularly of threat/control override content e.g. persecutory delusions, passivity delusions and thought insertion (Link and Stueve, 1994). These findings are in keeping with social psychology theory that violence in general is associated with an individual feeling under threat or losing control of his/her situation.

Based particularly on the work of Steadman and Monahan's group (Steadman et al, 1998) in the USA (the McArthur Foundation Violence Risk Assessment Study), the Royal College of Psychiatrists for the UK and Ireland in 1996, in their booklet *Assessment and Clinical Management of Risk of Harm to Other People,* detailed 'warning signs' that professionals should be aware of. These were:

- beliefs of persecution, or control by external forces;
- previous violence or suicide attempts;
- social restlessness;
- poor compliance with medication or treatment;
- substance abuse;
- hostility, suspiciousness and anger;
- threats.

Psychiatric patients tend to peak for violent offending at a later age than the general population. It is important to be aware that the oft-quoted 'best predictor of future behaviour is past behaviour' (after Kvaraceus, 1966) is based on non-psychiatric populations and, in any case, accounts for only five percent of the variance (Steadman et al, 1998). A history of previous violence is, of course, required for this to be relevant in any case. Among severely (psychotic) mentally ill people, delusions of threat/control override appear to be better predictors than past behaviour.

Among all individuals, including mentally ill people, a history of expressed threats (as opposed to generalised anger), substance misuse and a history of personal deprivation and/or abuse are all associated with violence. Indeed, it has been suggested that homicide rates in general may be reduced in the United Kingdom by coordinated multiagency responses and more policy and educational initiatives targetted specifically to counter domestic violence, child abuse, alcohol abuse and the carrying of knives and other weapons (Brookman and Maguire, 2003).

Law-breaking behaviour in general and violence in particular usually decrease when the basic needs of an individual are met. For instance, an individual with schizophrenia who kills often has a characteristic history of not only poor compliance with medication, leading to relapse of his or her mental illness, but also of being in a situation of social isolation and poor home conditions. Some individuals may even offend to remove themselves from their situation in the community to the security of prison or hospital. The risk of self-harm or suicide is, however, greater for people with schizophrenia, even if they have behaved seriously violently, than homicide or serious harm to others.

In summary, while no mental illness is characterised by serious violence, including homicide, the existing evidence suggests that there is a link between mental illness and violence. Mental illness is a risk factor, but not a large one, and the risk is increased by substance abuse.

Developments in brain scanning may elucidate this area further. Our research group has found evidence, using 31 phosphous magnetic resonance spectroscopy, of increased cerebral metabolism in male patients with schizophrenia who have dangerously offended, including by homicide (Puri et al, 2004). In a structural magnetic resonance imaging voxel based morphometry study (Puri et al, 2008), evidence of reduced grey matter volume bilaterally in the region around the supramarginal gyrus (Broadmann's areas 39 and 40), which are important in verbal working memory, and the cerebellum were found in those with schizophrenia who have violently offended, including by homicide, compared to matched individuals with schizophrenia who have not so offended.

Avoidable Deaths – The National Confidential Inquiry into Suicide and Homicide by People with Mental Illness, University of Manchester, England

This National Confidential Inquiry for England and Wales was set up in 1996 to collect detailed clinical information on homicides (and also suicides) by individuals in contact with mental health services (Appleby et al, 1999 and 2001).

Shaw et al (2006), using data from this Inquiry over a 5 year period from April 1999 to December 2003, identified 249 such cases of homicide from a total of 2670 homicides i.e. 9% of all homicides. This equated to 52 patient homicides a year. There was no evidence of a rise in homicides, including stranger homicides, by the mentally ill. The typical perpetrator of stranger homicides in England and Wales is a young male who has been drinking alcohol or abusing drugs (Shaw et al, 2004).

Those with schizophrenia were responsible for 30 patient homicides a year. Half were current or recent patients but one third had no previous contact with services.

Those with personality disorder and a history of current or previous contact with psychiatric services were responsible for 10 cases per year.

Rates of mental disorder in all perpetrators of homicide were as follows:

Life time mental disorder	30%
Schizophrenia (lifetime)	5%
Contact with mental health services	18%
Contact within 12 months	9%
Mental illness at time of offence	10%
Convicted of manslaughter on grounds of diminished responsibility (Section 2 Homicide Act 1957)	4%
Hospital order	6%

Fourteen per cent of homicides (7 per year) were considered 'most preventable' due to service failures e.g. lack of adequate supervision, poor compliance.

Recommendations resulting included:

(1) Ensure high risk patients receive enhanced care planning backed up by peer review. The lack of this was considered the cause of 53% of most preventable homicides.

(2) Respond robustly when a care plan breaks down. Lack of response were considered to have caused 18% of the most preventable homicides. Twenty five per cent of patient homicides were preceded by non-compliance.

(3) Develop services for dual diagnosis patients. Thirty-six per cent of homicide cases had dual diagnoses i.e. mental disorder and substance abuse.

A review of homicides by patients with severe mental illness was also conducted by Maden (2007). He looked at twenty-five cases from National Confidential Inquiry into Homicides by psychiatric patients between 1995 and 2007. Maden emphasised the value of structured clinical assessment of violence risk, especially the Historical Clinical Risk-20 (HCR-20) (Webster et al, 1997). The HCR-20 includes 20 items of historical (H) factors, which reflects long term risk, clinical (C) factors, which reflect current risk, and risk management (R) factors. It thus covers dynamic as well as actuarial risk factors. It can be used as an enquiry guide and prompt rather than a numerical rating scale. The cases reviewed by Maden resembled forensic psychiatric service cases with high H item scores, but most were under general psychiatric services at the time.

The lack of patient compliance and compulsory treatment in the community were seen by Maden as the major issues. The Mental Health Act 2007 for England and Wales has now introduced increased powers to treat patients compulsorily in the community. Risk assessment alone was deemed insufficient without such risk management.

A dual diagnosis with drug and alcohol misuse was present in 23 of 25 cases reviewed by Maden. Intoxication at the time of homicide offence was very frequent. Abstinence was therefore recommended as a condition of discharge from hospital. The need for setting limits and early intervention was highlighted. Clinicians should be clear where to draw a line for intervention. Maden also made the point that diagnosis is only one factor in the assessment of the risk of violence. Drug induced psychosis is just as dangerous as schizophrenia. The importance of involving carers was also emphasised as they are most at risk.

However, risk management does not equate to risk elimination and some violence, including homicides, by the mentally disordered is probably inevitable.

Inquiries into Homicides by Psychiatric Patients

These have been mandatory in England and Wales since 1994 (Department of Health, 1994), following a very critical and widely reported inquiry (Ritchie, Dick and Lingham, 1994) into the killing in 1992 of a Jonathan Zito by Christopher Clunis who suffered from chronic schizophrenia. Such inquiries have emphasised failures in care due to poor communication between professionals and agencies, downgrading of previous violence, failure to recognise and manage social restlessness and escalating problems, lack of contact of subjects with consultant psychiatrists, rigid catchment area practice, lack of resources e.g. lack of acute beds and trained staff, failure to use the Mental Health Act appropriately to detain for reasons of health before violence occurs, and lack of carer involvement, although the latter may raise issues of patient confidentiality. Non-compliance with treatment in the community has been perhaps the most common major factor characterising these cases. However, even Hippocrates noted patients tend not to take their prescribed treatments. Also, there can, of course, be no real ‘supervision’ in the community in the sense of continual observation.

Overall, such inquiries have highlighted not the limitations of risk assessment, as real as these are, but failure to communicate or manage known risk. Improving community psychiatric care may thus be more useful in reducing the risk of violence than attempts at perfecting risk assessment instruments. Certainly, the use of standardised structured risk assessment instruments would not alone prevent most homicides by psychiatric patients.

References

Applebaum, P.S., Robbins, P.C. and Monahan, J. (2000) Violence and delusions : data from the MacArthur Violence Risk Assessment Study. *American Journal of Psychiatry* 157 : 566-572.

Appleby, L., Shaw, J., Amos, T., McDonnell, R., Harris, C., McCann, K., Bickley H., Parsons, R., Kiernan, K. and Davies, S. (1999) *Safer services. Report of the National Confidential Inquiry into Suicide and Homicide by People with Mental Illness.* London: Stationery Office.

Appleby, L., Shaw, J., Sherratt, J., Amos, T., Robinson, J., McDonnell, R., McCann, K., Parsons, R., Burns, J., Bickley, H., Kiernan, K., Wren, J., Hunt, I., Davies, S and Harris, C. (2001) *Safety first. Report of the National Confidential Inquiry into Suicide and Homicide by People with Mental illness.* London: Stationery Office.

Bennett, D. (1996) Homicide, inquiries and scapegoating. *Psychiatric Bulletin* 20, 298 - 300

Brookman, F. and Maguire, M. (2003) *Reducing homicide : Summary of a review of the possibilities.* RDS Occasional Paper No. 84. London : Home Office.

Coid, J. (1983) The epidemiology of abnormal homicide and murder followed by suicide. *Psychological Medicine* 13 : 855 – 860.

Coleman, K., Hird, C., Povey, D. (2005). Violent Crime Overview, Homicide and Gun Crime 2004/5 (2nd edition). London: Home Office.

Dell, S. (1984) *Murder into Manslaughter : The Diminished Responsibility Defence in Practice* (Maudsley Monographs). Oxford : Oxford University Press.

Department of Health (1994) *Guidance on the Discharge of Mentally Disordered People and their Continuity of Care in the Community.* HSG (94) 27. London: NHS Executive.

Farrington, D.P. (1995) The Twelfth Jack Tizard Memorial Lecture : the development of offending and antisocial behaviour from childhood: Key findings from the Cambridge Study in Delinquent Development. *Journal of Child Psychology and Psychiatry and Allied Disciplines* 36: 929 – 64.

Gillies, H. (1965) Murder in the West of Scotland. *British Medical Journal* 111. 1087 -1094.

Green, C.M. (1981) Matricide by Sons. *Medicine, Science and the Law.* 21: 207 -214.

Kvaraceus, W. (1966) *Dangerous Youth.* Ohio: Columbus.

Large, M., Smith, G., Swinson, N., Shaw, J., Neeson, O. (2008) Homicide due to mental disorder in England and Wales over 50 years. *British Journal of Psychiatry.* 193: 130 – 137.

Lidz, C.W., Mulvey, E.P., Gardner, W. (1993) The accuracy of predictions of violence to others. *Journal of the American Medical Association* 269: 1007 – 11.

Link, B.G., Stueve, A. (1994). Psychotic symptoms and violent/illegal behaviour of mental patients compared to community controls. In: *Violence in Mental Disorder: Developments in Risk Assessment.* Eds Monahan, J. and Steadman, H.J. Chicago: Unverisity of Chicago Press. 137 – 160.

Maden, A. (2007) *Treating Violence: a guide to risk management in mental health* Oxford : Oxford University Press.

Ministry of Justice (2008) *Murder, manslaughter and infanticide : proposal for reform of the law.* Consultation paper CP19/08. London : Home Office.

Puri B.K., Counsell, S.J., Hamilton, G, Bustos, M.G., Horrobin, D.F., Richardson, A.J., Treasaden, I.H. (2004). Cerebral metabolism in male patients with schizophrenia who have seriously and dangerously offended : a 31P magnetic resonance spectroscopy study. *Prostaglandins, Leukotrienes and Essential Fatty Acids.* 70: 409 – 411

Puri, B.K., Counsell, S.J., Saeed, N., Bustos, M.G., Treasaden, I.H., and Bydder, G.M. (2008) Regional grey matter volumetric changes in forensic schizophrenia patients : an MRI study comparing the brain structure of patients who have seriously and violently offended with that of patients who have not. *BMC Psychiatry* 8 (suppl 1): S6.

Ritchie, J., Dick, D. and Lingham, R. (1994) *The Report of the Inquiry into the Care and Treatment of Christopher Clunis.* London: HMSO.

Royal College of Psychiatrists Special Working Party on Clinical Assessment and Management of Risk (1996) *Assessment and Clinical Management of Risk and Harm to Other People. Council Report CR53.* London: Royal College of Psychiatrists.

Shaw, J., Amos, T., Hunt, I.M., Flynn, S., Turnbull, P., Kapoor, N., Appleby, L. (2004) Mental illness in people who kill strangers : longitudinal study and national clinical survey. *British Medical Journal* 328 : 734 – 737.

Shaw, J., Hunt, I.M., Flynn, S., Meehan, J., Robinson. J., Bickley, H., Parsons, R., McCann, K., Burns, J., Amos, T., Kapoor, N., Appleby, L. (2006) Rates of mental disorder in people convicted of homicide : a national clinical survey. *British Journal of Psychiatry* 188 : 143 -147.

Shon, P.C.H. and Targonski, J.R. (2003) Declining trends in US parricides 1976 – 1998: Testing the Freudian assumptions. *International Journal of Law and Psychiatry* 26 : 387 – 402.

Steadman, H.J., Mulvey, E.P., Monahan, J., Robbins, P.C., Appelbaum P.S., Grisso, T., Loren, H., Roth, L.H., Silver, E. (1998) Violence by people discharged from acute psychiatric inpatient facilities and others in the same neighbourhoods. *Archives of General Psychiatry* 55: 393 – 401.

Swanson, J.W., Holzer, C.E., 3rd, Ganju, V.K., Jono, R.T. (1990) Violence and psychiatric disorder in the community: evidence from epidemiologic catchment area survey. *Hospitals and Community Psychiatry* 41: 761-70.

Taylor, P.J. and Gunn, J (1999) Homicides by people with mental illness: myth and reality. *British Journal of Psychiatry* 174, 9 – 14.

Treasaden, I. (2003) Assessment of violence in medium secure units. Chapter 2 in: *Dangerous Patients : a psychodynamic approach to risk assessment and management.* Edited by Doctor, R. London : Karnac. 21 – 31.

Webster, C.D, Douglas, K.S., Eaves, D., Hart, S.D. (1997) *HCR-20 Assessing risk of violence, Version 2*. Vancouver : Mental health, Law and Policy Institute, Simon Fraser University.

West, D.J. (1965) *Murder followed by suicide.* London: Macmillan.

In: Homicide: Trends, Causes and Prevention
Editor: Randal B. Toliver and Ulrich R. Coyne
ISBN 978-1-60741-625-8

Chapter 4

The Impact of Gun Control on Murder and Suicide in Canada

David Lester
The Richard Stockton College of New Jersey USA

The issue of whether the availability of firearms has an impact on the incidence of murder and suicide has long been debated, often with strong emotions on both sides of the debate. In the past, most of the research on this issue has been carried out on the United States, partly because the differing gun control laws in each of the 50 states provides a "natural experiment" to explore this issue (see Lester, 1984). However, the debate is also contentious in Canada (see Gabor, 2003), and several research studies have been conducted on Canadian data. The aim of the present essay is to review this research in order to see whether any sound conclusions can be drawn from it.

Chapdelaine and Maurice (1996) noted more than ten years ago that firearms cause more than 1,400 deaths annually in Canada with a cost to the nation of about \$6.6 billion. In Quebec, most deaths from gunshot wounds occur in the home, more often in rural areas than in urban areas, and from legally acquired hunting weapons which are often not stored in safely (in accordance with regulations in effect in Canada since January 1st 1993). However, firearms are also involved in other acts. Of the 12,850 robberies in Quebec in 1992, 4,320 (33%) involved firearms. Firearms are also used for suicide and, although many other methods are available for committing suicide, the mortality from suicidal actions involving firearms is 92% as compared to only 30% for suicidal actions involving drugs.

Miller (1995) estimated that the costs of gunshot wounds in Canada in 1991, using 1993 Canadian dollars, was \$6.6 billion - \$4.7 billion for suicide and attempted suicide, \$1.1 billion for homicides and assaults, and \$0.6 billion for unintentional shootings. Of this total amount, \$63 million was spend on medical and mental health care and \$10 million on public services. Productivity losses accounted for \$1.5 billion. The remaining costs represented the value attributed to pain, suffering and lost quality of life.

Canada has passed several gun control laws (Billl C-51 in 1977, Bill C-17 in 1991, and Bill C-68 in 1995), and a number of articles have appeared examining whether the passage of these laws had any impact on the incidence of suicide and murder in Canada and on the choice of method for committing suicide and murder. This essay will review this research to see whether any definitive conclusions can be drawn from the research. However, I will first briefly review some comparative studies on suicide and homicide in Canada and the United States.

Canada Versus the United States

For the period 1969-1988, suicide rates were higher in Canada than in the United States, whereas homicide rates were higher in the United States than in Canada (Leenaars & Lester, 1994a). Homicide and suicide rates were associated over time in the United States but unrelated in Canada. Furthermore, whereas the relative size of the youth cohort (ages 15-24) in the United States was associated with the suicide and homicide rates of this cohort, there was no similar association in Canada. Leenaars and Lester (1992) showed that the patterns of suicide rates by age and by sex also differed in the two countries for the period 1960-1988. For example, Canada experienced a much greater increase in the suicide rates of young men than did the United States in the period 1960 to 1988.

Lester (1990) reported that, in 1980, 37.8% of homicides in Canada were committed with guns compared to 64.8% of homicides in the United States. The suicide rates in 1980 for Canada by gun and by all other methods were 4.66 and 9.30 per 100,000 per year, respectively, and for the United States 6.76 and 5.04.

Finley et al. (2008) looked at all reported firearm injuries in Canada from 1999-2003 that were treated in trauma centers. Of the 784 incidents, 39.8% were fatal. About 28% of the incidents were suicide attempts, 60% assaults, 6% accidental and 6% unclassified. Men accounted for 94% of the incidents. Assaults were more common in young men and suicidal incidents in older adults. Death was predicted by the injury severity score, age over 45, non-accidental, and occurring at home.

Quan and Arboleda-Florez (1999) found that, in British Columbia in 1984-1995, 43.8% of men over the age of 55 used guns for completing suicide as compared to only 3.7% of women (for whom poisoning was the most common method for suicide).

Lester and Leenaars (1998) argued that there was a subculture of violence in Canada in 1975-1985 by showing that the suicide, homicide and accidental heath rates using guns in the Canadian provinces were all strongly associated. Provinces that a high firearm death rate from one cause also had high firearm death rates from the other two causes.

Sloan, et al. (1988, 1990) compared suicide and homicide in Vancouver in Canada and Seattle in the United States, cities of roughly the same size. The suicide rates were of similar magnitude - 15.55 per 100,000 per year and 15.12 in Vancouver and Seattle, respectively. Although the rate of suicide by firearm was lower in Vancouver than in Seattle (2.87 versus 6.73), the suicide rates by all other methods were higher in Vancouver than in Seattle (12.68 and 8.39, respectively). The higher homicide rate in Seattle than in Vancouver (11.3 versus 6.9) was mostly accounted for by the higher firearm homicide rate in Seattle than in Vancouver (4.8 versus 1.0). Similarly, the higher rate of aggravated assault in Seattle than in Vancouver (486 versus 420) was mostly accounted for the higher rate using firearms (88 versus 11).

Mauser (1990; Mauser & Margolis, 1992) compared the attitudes of Canadians and Americans toward guns in the 1970s and 1980s. The citizens of both nations favored both gun control legislation and their right to own guns. The primary reason for gun ownership in both countries was for hunting. However, Canadians were more in favor of stricter gun control laws such as the registration of guns (83% versus 67% in Canada and the United States, respectively) and the banning of pistols and revolvers (81% and 45%). About the same proportion of households in both countries possess rifles, and the majority in both nations felt that store owners were justified in using guns to protect their stores in some circumstances. The predictors of support for gun control laws were similar in the two countries. In Canada, support was associated positively with the perception of the effectiveness of gun control laws and living in rural areas and negatively with being male and gun ownership. In America, support was associated in a similar fashion with these variables with one exception – rural living was no longer associated with support for gun control.

Mauser (1996) compared surveys of Canadian and American household around the year 1990 that inquired about the defensive use of firearms. 3.1% of Canadians and 4.1% of American had used firearms against human and animal threats in the prior five years. For human threats alone, the percentages were 1.6% and 3.9% for Canada and the United States. Mauser commented that the percentages for Canada were higher than many had believed.

GUN AVAILABILITY IN CANADA

Chapdelaine, et al. (1991) reported data from a government-sponsored poll of over 10,000 Canadian households published in 1991. There were an estimated 5.9 million firearms privately owned in 2.2 million households. Of these firearms, 51% were rifles (24% semi-automatic), 39% shotguns (17% semi-automatic), 7% handguns and 3% "other". The purpose of ownership was 67% hunting, 13% collecting, 12% target shooting, 2% employment, 1% for self-protection, and 5% unknown.

Men accounted for 85% of the firearm owners, and 45% of the households with at least one firearm had an income over $40,000 and 11% less than $20,000 (as compared with 17% of the Canadian population). No household member had received instruction in the safe care and handling or firearms in the prior 5 years in 51% of the households, and 50% of the households had not used the firearm in the past year.

PROXY MEASURES OF GUN AVAILABILITY

Suicide

Cook (1982) poposed that the percentage of suicides or homicides using firearms could be used as an indirect measure of gun availability, as could the accidental death rate from firearms. In a study of the Canadian provinces in 1980, Lester (1994) found that the accidental death rate from firearms was positively associated with the suicide rate using firearms and to the proportion of suicides using firearms, but negatively to the suicide rate by all other methods. Thus, gun availability did appear to be associated with the use of guns for suicide. However, the percentage of homicides using firearms did not show these same associations.

Lester (2000b) examined changes in the suicide rate in Canada for 1970-1995. Lester used the percentage of suicides plus homicides using guns as a proxy measure of gun availability. This measure was positively associated with the firearm suicide rate and negatively with the suicide rate by all other methods. It was not significantly associated with the total suicide rate. These results indicate that switching of methods for suicide may have occurred when guns were relatively less available.

Lester also used the accidental firearm death rate as a proxy measure of gun availability. This measure was not significantly associated with the firearm suicide rate but was negatively associated with the suicide rate by all other methods and with the total suicide rate. The results from the two proxy measures clearly contradict each other.

Lester (2001) reported that, for 1970-1995, the accidental firearm mortality rate was associated with percentage of suicides using firearms for the total population, men and women, and for all age groups except those aged 55+. Bridges (2002) extended Lester's analysis for the period 1970-1998 and replicated his results.

Bridges and Kunselman (2004) examined a different time period (1974-1999) and compared the results using homicide versus murder rates. The accidental firearm death rate was positively associated with the suicide rate by firearms and negatively with the suicide rate by all other methods (and not significantly associated with the overall suicide rate). Similar results were obtained for the percentage of suicides and homicide by gun and the percentage of suicides and murders by gun. For this time period, the evidence for switching was stronger than that in Lester's studies.

For Quebec, Simon, et al. (1996) used the number of hunting licenses issued in each region as a proxy measure of gun availability. They found a large, positive association between the number of licenses issued in each region and the firearm suicide rate. They also found a strong association between the firearm suicide rate and the overall suicide rate.

Carrington and Moyer (1994b) looked at suicide rates in the Canadian provinces for three years (1987-1989), providing a panel data-set.[1] They used data (for one year) on percent households owning guns (obtained from household surveys) and the percent urbanized in correlation and regression analyses. They found that gun ownership predicted the firearm suicide rate and the overall suicide rate but not the suicide rate by all other methods. In contrast, urbanization predicted the suicide rate by all other methods and the overall suicide rate, but not the firearm suicide rate. Carrington and Moyer concluded that firearm availability was associated with a higher use of guns for suicide with no evidence of switching methods.

Homicide

Lester (2000b) examined changes in the homicide rate in Canada for 1970-1995. The accidental firearm death rate was positively associated with the firearm homicide rate and negatively with the homicide rate by all other methods. The total homicide rate was not

[1] This technique simply increased the sample size by a factor of three, resulting in significant associations whereas the associations might not have been significant if data from a single year had been used.

associated with the accidental firearm mortality rate. These results indicate that switching of methods was taking place.

Lester also used the percentage of suicides plus homicides using guns as a proxy measure of gun availability. This measure was positively associated with the firearm homicide rate and the total homicide rate but not with the homicide rate by all other methods. These results indicate that switching of methods did not occur. The results from the two proxy measures clearly contradict each other.

Lester (2001) reported that, for 1970-1995, the accidental firearm mortality rate was associated with percentage of homicides using firearms for the total population, men and women, and for all age groups except those aged 55+. Bridges (2002) extended Lester's analysis for the period 1970-1998 and replicated his results.

Bridges and Kunselman (2004) examined a different time period (1974-1999) and compared the results using homicide versus murder rates. The accidental firearm death rate was positively associated with the homicide and the murder rates by firearms and the overall homicide and murder rates. The accidental firearm death rate was also positively associated with the homicide and murder rates by all other methods, but not significantly. Similar results were obtained using the proxy measures of the percentage of suicides and homicide by firearm and the percentage of suicides and murders by gun. These results provide no evidence for switching methods.

Armed Robbery

Lester (2000a) looked at robbery rates in Canada for 1974-1995. Using the accidental death rate from firearms as a proxy measure of gun availability, Lester found that this measure was positively associated with the robbery rate using firearms and negatively associated with the robbery rates with other weapons and with no weapons. The same pattern was found using the percentages of suicides plus homicides by gun as a proxy measure of gun availability. Lester concluded that gun availability was associated with robbers switching to guns for their crimes, weapons which have a greater probability of resulting in death to the robbery victims.

Bill C-51 was passed during this period. The two proxy measure of gun availability were strongly associated with each other ($r = 0.91$) and negatively with the year, indicating that guns became less available over this time period. The robbery rate by firearms declined over the period, while the robbery rates with other weapons and with no weapon increased.

Accidental Deaths

Gabor, et al. (2001) found a strong association between measures of gun availability as measured by household surveys in the Canadian provinces and territories in 1988-1997 and the mortality rate from unintentional firearms deaths.

Bill C-51

Centerwall (1991) compared Canadian provinces and American states that are close to the border between the two countries, such as Manitoba and Minnesota. He noted that estimates of handgun ownership in America were 4 to 10 times higher than in Canada, while ownership of long guns was similar in two sets of regions. Murder rates were similar in the two sets of regions, but the murder rate using handguns was much higher in the American states than in the Canadian provinces. Centerwall concluded that, "In the relative absence of handguns, dangerously violent Canadians commit their assaults using other mean which are, on the average, as lethal as handguns" (p. 1259).

Sproule and Kennett (1989) noted that gun control laws were stricter in Canada than in the United States. Infractions were federal offenses, whereas each state in the United States has its own laws. Gun control laws can be by-passed in the United States by driving to a state with weak gun controls laws. In addition, handguns are more severely regulated in Canada, being available only to police and security personnel, members of bonafide gun clubs and bonafide gun collectors. Although demonstrating a need for protection is a possible reason for a permit, it is rarely, if ever, granted. For the period 1977 to 1983, the murder rates per 100,000 per year were:

	handguns	other guns	other methods
Canada	0.28	0.67	1.79
USA	4.05	1.32	3.31

It can be seen clearly that handguns were used proportionately more often for murder in the United States than in Canada.

Sproule and Kennett (1988) noted that the Canadian parliament introduced a stricter gun control law in 1977 (Bill C-51), which was implemented fully in 1979, and abolished the death penalty at the same time. Sproule and Kennett compared homicide rates in 1972-1976 and 1977-1982. The overall homicide rate did not change significantly, but the homicide rate using firearms did decline from the first to the second time period. They also noted that the average number of victims per murder was greater in both time periods when the murderer used a gun.

Mundt (1990) also presented a study of the impact of Bill C-51. Bill C-51 mandated the purchase of a certificate for buying any gun, strengthened the registration requirements for handguns and other restricted weapons already imposed in 1968, prohibited automatic weapons and sawed-off shotguns and rifles, and imposed mandatory prohibitions on serious criminals. Mundt carried out no statistical analysis but merely provided graphs of firearm incidents in Canada and the United States: (1) Homicide trends in Canada showed no trend from 1974 to 1987; (2) the percentage of homicides using guns in general and handguns declined from 1974 on; (3) there were no clear trends in the rate of armed robbery, although the percentage of armed robberies declined; (4) both the total suicide rate and the suicide rate using firearms declined after 1979; and (5) the accidental death rate from firearms declined from 1974 on. The conclusion is that the decreased use of guns seems to have been apparent from 1974 on, and did not change noticeably after 1979. However, as mentioned above, Mundt carried out no statistical tests on the data.

Hung 1993) pointed out factual inaccuracies, logical inconsistencies and methodological fallacies in Mundt's article but did not perform any statistical tests of the data. Lester and Leenaars (1994) also commented on Mundt's article, but for the first time presented data and statistical tests. Their study, and their subsequent studies, will be discussed in the next section.

However, before moving on, it is important to note that gun legislation was passed in Canada in 1968, and this legislation may already have had impact on the use of guns for suicide and murder prior to the passage of Bill C-51 in 1977.

Methodologically Sound Research

Lester and Leenaars have carried out a series of studies on the impact of Bill C-51 on suicide, homicide and accidental death rates in Canada, and the data on which they base their studies are shown in Table 1.

Table 1. Suicide, homicide and accidental death rates in Canada

	Suicide				Homicide			% by gun	Accidental death rate by gun
	total	guns	Other methods	% by gun	total	guns	Other methods		
1969	10.91	3.57	7.34	32.7	1.79	0.74	1.04	41.6	
1970	11.33	3.74	7.59	33.0	1.98	0.86	1.12	43.7	0.606
1971	11.86	4.28	7.58	36.1	2.12	0.88	1.24	41.5	0.663
1972	12.19	4.29	7.90	35.2	2.32	0.93	1.39	40.2	0.468
1973	12.58	4.31	8.27	34.3	2.40	1.20	1.43	40.8	0.558
1974	12.98	4.57	8.41	35.2	2.43	1.16	1.23	49.5	0.546
1975	12.37	4.64	7.73	37.5	2.66	0.96	1.50	43.5	0.489
1976	12.76	4.76	8.00	37.3	2.42	1.10	1.46	39.6	0.387
mean	12.12	4.27	7.85	35.2	2.26	0.96	1.30	42.6	
SD	0.72	0.42	0.42	1.8	0.28	0.15	0.17	3.2	
b	0.26*	0.16*	0.10	0.61*	0.10*	0.05*	0.06*	0.11	
1977	14.26	5.46	8.80	38.3	2.57	0.98	1.58	38.4	0.430
1978	14.80	5.48	9.32	37.0	2.43	0.98	1.45	40.2	0.383
1979	14.18	4.65	9.53	32.8	2.46	0.79	1.67	32.2	0.300
1980	14.03	4.68	9.35	33.4	2.07	0.78	1.29	37.8	0.309
1981	13.98	4.81	9.17	34.4	2.30	0.75	1.55	32.7	0.253
1982	14.30	4.88	9.42	34.1	2.42	0.86	1.56	35.7	0.227
1983	15.09	4.97	10.12	33.0	2.38	0.80	1.58	33.6	0.165
1984	13.69	4.19	9.50	30.6	2.31	0.86	1.45	37.3	0.239
1985	12.85	4.10	8.75	31.9	2.12	0.71	1.41	33.3	0.248
mean[2]	14.11	4.72	9.40	33.4	2.31	0.82	1.49	35.3	
SD	0.68	0.44	0.38	1.9	0.15	0.08	0.12	3.0	
B	-0.15	-0.13*	-0.02	-0.57*	-0.02	-0.02	-0.01	-0.39	

[2] These means are based on the years 1978-1985.

Table 1. (Continued)

t before/after	5.70*	2.09*	4.81*	1.91	0.41	2.38*	2.66*	4.79*	
1986	14.50	4.69	9.81	32.3	2.17	0.67	1.50		0.198
1987	14.03	4.39	9.63	31.3	2.42	0.75	1.67		0.234
1988	13.05	3.97	9.08	30.4	2.14	0.63	1.51		0.223
1989	12.75	3.93	8.82	30.9	2.40	0.80	1.60		0.281
1990	12.16	3.79	8.37	31.2	2.37	0.71	1.66		0.237
1991	12.78	3.94	8.83	30.8	2.69	0.96	1.73		0.235
1992	12.99	3.67	9.32		2.56	0.87	1.69		0.221
1993	13.14	3.64	9.50		2.17	0.67	1.50		0.152
1994	12.82	3.33	9.49		2.04	0.67	1.37		0.130
1995	13.41	3.08	10.33		1.99	0.59	1.40		0.166

Males

	total	guns	other methods	% by gun	total	guns	other methods	% by gun	accidental death rate
1969	15.58	6.50	9.08	41.7	2.42	1.10	1.32	45.6	1.130
1970	16.23	6.73	9.50	41.5	2.45	1.24	1.21	50.6	1.115
1971	17.29	7.85	9.44	45.4	2.77	1.20	1.57	43.5	1.213
1972	17.43	7.92	9.51	45.4	2.94	1.30	1.64	44.2	0.862
1973	18.03	8.01	10.02	44.4	3.09	1.35	1.74	43.8	1.008
1974	18.85	8.39	10.46	44.5	3.06	1.68	1.38	55.0	1.022
1975	17.94	8.56	9.38	47.7	3.53	1.63	1.90	46.1	0.875
1976	18.41	8.79	9.62	47.7	3.21	1.40	1.81	43.6	0.690
mean	17.47	7.84	9.63	44.79	2.93	1.36	1.57	46.55	0.989
SD	1.10	0.83	0.43	2.33	0.38	0.20	0.25	4.14	0.172
b	0.40*	0.32*	0.08	0.82*	0.14*	0.07*	0.08*	-0.03	-0.56*
1977	21.25	10.09	11.16	47.5	3.45	1.45	2.00	42.1	0.743
1978	22.36	9.96	12.40	44.6	3.33	1.43	1.90	42.9	0.651
1979	21.42	8.70	12.72	40.6	3.20	1.14	2.06	35.5	0.544
1980	21.32	8.69	12.63	40.8	2.78	1.12	1.66	40.2	0.580
1981	21.30	8.95	12.35	42.0	2.87	1.04	1.83	36.4	0.447
1982	22.33	9.05	13.28	40.5	3.26	1.22	2.04	37.4	0.418
1983	23.41	9.37	14.04	40.0	3.12	1.13	1.99	36.2	0.308
1984	21.40	7.89	13.51	36.9	3.18	1.31	1.87	41.2	0.434
1985	20.46	7.74	12.72	37.8	2.71	1.00	1.71	36.8	0.478
mean	21.75	8.79	12.94	40.40	3.06	1.17	1.88	38.32	0.482
SD	0.91	0.73	0.61	2.38	0.24	0.14	0.15	2.73	0.107
b	-0.07	-0.21	0.14	-0.83*	-0.04	-0.02	-0.01	-0.30	-0.31*
t before/after	8.50*	2.44*	12.60*	3.72*	0.78	2.16*	3.06*	4.69*	7.09*

Females

	total	guns	other methods	% by gun	total	guns	other methods	% by gun	accidental death rate
1969	6.21	0.62	5.59	10.0	1.15	0.38	0.77	33.3	0.134
1970	6.41	0.73	5.68	11.5	1.50	0.49	1.01	32.5	0.094
1971	6.43	0.71	5.72	11.1	1.48	0.56	0.92	37.7	0.111
1972	6.94	0.66	6.28	9.5	1.69	0.56	1.13	33.2	0.073
1973	7.14	0.62	6.52	8.6	1.71	0.58	1.13	33.9	0.109
1974	7.13	0.76	6.37	10.6	1.79	0.72	1.07	40.3	0.071
1975	6.83	0.73	6.10	10.8	1.80	0.69	1.11	38.5	0.105
1976	7.16	0.77	6.39	10.8	1.63	0.52	1.12	31.7	0.087
mean	6.78	0.70	6.08	10.36	1.59	0.56	1.03	35.14	0.098
SD	0.38	0.06	0.37	0.95	0.22	0.11	0.13	3.21	0.021
b	0.13*	0.01	0.12*	-0.01	0.07*	0.03	0.04*	0.32	-0.04
1977	7.34	0.88	6.46	12.0	1.69	0.52	1.17	30.8	0.120
1978	7.33	1.05	6.28	14.3	1.53	0.53	1.00	34.3	0.119
1979	7.02	0.64	6.38	9.1	1.73	0.45	1.28	26.2	0.059
1980	6.84	0.73	6.11	10.7	1.36	0.45	0.91	32.9	0.041
1981	6.79	0.75	6.04	11.0	1.74	0.46	1.28	26.6	0.065
1982	6.41	0.78	5.63	12.2	1.56	0.51	1.05	33.0	0.040
1983	6.92	0.66	6.26	9.5	1.65	0.48	1.17	29.0	0.024
1984	6.14	0.56	5.58	9.1	1.45	0.42	1.03	28.8	0.047
1985	5.41	0.54	4.87	10.0	1.54	0.42	1.12	27.4	0.023
mean	6.61	0.71	5.89	10.74	1.57	0.46	1.10	29.77	0.052
SD	0.60	0.16	0.51	1.79	0.13	0.04	0.13	3.18	0.031
b	-0.21*	-0.05*	-0.16*	-0.39	-0.01	-0.01	0.01	-0.48	-0.10*
t before/ after	0.69	0.23	0.83	0.52	0.28	2.40*	1.11	3.36*	3.47*

These data were calculated from raw data obtained from Statistics Canada. The results of the statistical analyses by Leenaars and Lester are also shown in Table 1.

Suicide

Lester and Leenaars (1993, 1994) noted that, in 1969-1976, prior to the passage of Bill C-51, the suicide rate by firearms was increasing (the unstandardized regression coefficient [b] was +0.16, p = .0003), as were the total suicide rate (b=0.26, p = .003) and the proportion of suicides using guns (b=0.61, p = .01). The suicide rate by all other methods did not change significantly (b = 0.10, p > .05).

For the eight years after the passage of Bill C-51, 1978-1985, the suicide rate by firearms decreased (b = -0.13, p = .04), as did the percentage of suicides using firearms (b = -0.57, p = .03), while the suicide rate by all other methods did not change significantly (b = -0.02, p > .05), nor did the total suicide (b = -0.15, p > .05). Lester and Leenaars concluded that Bill C-51 was followed by a decrease in the use of guns for suicide without there being any increase in suicide by all other methods. Substitution of method (or switching) did not occur. The data showed that the effect persisted into the period 1986-1991

Leenaars and Lester (1996) noted that the total suicide rate increased from the period 1969-1976 to the period 1978-1985, as did the suicide rate by all other methods. The suicide rate by firearms increased, but not significantly, while the percentage of suicides using firearms decreased, but not significantly. Thus, the passage of Bill C-51 seems to have lessened the increasing suicide rate by guns in Canada.

Leenaars and Lester (1996) looked at these effects by sex. Looking at the results, for men, suicide rates rose by firearms and by all other methods after the passage of Bill C-51. This, this seems to have been a period on increasing suicide rates for men. However, the percentage of men using guns for suicide decreased after the passage of Bill C-51, and the regression coefficients indicated that the use of guns for suicide for 1978-1985 stopped increasing in the way that it had been in the period 1969-1976.

For women, there were no changes in the suicide rates by firearms and by all other methods after the passage of Bill C-51. After 1978, the suicide rates by firearms and by all other methods both began to decrease (as seen from the regression coefficients), and so this seems to have been a period of decreasing suicide rates for women. In summary, for suicide, the passage of Bill C-51 seems to have led men to switch from firearms as a method for suicide to the use of other methods but to have had no impact on women.

Leenaars and Lester (1997b) looked at the impact of Bill C-51 by age. The firearm suicide rate decreased after passage of Bill C-51 only for suicides aged 35-64; the firearm suicide rate increased for those aged 15-34 and over the age of 65. The percentage of suicides using firearms declined only for those aged 15-64 while it increased for those over the age of 65. Switching to other methods for suicide was apparent in those aged 15-34 and those over the age of 75. The change in linear trends in the two periods (1969-1976 and 1978-1985) from an increasing trend prior to the passage of the bill to a declining trend after passage of the bill was apparent for those aged 15-44.

Carrington (1999), commenting on an earlier report by Leenaars and Lester (1996) looked at the slopes of the regression lines before and after the passage of Bill C-51, for suicide and for homicide and for both combined and for males and females separately. Most of the trends prior to the passage of Bill C-51 were positive (increasing rates) and statistically significant. Afterwards, most of the slopes were negative and the changes were significant. For both men and women, there was no evidence for switching methods.

During this time period, many social changes were taking place in Canada aside from changes in gun control laws. Leenaars, et al. (2003; Leenaars & Lester, 1999) ran multiple regressions for the period 1969-1985 using the passage of Bill C-51 (as a dichotomous variable – before versus after), the percentage of young men aged 15-24, the birth rate, the marriage rate, the divorce rate, the unemployment rate and the median family income to predict the suicide rates overall and for males and for females. In full multiple regressions, Bill C-51 had a significant beneficial impact on the firearm suicide rate overall and for both men and women. A similar beneficial impact was found for the percentage of suicides using firearms. The suicide rate by all other methods increased significantly for men but declined (non-significantly) for women. The total suicide rate declined for women (non-significantly) and increased (significantly) for men. Thus, switching appears to have occurred for men, but not for women.

Lester, et al. (2003) noted that an alternative method of statistical analysis (other than comparing pre- and post-periods after a change) is to use an interrupted time-series analysis. This analysis for the period 1969-1985 indicated that the passage of Bill C-51 had no impact on the total suicide rate, but the upward trend in the total suicide rate was less steep after the passage of the Bill. Similar results were obtained for the firearm suicide rate. For both the total suicide rate and the firearm suicide rate, these trends were greater for men than for women. The data for suicide by all other methods showed evidence of displacement for men but not for women.

Bridges (2004) explored the impact of two later gun control laws, Bill C-17 (passed in 1991) and Bill C-68 (passed in 1995) on the suicide rate, using the same technique as Leenaars and Lester. Bill C-17 banned semi-automatic firearms that could be converted to full automatic fire, raised the requirements for screening to obtain a certificate to purchase a firearm, mandated safe storage policies, and banned large-capacity magazines; Bill C-68 required a license to own and to purchase a firearm and to purchase ammunition, banned semi-automatic military assault weapons, as well as short-barreled and small caliber handguns (Cukier, 2000).

Bridges compared the time periods 1984-1990 and 1991-1998. After 1990, the suicide rate by firearms and the percentage of suicides using firearms decreased significantly, whereas the suicide rate by all other methods increased significantly, leaving the overall suicide rate unchanged. After 1990, the suicide rate by firearms and the percentage of suicides using firearms showed a steady, significant decline. These results suggest that the reduced availability of guns led potential suicides to choose other methods for suicide (that is, switching occurred).

Provincial Suicide Rates

Rich, et al. (1990) examined the impact on Bill C-51 on suicides in Ontario as a whole and in Toronto Ontario, comparing the periods 1973-1978 and 1979-1983. They found no change in the overall suicide rate in Ontario or in Toronto. There was a significant decrease in the proportion of male suicides using guns in Toronto. (Too few women used guns for the analysis to be meaningful.)

Carrington and Moyer (1994a) compared the periods of 1973-1977 and 1979-1983 as well as 1965-1977 and 1979-1989. They used both crude and age-standardized suicide rates whereas Rich, et al. used crude suicide rates. They confirmed that the overall suicide rate in Ontario did not change from the first to the second period. However, looking at trends in the before and after periods, they found that, before the passage of Bill C-51, the overall suicide rate, the firearm suicide rate and the suicide rate using other methods were increasing. After passage of the bill, all three suicides rates showed a declining trend. The use of age-standardize rates gave results similar to those for crude suicide rates. The fact that suicide by methods other than firearms showed a declining trend after the passage of the bill suggests that there were societal changes other than the passage of the bill that may have led to this declining trend.

Carrington and Moyer (1994b) carried out an analysis similar to those conducted by Leenaars and Lester, using the periods 1965-1977 and 1979-1989 for Canada as a whole and for each province. Nine of the ten Canadian provinces had significantly increasing trends in firearm suicide rates and the total suicide rate for 1965-1977. After the passage of Bill C-51, all ten provinces had either stable or decreasing firearm suicide rates and total suicide rates. None of the provinces had a significant increase in the suicide rate by all other methods for 1979-1989, and so switching methods did not occur.

Caron (2004) examined the impact of the implementation of Bill C-17 in 1992 in the Abitibi-Temiscamingue region of Quebec. While the firearm suicide rate decreased significantly, the suicide rate by all other methods and the overall suicide rate both increased. These trends were found for both men and women. The decrease in the firearms suicide rate was not, however, found for men over the age of 45. Caron concluded that switching of methods occurred, especially to hanging for young adults and to poisoning for women.

Caron, et al. (2008) carried out a detailed analysis of suicide rates by method in Quebec for the period 1987-2001, spanning the passage of Bill C-17. Caron, et al. examined the periods before and after Bill C-17 was implemented beginning in 1992, looked at trends in the suicide rates before and after 1992, carried out an interrupted time-series analysis, and examined the results of a multivariate regression analysis including divorce and unemployment rates. Their conclusion was that firearm suicide rates decreased after 1992, whereas the overall suicide rate and the suicide rate by all other methods increased, both for the total population and for men and women separately. However, a decreasing trend in firearm suicide rates was apparent prior to 1992, and so the decreasing trend afterwards appears to have been part of this long-term trend and not a result of the passage of Bill C-17. Caron, et al. concluded that the passage of Bill C-17 had no impact on the firearm suicide rate in Quebec. The passage of Bill C-17 also appeared to have no impact on the increasing trends in the overall suicide rate or the suicide rate by all other methods in Quebec.

Homicide

It must be noted that the rates and percentages in this section are based on data from victims of homicide, not from murderers.

Leenaars and Lester (1994b, 1996, 1997a, 1997b, 2001) examined the homicide rate in Canada before and after the passage of Bill C-51. Leenaars and Lester (1994b) found that the total homicide rate did not change from 1969-1976 to 1978-1985, but the homicide rate by firearms decreased significantly, as did the percentage of homicide using firearms, while the homicide rate using all other methods increased significantly. Since the total homicide rate did not change after the passage of Bill C-51, it appears that switching of methods for homicide occurred. Leenaars and Lester (2001) extended this preliminary report. They noted that the total homicide rate and the homicide rates by firearms and by all other methods were all increasing in the period 1969-1976 ($b = 0.10$, 0.05 and 0.08, respectively), but after the passage of Bill C-51, for the period 1978-1985, all three rates stayed at the same level.

Leenaars and Lester (1996) looked at these effects by sex. For male victims, the passage of Bill C-51 led to a reduced use of firearms for homicide and a greater use of all other methods. However, the use of firearms for murdering men stopped increasing after 1977 (as seen from the non-significant regression coefficients). For female victims, the firearms homicide rate decreased after the passage of Bill C-51, with no evidence of switching to other methods for homicide. Furthermore, the percentage of women killed with firearms declined after the passage of Bill C-51. In summary, the passage of Bill C-51 seems to have a more beneficial impact on female victims than on male victims.

As was noted above, Carrington (1999), commenting on an earlier report by Leenaars and Lester (1996) looked at the slopes of the regression lines before and after the passage of Bill C-51, for suicide and for homicide and for both combined and for males and females separately. Most of the trends in homicide prior to the passage of Bill C-51 were positive (increasing rates) and statistically significant. Afterwards, most of the slopes were negative and the changes were significant. For both men and women, there was no evidence for switching methods.

Leenaars and Lester (1997b, 2001) looked at the effects of Bill C-51 by the age of the victim. Comparing the periods 1969-1976 and 1978-1985, the percentage of homcides by firearms decreased for all age groups, significantly so for five of the seven age groups. The firearm homicide rate declined also for all age groups, significantly for five of the seven age groups. However, the homicide rate by all other methods increased only for those 54 years of age or younger while declining for those aged 55+, although not significantly so. The total homicide rates declined for all groups, but significantly so for only those aged 55-64. Thus, switching of methods appears to have taken place for homicide victims under the age of 54, but not for those 55 years of age and older. The linear trends for the two time periods by the age of the homicide victim were inconsistent. However, none of the regression coefficients for the firearm homicide rate by the age of the victim were significantly different from zero, indicating no consistent significant trends within each period even though the average homicide rate dropped for the first period (1969-1976) to the second period (1978-1985).

As noted above, during this time period, many social changes were taking place in Canada aside from changes in gun control laws. Leenaars and Lester (2001; Leenaars & Lester, 1999) ran multiple regressions for the period 1969-1985 using the passage of Bill C-51 (as a dichotomous variable), the percentage of young men aged 15-24, the birth rate, the marriage rate, the divorce rate, the unemployment rate and the median family income to predict the homicide rates by method. In full multiple regressions, the regression coefficient for Bill C-51 was negative for the total homicide rate, the rate by firearm, the rate by all other methods and the percentage of homicides using firearms, but statistically significant only for the total homicide rate. The results by sex (of the victim) were similar, except that, for men, the negative regression coefficient for the percentage of homicides using firearms was also significant along with that for the total homicide rate.

Bridges (2004) explored the impact of two later gun control laws, Bill C-17 (passed in 1991) and Bill C-68 (passed in 1995) on the homicide rate, using the same technique as Leenaars and Lester. Bridges compared the time periods 1984-1990 and 1991-1998. After 1990, the homicide rate using firearms declined, but so did the overall homicide rate and the homicide rate by all other methods. The percentage of homicides using firearms did not change significantly. After 1990, all three homicide rates continued to decline significantly. These results appear to indicate other social forces impacting on homicide rates other than the passage of gun control laws.

Mauser and Holmes (1992) used panel data – for nine of the ten provinces for each year from 1968 to 1988. The association of the passage of Bill C-51 in 1977 was associated with a decline in the homicide rate but not significantly. A multiple regression analysis with five other variables (such as the proportion of males aged 15-24 and the unemployment rate) showed that the effect of the gun control law was statistically significant. However, Mauser and Holmes noted that the homicide rate was declining in Canada from 1973 on and, to correct for that, they added a time variable (year). After this correction, the effect of the gun control law in the multiple regression was no longer statistically significant. Mauser and Holmes concluded that the passage of Bill C-51 had no impact on the homicide rate in Canada.

Accidental Deaths

Leenaars and Lester (1997) examined the impact of Bill C-51 on accidental deaths from firearms for men and women separately. The accidental death rate from firearms decreased in 1969-1976 after the passage of Bill C-51 for both men and women. Males showed a decreasing trend in mortality both before (1969-1976) and after (1978-1985) the passage of Bill C-51, while females showed a decreasing trend only after the passage of the bill. To explore the impact of unemployment and divorce rates, these two variables along with before versus after the passage of Bill C-51 were entered into a multiple regression, and the impact of the bill was negative on the mortality rate as expected (b = -1.38 for men and –0.32 for women) but not statistically significant.

Leenaars and Lester (1999) ran a multiple regression for the period 1969-1985 using divorce and unemployment rates and the passage of Bill C-51 to predict the accidental mortality from firearms. All three predictor variables were negative and statistically significant, indicating the gun control law reduced accidental mortality from firearms even after controls for divorce and unemployment rates.

Armed Robbery

Mauser and Maki (2003) formed a panel data set (pooled time series and cross-sectional data) for all ten Canadian provinces and the two territories for an 18-year period. In an econometric multiple regression analysis, with nine independent variables, the passage of Bill C-51 did not have a significant impact on the rates of robbery, armed robbery or firearm robbery.

The Implementation of Gun Control Laws

Laws may be passed, but they may not be obeyed or enforced. Lavoie, et al. (1994) evaluated the enforcement of Bill C-17 in Quebec. In a random community survey, they found that 99.6% of the firearms were kept unloaded, 70% were inoperative (that is, they had a locking mechanism) or inaccessible (locked up), and 91% had the ammunition safely stored. Sixty-five percent of gun owners had followed all three criteria.

Discussion

This essay has reviewed a large number of papers, the majority of which are based on the same limited set of data, most of which are shown in Table 1. Thus, the differences in the conclusions of the studies depend mostly on the statistical technique used and the subgroup of the Canadian population studied.

All of the studies are, by necessity, correlational, and so cause-and-effect conclusions cannot be drawn. However, nations rarely, if ever, introduce changes in public policy in a way that permits an experimental design. This could be done, for example, by introducing a change in public policy in some regions but not in others. (Ideally, the two sets of regions should be chosen randomly.) Political reality prevents such experiments.

The Canadian situation is complicated by the passage of several gun control bills – in 1968, 1977, 1991 and 1995. During this time period, many social and economic changes also occurred, thereby complication and possibly confounding the impact of any one variable.

The results are also complicated by the technique of analysis used. In a meta-analysis of studies on the impact of executions on the homicide rate, Yang and Lester (2008) found that the conclusions were different for time-series, ecological and panel data sets. The studies reviewed in this essay on gun control have employed all three methodologies and, therefore, it would not be surprising if the results depended on the methodology used.

For studies of gun control, it is also important to explore the enforcement of the laws. In the study of the deterrent effect of the death penalty, in the 1970s, the focus switched from the study of the existence or passage of a death penalty law to the study of the impact of actual executions. Only one study was identified that explored whether Canadians obey the gun control laws, and no studies were identified on the enforcement of the gun control laws.

One conclusion from this body of research is that gun control appears to reduce the use of firearms for suicide and murder. The evidence as to whether individuals switch to other means for killing themselves or murdering others is contradictory. The conclusion depended on the time period studied, the methodology used, and the particular subgroup of the population that is the focus of the study.

Public policy is rarely made on the basis of social science research. However, an examination of the situation in Canada suggests that both opponents and advocates of gun control could agree on provisions such as the safe storage of firearms and safety training for those who purchase and own guns.

The provision of licenses for purchasing and registering a gun is more controversial, but the requirements that people obtain licenses to drive cars and that cars must be registered do not have any significant impact on people's ownership of cars. Objections to similar requirements for firearms seem to rest on fears of a "slippery slope," that is, that passing such requirements is just the first step to much more stringent requirements. Similarly, restrictions on the type of firearm permitted are reasonable. After all, it is unlikely that any government would permit citizens to own missile launchers and missiles. The difficulty is in negotiating what firearms are allowed and which are not, and assuaging fears of a "slippery slope" in this area.

References

Bridges, F. S. (2002). Gun availability and use of guns for murder and suicide in Canada. *Psychological Reports*, 90, 1257-1258.

Bridges, F. S. (2004). Gun control law (Bill C-17), suicide, and homicide in Canada. *Psychological Reports*, 94, 819-826.

Bridges, F. S., & Kunselman, J. C. (2004). Gun availability and use of guns for suicide, homicide, and murder in Canada. *Perceptual & Motor Skills*, 98, 594-598.

Caron, J. (2004). Gun control and suicide. *Archives of Suicide Research*, 8, 361-374.

Caron, J., Julien, M., & Huang, J. H. (2008). Changes in suicide methods in Quebec between 1987 and 2000. *Suicide & Life-Threatening Behavior*, 38, 195-208.

Carrington, P. J. (1999). Gender, gun control, suicide and homicide in Canada. *Archives of Suicide Research*, 5, 71-75.

Carrington, P. J., & Moyer, S. (1994a). Gun control and suicide in Ontario. *American Journal of Psychiatry*, 151, 606-608.

Carrington, P. J., & Moyer, S. (1994b). Gun availability and suicide in Canada. *Studies on Crime & Crime Prevention*, 3, 168-178.

Centerwall, B. S. (1991). Homicide and the prevalence of handguns. *American Journal of Epidemiology*, 134, 1245-1260.

Chapdelaine, A., & Maurice, P. (1996). Firearms injury prevention and gun control in Canada. *Canadian Medical Association Journal*, 155, 1285-1289.

Chapdelaine, A., Samson, E., Kimberley, M. D., & Viau, L. (1991). Firearm-related injuries in Canada. *Canadian Medical Association Journal*, 145, 1217-1223.

Cook, P. J. (1982). The role of firearms in violent crime. In M. E. Wolfgang & M. E. Weiner (Eds.) *Criminal violence*, pp. 236-291. Beverly Hills, CA: Sage.

Cukier, W. (2000). Firearms regulation. *Chronic Diseases in Canada*, 19(1), 25-34.

Finley, C. J., Hemenway, D., Clifton, J., Brown, D. R., Simons, R. K., & Hameed, S. M. (2008). The demographics of significant firearm injury in Canadian trauma centers and the associated predictors of inhospital mortality. *Canadian Journal of Surgery*, 51, 197-203.

Gabor, T. (2003). Universal firearm registration in Canada: Three perspectives. *Canadian Journal of Criminology & Criminal Justice*, 45, 465-471.

Gabor, T., Roberts, J. V., Stein, K., & DiGiulio, L. (2001). Unintentional firearms deaths. *Canadian Journal of Public Health*, 92, 396-398.

Hung, C. K. (1993). Comments on the article…"Gun control and rates of firearms violence in Canada and the United States" by Robert J. Mundt. *Canadian Journal of Criminology*, 35, 37-41.

Lavoie, M. Cardinal, L., Chapdelaine, A., & St-Laurent, D. (1994). L'état d'entreposage des armes à feu longues gardées à domicile au Quebec. *Maladies Chroniques au Canada*, 22, 26-32.

Leenaars, A. A., & Lester, D. (1992). Comparison of rates and patterns of suicide in Canada and the United States, 1960-1988. *Death Studies*, 16, 417-430.

Leenaars, A. A., & Lester, D. (1994a). Suicide and homicide rates in Canada and the United States. *Suicide & Life-Threatening Behavior*, 24, 184-191.

Leenaars, A. A., & Lester, D. (1994b). Effects of gun control on homicide in Canada. *Psychological Reports*, 75, 81-82.

Leenaars, A. A., & Lester, D. (1996). Gender and the impact of gun control on suicide and homicide. *Archives of Suicide Research*, 2, 223-234.

Leenaars, A. A., & Lester, D. (1997a). The effects of gun control on the accidental death rate from firearms in Canada. *Journal of Safety Research*, 28, 119-122.

Leenaars, A. A., & Lester, D. (1997b). The impact of gun control on suicide and homicide across the life span. *Canadian Journal of Behavioural Sciences*, 29, 1-6.

Leenaars, A. A., & Lester, D. (1999). Gender, gun control, suicide and homicide. *Archives of Suicide Research*, 5, 77-79.

Leenaars, A. A., & Lester, D. (2001). The impact of gun control (Bill C-51) on homicide in Canada. *Journal of Criminal Justice*, 29, 287-294.

Leenaars, A. A., Moksony, F., Lester, D., & Wenckstern, S. (2003). The impact of gun control (Bill C-51) on suicide in Canada. *Death Studies*, 27, 103-124.

Lester, D. (1984). *Gun control: Issues and answers*. Springfield, IL: Charles Thomas.

Lester, D. (1990). The availability of firearms and the use of firearms for suicide. *Acta Psychiatrica Scandinavica*, 81, 146-147.

Lester, D. (1994). Use of firearms for suicide in Canada. *Perceptual & Motor Skills*, 79, 962.

Lester, D. (2000a). Armed robbery and the availability of firearms in Canada. *EuroCriminology*, 14, 113-115.

Lester, D. (2000b). Gun availability and the use of guns for suicide and homicide in Canada. *Canadian Journal of Public Health*, 91, 186-187.

Lester, D. (2001). Gun availability and use of guns for murder and suicide in Canada. *Psychological Reports*, 89, 624.

Lester, D., & Leenaars, A. A. (1993). Suicide rates in Canada before and after tightening firearm control laws. *Psychological Reports*, 72, 787-790.

Lester, D., & Leenaars, A. A. (1994). Gun control and rates of firearms violence in Canada and the United States. *Canadian Journal of Criminology*, 36, 463-464.

Lester, D., & Leenaars, A. A. (1998). Is there a regional subculture of firearm violence in Canada? *Medicine, Science & the Law*, 38, 317-320.

Mauser, G. A. (1990). A comparison of Canadian and American attitudes towards firearms. *Canadian Journal of Criminology*, 32, 573-589.

Mauser, G. A. (1996). Armed self-defense. *Journal of Criminal Justice*, 24, 393-406.

Mauser, G. A, & Holmes, R. A. (1992). An evaluation of the 1977 Canadian firearms legislation. *Evaluation Review*, 16, 603-617.

Mauser, G. A., & Maki, D. (2003). An evaluation of the 1977 Canadian firearm legislation. *Applied Economics*, 35, 423-436.

Mauser, G. A., & Margolis, M. (1992). The politics of gun control. *Government & Policy*, 10, 189-209.

Miller, T. R. (1995). Costs associated with gunshot wounds in Canada in 1991. *Canadian Medical Association Journal*, 153, 1261-1268.

Mundt, R. J. (1990). Gun control and rates of firearms violence in Canada and the United States. *Canadian Journal of Criminology*, 32, 137-154.

Quan, H., & Arboleda-Florez, J. (1999). Elderly suicide in Alberta. *Canadian Journal of Psychiatry*, 44, 762-768.

Rich, C. L., Young, J. G., Fowler, R. C., Wagner, J., & Black, N. A. (1990). Guns and suicide. *American Journal of Psychiatry*, 147, 342-346.

Simon, R., Chouinard, M., & Gravel, C. (1996). Suicide and firearms. In J. L. McIntosh (Ed.) *Suicide '96*, pp.35-37. Washington, DC: American Association of Suicidology.

Sloan, J. H., Kellerman, A. L., Reay, D. T., Ferris, J. A., Koepsell, T., Rivara, F. P., Rice, C., Gray, L., & LoGerfo, J. (1988). Handgun regulations, crime, assaults, and homicide. *New England Journal of Medicine*, 319, 1256-1262.

Sloan, J. H., Rivara, F. P., Reay, D. T., Ferris, J. A., & Kellerman, A. L. (1990). Firearm regulations and rates of suicide. *New England Journal of Medicine*, 322, 369-373.

Sproule, C. F., & Kennett, D. J. (1988). The use of firearms in Canadian homicides 1972-1982. *Canadian Journal of Criminology*, 30, 31-37.

Sproule, C. F., & Kennett, D. J. (1989). Killing with guns in the USA and Canada 1977-1983. *Canadian Journal of Criminology*, 31, 245-251.

Yang, B., & Lester, D. (2008). The deterrent effect of executions. *Journal of Criminal Justice*, 36, 453-460.

In: Homicide: Trends, Causes and Prevention
Editor: Randal B. Toliver and Ulrich R. Coyne ISBN 978-1-60741-625-8

Chapter 5

Mass Murderer, Unwilling Executioner, or Something Else: A Case Study of a Serbian Soldier

Mark A. Winton
Department of Criminal Justice and Legal Studies,
University of Central Florida, Orlando, FL 32816-1600, USA

Abstract

The purpose of this paper is to examine accounts of a Serbian soldier who participated in the execution of civilians during the Bosnian genocide. The application of Lonnie Athens' violentization theory (Athens, 2003) and the circumplex theory from family therapy (Olson, 1995, 2000) are used to examine the case study. Following Winton's (2008) and Winton and Unlu's (2008) model, the theories are consistent with the data. Suggestions for further research are addressed.

Keywords: Genocide, circumplex model, violentization theory, Balkans, war crimes.

Genocide has been neglected in the criminology and sociology literature (Day and Vandiver, 2000; Morrison, 2004; Yacoubian, 2000). The purpose of this study is to use two theoretical models to explain genocidal behavior (Winton and Unlu, 2008). One soldier's account of his participation in the Bosnian genocides is analyzed using Lonnie Athens' violentization theory (Athens, 2003) and Olson's (1995, 2000) circumplex model. This will allow for an integration of perspectives to address both structural and agency factors (Winton and Unlu, 2008).

The circumplex model of family functioning focuses on patterns of cohesion, flexibility, and communication (Olson, 2000; Olson, 1995; Olson and DeFrain, 1997). Families may be classified as balanced or unbalanced. High (enmeshed) or low (disengaged) levels of cohesion are related to family problems as are high (chaotic) or low (rigid) levels of flexibility (Olson,

2000; Olson, 1995; Olson and DeFrain, 1997). Winton and Unlu (2008) used the circumplex model to address the structural features of Balkan society during the 1990s genocide.

Athens (2003) developed an interpretive approach to represent how violent actors explain their situations. According to Athens (1992, 1997, 2003) there are four stages of the violentization process: brutalization (witnessing and experiencing violence), defiance (using violence to prevent or stop violence), violent dominant engagements (engaging in violent behavior), and virulency (defining oneself as a violent and dangerous person). Both of these theories will be used together to examine the case study of a Serbian soldier who killed over 70 civilians during the genocide.

Methods

The case study of Drazen Erdemovic was selected from The International Criminal Tribunal for the former Yugoslavia (ICTY) court transcripts and was used as data of the perpetrator's account of the mass killings. These transcripts provided information about the organization and implementation of the massacres. Directed qualitative content analytic procedures were used to analyze how the perpetrator constructed his participation in the killings and to assess how the data fit the theories (Hsieh and Shannon, 2005; see Winton and Unlu).

Data Sources

While multiple databases were consulted (e.g. Criminal Justice Abstracts, Academic Search Premier, JSTOR, Political Science Abstracts, PsychINFO, and Sociological Abstracts), the main data source consisted of The International Criminal Tribunal for the former Yugoslavia (ICTY) court transcripts. Previous work by Winton (2008) and Winton and Unlu (2008) were also used.

Data Analysis

Qualitative content analysis was used to determine if the theories could explain the case study through an analysis of "the content of text data through the systematic classification process of coding and identifying themes or patterns" (Hsieh and Shannon, 2005, p. 1278). The application of this method is explained in Winton and Unlu (2008) and Winton (2008). The codes have been established based on the violentization and circumplex model theories.

Balkan society was previously classified as rigidly enmeshed during the genocide (Winton and Unlu, 2008). According to the circumplex model, a rigid social structure included an authoritarian leadership style with strict codes of conduct (Olson, 1995; Olson and Defrain, 1997; Olson 2000; Winton, 2008). In this type of environment, people avoid questioning authority figures. In addition, there is a failure to adapt to societal changes. Enmeshed cohesion consisted of high levels of group loyalty, emotional closeness, dependency, and fears of negative sanctions for disagreeing with the perpetrator ideology (Winton, 2008).

For violentization theory, Athens' (1992, 1997, 2003) work was used. The stages of violentization are as follows:

- Brutalization- This initial stage consisted of teaching and modeling violent behavior through threatening, observing, and demonstrating how to use physical force (Athens, 1992, 1997, 2003; Winton and Unlu, 2008).
- Defiance-This second stage focused on the development of a belief system that supports using violence in order to reduce threats to the self (Athens, 1992, 1997, 2003; Winton and Unlu, 2008).
- Violent Dominant Engagements-In the third stage, the perpetrators are acting out in violent ways (Athens, 1992, 1997, 2003). The two previous stages have been internalized.
- Virulency- The fourth stage focused on the perpetrators defining themselves as violent and dangerous (Athens, 1992, 1997, 2003).
- Extreme Virulency-Extreme virulency was added by Winton (2008) to code for violence that included torture, mutilation, sexual assault, and slavery.

RESULTS

As previously mentioned, Balkan society had become rigidly enmeshed during the genocide (Winton and Unlu, 2008). As will be demonstrated, the "we must kill or be killed" genocidal script had been implemented during the massacre (Winton, 2008).

According to The International Criminal Tribunal for the former Yugoslavia (ICTY),

> The accused, Drazen Erdemovic, came into the custody of the International Tribunal for the Prosecution of Persons Responsible for Serious Violations of International Humanitarian Law Committed in the Territory of the former Yugoslavia since 1991, hereinafter referred to as the "International Tribunal" (Prosecutor v. Drazen Erdemovic, 1998, paragraph 1). At his initial appearance before Trial Chamber I on 31 May 1996, the accused pleaded guilty to the count of a crime against humanity. That Trial Chamber accepted the accused's guilty plea and dismissed the alternative count of a violation of the laws or customs of war. Due to concerns about the state of health of the accused, the Trial Chamber commissioned psychiatric and psychological evaluation. The expert medical commission reported that the accused was suffering from post-traumatic stress of such severity that he was unable to stand trial and recommended that a second examination be held in six months' time. At a status conference on 4 July 1996, the accused affirmed that he wished to continue to plead guilty (Prosecutor v. Drazen Erdemovic, 1998, paragraph 5).
>
> On 14 January 1998, this Trial Chamber took a fresh plea from the accused. He pleaded guilty to the charge of a violation of the laws or customs of war. The Prosecutor withdrew the alternative count of a crime against humanity. Thereafter, the Chamber heard submissions on sentencing at the pre-sentencing hearing (Prosecutor v. Drazen Erdemovic, 1998, paragraph 8).

Erdemovic instructed the court to use his previous statements that are summarized below. It was agreed that Erdemovic committed the killings while under orders and threat of death. According to court transcripts:

> Between 13 July 1995 and approximately 22 July 1995, thousands of Bosnian Muslim men were summarily executed by members of the Bosnian Serb army and Bosnian Serb police at divers locations including, but not limited to a warehouse at Kravica, a meadow and a dam near Lazete and divers other locations. (Prosecutor v. Drazen Erdemovic, 1998, paragraph 8).
>
> On or about 16 July 1995, *DRAZEN ERDEMOVIC* and other members of his unit were informed that bus loads of Bosnian Muslim civilian men from Srebrenica, who had surrendered to Bosnian Serb military or police personnel, would be arriving throughout the day at this collective farm (Prosecutor v. Drazen Erdemovic, 1998, paragraph 10).
>
> On or about 16 July 1995, buses containing Bosnian Muslim men arrived at the collective farm in Pilica. Each bus was full of Bosnian Muslim men, ranging from approximately 17-60 years of age. After each bus arrived at the farm, the Bosnian Muslim men were removed in groups of about 10, escorted by members of the 10th Sabotage Detachment to a field adjacent to farm buildings and lined up in a row with their backs facing *DRAZEN ERDEMOVIC* and members of his unit (Prosecutor v. Drazen Erdemovic, 1998, paragraph 11).
>
> On or about 16 July 1995, *DRAZEN ERDEMOVIC*, did shoot and kill and did participate with other members of his unit and soldiers from another brigade in the shooting and killing of unarmed Bosnian Muslim men at the Pilica collective farm. These summary executions resulted in the deaths of hundreds of Bosnian Muslim male civilians." (Prosecutor v. Drazen Erdemovic, 1998, paragraph 12). However, the Trial Chamber also accepts that the accused committed the offence in question under threat of death. At different stages in the previous proceedings, he testified as follows:
>
> "Your Honour, I had to do this. If I had refused, I would have been killed together with the victims. When I refused, they told me: "If you are sorry for them, stand up, line up with them and we will kill you too". I am not sorry for myself but for my family my wife and son who then had nine months, and I could not refuse because they would have killed me..."
>
> "Q. What happened to those civilians? A. We were given orders to fire at those civilians, that is, to execute them. Q. Did you follow that order? A. Yes, but at first I resisted and Brano Gojkovic told me if I was sorry for those people that I should line up with them; and I knew that this was not just a mere threat but that it could happen, because in our unit the situation had become such that the Commander of the group has the right to execute on the spot any individual if he threatens the security of the group or if in any other way he opposes the Commander of the group appointed by the Commander Milorad Pelemis..."
>
> "It was so difficult for me, but I had no choice. I had no choice..."
>
> "The Lieutenant Colonel took us to a farm. I did not know the name of that farm. I just explained the location. I knew that the village of Pilica was there, but it was only when we got there that I learned what was happening. They told us that a bus load of civilians would come from Srebrenica. I said immediately that I did not want to take part in that and I said, "Are you normal? Do you know what you are doing?" But nobody listened to me and they told me, "If you do not wish to, if you ....you can just go and stand in the line together with them. You can give us your rifle."
>
> I told you last time, if I had been alone, if I had not had my wife and a son, I would have fled and something else would have happened. I had to do that. I was forced to do that" (Prosecutor v. Drazen Erdemovic, 1998, paragraph 14).

It appears from the above statements that Erdemovic participated in the massacre under the threat of death. He was in the "kill or be killed" situation described in other genocides

(Winton, 2008). Erdemovic pointed out that his commander could execute any of the soldiers on the spot if he felt it was necessary for soldier safety. While Erdemovic tried to verbally persuade his comrades to avoid the massacre, he was given a choice-"kill or be killed."

He provided an example of the "kill or be killed" situation as follows:

> "Q. Did you know at the time of anyone who was shot for having disobeyed orders?
>
> A. You know, I will tell you, I am sure that I would have been killed had I refused to obey because I remember that Pelemis had already ordered one man to slaughter another man and I am familiar with some other orders, I mean, what a Commander was entitled to do if he was disobeyed; he could order this person's liquidation immediately. I had seen quite a bit of that over those few days and it was quite clear to me what it was all about" (Prosecutor v. Drazen Erdemovic, 1998, paragraph 14).

Aggravating circumstances are presented in the court transcripts as follows:

> The Trial Chamber accepts that hundreds of Bosnian Muslim civilian men between the ages of 17 and 60 were murdered by the execution squad of which the accused was part. The Prosecution has estimated that the accused alone, who says that he fired individual shots using a Kalashnikov automatic rifle, might have killed up to a hundred (100) people. This approximately matches his own estimate of seventy (70) persons. No matter how reluctant his initial decision to participate was, he continued to kill for most of that day. The Trial Chamber considers that the magnitude of the crime and the scale of the accused's role in it are aggravating circumstances to be taken into account in accordance with Article 24(2) of the Statute of the International Tribunal (Prosecutor v. Drazen Erdemovic, 1998, paragraph 15).

Demographic and personal data about Erdemovic was also presented in the trial transcripts. Erdemovic was 23 years old during the time of the massacre. Based on his confession, remorse, and family situation, the Trial Chamber believed that he is "reformable and should be given a second chance to start his life afresh upon release, whilst still young enough to do so" (Prosecutor v. Drazen Erdemovic, 1998, paragraph 16). The court transcripts continue with a description of his family background and character and how he attempted to avoid becoming a killer:

> The accused has a wife, who is of different ethnic origin, and the couple have a young child who was born on 21 October 1994. Defence Counsel has submitted that the accused's family has fallen on hard times and will suffer hardship due to his serving a prison sentence. The accused is a locksmith by training and was drawn into the maelstrom of violence that engulfed the former Yugoslavia. He has professed pacifist beliefs and claims to have been against the war and nationalism. He claims that he had to join the BSA in order to feed his family. In July 1995, he was a private in the 10th Sabotage Detachment where he was not in a position of command. He was, apart from a two month period as a sergeant in that unit, a mere footsoldier whose lack of commitment to any ethnic group in the conflict is demonstrated by the fact that he was by turns a reluctant participant in the Army of the Republic of Bosnia-Herzegovina, hereinafter referred to as the "ABH", the Croatian Defence Council, hereinafter referred to as the "HVO", and the BSA. The possibility of his being a soldier of fortune has not been suggested by any of the parties.
>
> The 10th Sabotage Detachment was involved with reconnaissance in enemy territory and placing explosives in the artillery of the areas controlled by the ABH. According to the accused, he chose this unit because "it did not involve the loss of human lives. It involved

artillery, old iron." In addition, he chose it as there were other non-Serb soldiers in it and it did not have a reputation for brutality at the material time. (Prosecutor v. Drazen Erdemovic, 1998, paragraph 16).

In describing his character, court transcripts indicated that:

> The Prosecution stated that they found no inconsistencies with the information which he gave them; their investigations have confirmed much of what he told them, indicating that the accused is of an honest disposition. This is supported by his confession and consistent admission of guilt, in particular by the fact that he came forward voluntarily and told of his part in the massacres before his involvement was known to any investigating authorities. In his submissions, the Defence Counsel portrayed the accused as an easygoing young man showing no signs of bigotry or intolerance, with a desire to help others in difficulty. The accused's upbringing was steeped in values of tolerance for others, and this is reflected in the fact that he chose to marry a woman from another ethnic group. Defence Counsel sees the accused as a victim of the whirlwind of war and a victim of his own deeds. Whilst the Commission of Medical Experts made a finding of emotional immaturity, which is noted, there is nothing to substantiate Defence Counsel's submission to Trial Chamber I (which was not raised again before this Trial Chamber) that when the accused committed the killings, he "lacked mental responsibility because he suffered a temporary mental disorder or, at best, his mental responsibility was significantly diminished also…"
>
> Witness Y, who also testified before Trial Chamber I, met the accused in 1993 and they were part of a group of multi-ethnic friends. According to this witness, the accused was not a nationalist. He was a popular, vivacious and outgoing person who was non-confrontational. Witness Y was certain that the accused hated the war and the army but believed that he simply had to do all of it; he was not the sort of person to kill of his own free-will. According to the evidence of the accused before Trial Chamber I, admitted by this Trial Chamber, he had helped a family of Serb civilians, mainly women and children, to escape from the Tuzla area to Republika Srpska, which led to his being assaulted by soldiers from the HVO. He also appears to have been imprisoned as a result. The accused has told the International Tribunal that during the killings at the Pilica collective farm, he tried to save a man, but was not able to do so because his commander, Brano Gojkovic, said that he did not want to have any witnesses to that crime. (Prosecutor v. Drazen Erdemovic, 1998, paragraph 16).

Erdemovic expressed feelings of guilt over his participation in the massacre although his guilt is expressed in an ambivalent manner. He expressed global guilt over the genocide but did not feel guilty for the specific crimes that he committed. In other words, the "kill or be killed" scenario removed or reduced his individual guilt.

The accused told Trial Chamber I that:

> "I only wish to say that I feel sorry for all the victims, not only for the ones who were killed then at that farm. I feel sorry for all the victims in the former [sic] Bosnia and Herzegovina regardless of their nationality."
>
> On 24 June 1996, the Commission of Medical Experts noted that the accused had an ambivalent feeling about his guilt. "He knew he killed innocent civilians, but he had no choice himself. There were other people who ordered him to shoot people. In a legal sense he doesn't feel guilty of the crimes he is accused of." The post-traumatic stress which the accused suffered from in the aftermath of the Srebrenica atrocities demonstrates how he himself has suffered from being forced to commit the killings against his will. (Prosecutor v. Drazen Erdemovic, 1998, paragraph 16).

His cooperation aided the court system in various ways:

> Whilst the OTP knew in general terms of the killings committed in Srebrenica, the testimony of the accused was particularly valuable for providing them with details of four incidents of which they did not previously know: the killings at the Pilica collective farm, those at the Pilica cultural hall, the killing of an unidentified civilian male of military age in Srebrenica as the accused entered the town, and a killing in Vlasenica on 13 July 1996 after he returned to Bijeljina, by soldiers who, under orders, cut the throat of a prisoner. Prior to the testimony of the accused, the OTP had no knowledge of these incidents. The accused provided substantial details in connection with the aforementioned incidents such as the identification of his commanders and fellow executioners, as well as information on the Drina Corps, the structure of the BSA and the units that were involved in the takeover of Srebrenica such as the 10th Sabotage Detachment and the Bratunac Brigade. On 5 July 1996, the accused gave evidence in the Rule 61 hearing of the case brought against Radovan Karadzic and Ratko Mladic. His testimony was significant in two respects: it contributed to the decision of the Rule 61 Chamber to issue international arrest warrants for the two, and secondly, his testimony, that of an insider in the BSA, is evidence of what happened in Srebrenica (Prosecutor v. Drazen Erdemovic, 1998, paragraph 16).

In regard to duress that Erdemovic faced, the Trial Chamber stated,

> "*duress does not afford a complete defence to a soldier charged with a crime against humanity and/or a war crime involving the killing of innocent human beings*". It may be taken into account only by way of mitigation. (Prosecutor v. Drazen Erdemovic, 1998, paragraph 17). It has been accepted by the parties and the Trial Chamber that there was duress in this case. The earlier testimony of the accused has been cited above. Mr. Ruez has testified of the circumstances of a very vicious and cruelly fought war, the brutal nature of the battle for Srebrenica, the attendant environment of soldiers killing pursuant to superior orders, the accused's vulnerable position as a Bosnian Croat in the BSA and his history of disagreements with his commander, Milorad Pelemis, and subsequent demotion. He feels that had the accused refused to shoot, "most certainly, he would get into very deep trouble. . ."(Prosecutor v. Drazen Erdemovic, 1998, paragraph 17).
>
> The accused displays a tendency to feel the helpless victim; there are several references in his testimonies to his having no choice in a variety of situations. He speaks of his having to become a soldier, that he had no choice in leaving the Republic of Croatia for Republika Srpska, that he had to join the BSA "to feed my family", that he "simply had to" go to the military barracks and leave behind his bedridden wife and sick child, that he had no choice in taking part in the Srebrenica operation, and that he "had to shoot those people" murdered in the Pilica collective farm massacre. On the other hand, he has provided testimony of incidents when he broke out of this chain of helplessness and took positive action; such as when he saved some Serbs in Tuzla, when he saved Witness X, when he refused to comply with the orders of Lieutenant Milorad Pelemis, when he tried to refuse to kill at the collective farm and when he refused to kill at the hall in Pilica. Thus, he was capable of taking positive action, once he had weighed up his options. The risks that he took appear to have been calculated and considered. (Prosecutor v. Drazen Erdemovic, 1998, paragraph 17).

While duress is examined during the violentization process, the victim experience is brought into the sentencing. Erdemovic helped to identify other perpetrators and crimes that would not have come to the attention of the court system. By doing this, he also would be putting himself at risk of retaliation by the perpetrators or their supporters. Erdemovic presented himself as a victim. In this case the individual is constructed as a victim and a perpetrator. This fits within the violentization paradigm.

> The evidence reveals the extremity of the situation faced by the accused. The Trial Chamber finds that there was a real risk that the accused would have been killed had he disobeyed the order. He voiced his feelings, but realised that he had no choice in the matter: he had to kill or be killed. (Prosecutor v. Drazen Erdemovic, 1998, paragraph 17).
>
> In addition to the aggravating and mitigating circumstances already discussed, the sentence determined by the Trial Chamber has taken into account the circumstances of the killings, looking in particular at the degree of suffering to which the victims of the massacre were subjected before and during the killings, the means used by the accused to kill and his attitude at the time. The atmosphere of terror and violence has been well-illustrated to the Trial Chamber by the accused and Mr. Ruez; the victims were, in particular after the arrival on the scene of members of the Bratunac Brigade, subjected to physical assault, humiliation and verbal abuse. For the victims who arrived after the first set of killings, there was the certain knowledge of death, as they will have seen the bodies of those already murdered and heard the gunshots fired by the accused and his fellow executioners. The degree of suffering of these people cannot be overlooked. But the accused's reluctance to participate and his reaction to having to perform this gruesome task have already been discussed elsewhere in this Judgement. It is clear that he took no perverse pleasure from what he did. (Prosecutor v. Drazen Erdemovic, 1998, paragraph 20).

The outcome of this case is as follows:

> FOR THE FOREGOING REASONS, having considered all of the evidence and the arguments of the parties and the jurisprudence of the International Tribunal, THE TRIAL CHAMBER, in accordance with the Statute and Rules of Procedure and Evidence, imposes on Drazen Erdemovic the sentence of five (5) years' imprisonment for the VIOLATION OF THE LAWS OR CUSTOMS OF WAR to which he pleaded guilty on 14 January 1998, with credit to be given for his time in detention since 28 March 1996. (Prosecutor v. Drazen Erdemovic, 1998, paragraph 23).

Discussion and Conclusions

The purpose of this study was to examine the accounts of a Serbian soldier who killed over 70 civilians during the Bosnian genocide and to determine if the circumplex model and violentization theory can explain this genocidal situation. Specifically, the model presented by Winton and Unlu (2008) was applied to this case study.

In the case of Erdemovic, an apparently well adjusted, married father, with no apparent history of violence, and without previous nationalistic biases found himself in a "kill or be killed" scenario. He had a choice to kill those defined as the enemy or be killed himself. This 23 year old soldier did not plan to execute over 70 innocent civilians. Erdemovic plead guilty and provided additional information about his crimes and those of his superiors. He stated that he had no choice but to kill. He tried to avoid having to kill and asked his superior officers to think about what they were doing and spare the lives of the civilians. Despite being diagnosed with Post Traumatic Stress Disorder (after the massacre), he appeared to free of other major mental disorders.

Erdemovic went through part of the violentization process within a rigidly enmeshed environment. Erdemovic went through the brutalization stage as he was taught how to use violent strategies during his military training, witnessed violence against others, and received coaching to engage in violent behavior by his peers and superiors during the conflict. The military provided training and permission to engage in violent behavior (see Sanborn, 2003).

During the defiance stage, Erdemovic tried to stop the massacre by telling his colleagues to think about what they were going to do. During this stage, Erdemovic believed that he would be killed along with his family if he did not engage in violent behavior. This situation apparently encouraged him to use violent behavior by participating in the massacre to reduce the threat to himself and his family. During the violent dominant engagements stage, Erdemovic reluctantly engaged in violent behavior by killing over 70 innocent civilians.

He does not progress to the virulency stage as he feels guilty about what has occurred, does not want to participate in any additional violence, and feels sick over his behavior (Drakulić, 2004). Drakulić states, "Drazen had never felt so alone, alone with twelve hundred dead bodies that would follow him wherever he went" (p. 120). He does not define himself as a violent and dangerous person.

Browning (1998) found that the group of Nazis in the Reserve Police Battalion 101 consisted of some who were eager to kill, others that killed reluctantly, and some who refused to kill, but a majority of the group did become killers. One difference in Browning's case study was that the Police Battalion participants could avoid participating in the killings without major threat to their safety. According to Browning (1998), "if the men of Reserve Police Battalion 101 could become killers under such circumstances, what group of men cannot" (p. 189)?

In contrast, Rhodes (2002) found that the Nazi task forces were predisposed toward violent behavior and went through the violentization process outlined by Athens (1992). Rhodes model appears to be more consistent with this case study.

There are several limitations to this study. First, one case was presented of an individual who was very forthcoming with information about his participation in the genocide. Second, using secondary sources precluded asking the individual direct questions related to the theories. Third, the use of court transcripts may exclude other relevant information from the analysis. Finally, a comparative analysis with other cases studies was not provided.

Genocide is often a neglected topic in criminology, sociology, and criminal justice courses and research. Perhaps it is very difficult to integrate genocide into criminological or sociological theories. More interest may be generated from recent and current genocides (e.g. Sudan). This is a prime area of interdisciplinary study with the potential for communication across fields as understanding genocide may require the integration of theories from various disciplines (e.g. anthropology, sociology, political science, psychology, and neurology).

What drives people to commit genocide? While greatly disturbed individuals may engage in violent behavior, this research, as well as other studies have shown that "normal" people engage in genocide. Future research of this nature may provide information about the deviolentization process (Ulmer, 2003). Hopefully, further research on genocide will be conducted from criminological and sociological perspectives with direct policy implications for prevention and intervention.

References

Athens, L. H. (1992). *The creation of dangerous violent criminals*. Urbana: University of Illinois Press.

Athens, L. (1997). *Violent criminal acts and actors revisited.* Urbana: University of Illinois Press.

Athens, L. (2003). Violentization in larger social context. In L. Athens and J. T. Ulmer (Eds.), *Violent acts and violentization: assessing, applying, and developing Lonnie Athens' theories* (pp. 1-41). Boston: Elsevier Science.

Browning, C.R. (1998). *Ordinary men: reserve police battalion 101 and the final solution in Poland.* New York: HarperPerennial.

Day, L. E., and Vandiver, M. (2000). Criminology and genocide studies: notes on what might have been and what still could be. *Crime, Law and Social Change, 34*, 43-59.

Drakulić, S. (2004). *They would never hurt a fly: war criminals on trial in the Hague.* New York: Penguin.

Dulić, T. (2006). Mass killing in the independent state of Croatia, 1941–1945: a case for comparative research. *Journal of Genocide Research, 8*, 255–281.

Hsieh, H., and Shannon, S.E. (2005). Three approaches to qualitative content analysis. *Qualitative Health Research, 15*, 1277-1288.

Morrison, W. (2004). 'Reflections with memories': everyday photography capturing genocide. *Theoretical Criminology, 8*, 341-358.

Olson, D. H. (1995). Family systems: Understanding your roots. In R. D. Day, K. R. Gilbert, B. H. Settles, and W. R. Burr (Eds.), *Research and theory in family science* (pp. 131-153). Pacific Grove, CA: Brooks/Cole.

Olson, D. H. (2000). *Clinical Rating Scale (CRS) for the Circumplex Model of Marital and Family Systems* [Brochure]. Minneapolis: Life Innovations.

Olson, D. H., and DeFrain, J. (1997). *Marriage and the family: diversity and strengths* (2nd ed.). Mountain View, CA: Mayfield.

Prosecutor v. Drazen Erdemovic, Sentencing Judgement, 5 March 1998, Case No. IT-96-22. Retrieved January 18, 2007, from http://www.un.org/icty/erdemovic/trialc/judgement/erd-tsj980305e.htm.

Rhodes, R. (2002). *Masters of death: the SS-Einsatzgruppen and the invention of the Holocaust.* New York: Vintage Books.

Sanborn, J. (2003). The short course for murder: How soldiers and criminals learn to kill. In L. Athens and J. T. Ulmer (Eds.), *Violent acts and violentization: assessing, applying, and developing Lonnie Athens' theories* (pp. 107-124). Boston: Elsevier Science.

Ulmer, J. T. (2003). Afterword: Where does violentization go from here? In L. Athens and J. T. Ulmer (Eds.), *Violent acts and violentization: assessing, applying, and developing Lonnie Athens' theories* (pp. 175-183). Boston: Elsevier Science.

Winton, M. A. (2008). Dimensions of genocide: the circumplex model meets violentization theory. *The Qualitative Report, 13*(4), 605-629. Retrieved from http://www.nova.edu/sss/QR/QR13-4/winton.pdf.

Winton, M.A. and Unlu, A. (2008). Micro-macro dimensions of the Bosnian genocides: The circumplex model and violentization theory. Aggression and Violent Behavior, 13, 45-59.

Yacoubian, G. S. (2000). The (in)significance of genocidal behavior to the discipline of criminology. *Crime, Law and Social Change, 34*, 7-19.

In: Homicide: Trends, Causes and Prevention
Editor: Randal B. Toliver and Ulrich R. Coyne
ISBN 978-1-60741-625-8

Chapter 6

HOMICIDE TRENDS IN DELHI, INDIA

Anil Kohli and Arvind Kumar
Department of Forensic Medicine
University College of Medical Sciences
Delhi, India

ABSTRACT

Pattern of homicides in Delhi, India was studied over a two year period from November 1991 to October 1993 and repeated over a two year period from January 2006 to December 2007. Both the studies were carried out in a tertiary care teaching hospital catering to North-east district of Delhi, India. The aim was to assess the pattern of homicides in Delhi and to look for any changes in the homicide pattern in Delhi over a period of time (fifteen years).

Delhi, the capital of India, currently has a population of about fourteen million. The murder crime rate for Delhi in1991 was 5.1 and in 2006 was 2.9.The culpable homicide not amounting to murder crime rate for Delhi in 1991 was 0.65 and in 2006 was 0.45. In the two year period of 1991-1993 homicides comprised 12.8% of the total cases brought for autopsy whereas in the two year period 2006-2007 they comprised 6.3% of the total cases brought for autopsy.

The studies took into account the age and sex of the victims, survival time after the incident, types of fatal injuries and the body organs involved. Males were the predominant victims in 1991-1993 and 2006-2007 (79% and 83.6% respectively). Spot deaths and victims brought dead to the hospital constituted a large number of cases (60.4% in 1991-1993 and 59.6% in 2006-2007). The maximum number of victims were in the age group of 21-30 years constituting 45.5% of the total cases in 1991-1993 and 34.9% of the total cases in 2006-2007. Deaths due to stabbing by sharp edged weapons were the commonest in 1991-1993 comprising 41% of the total cases. Deaths due to firearm injuries constituted 10.4% of cases and those due to blunt force injuries made up 15.7% of the cases. Interestingly in 2006-2007 deaths due to stabbing by sharp edged weapons occurred only in 24% of the cases, whereas death due to firearm injuries and blunt force injuries comprised 24% and 28.4% of the cases respectively. Some of the major motives for the homicides in our study were gain, property disputes, personal vendetta, love affairs/sexual causes and dowry. Reasons for the changing trends in Delhi are discussed in the chapter. Homicide trends in Delhi are also compared to the trends seen in other cities of India.

INTRODUCTION

Homicide (Latin homicidium, homo human being + caedere to cut, kill) refers to the act of killing another human being. The term applies to all such killings, whether criminal or not. Homicide is not always an illegal act. Homicide is considered non criminal in situations like deaths as the result of war or putting someone to death by the valid sentence of a court. Killing may also be legally justified or excused, as it is in cases of self-defense or when someone is killed by another person who is attempting to prevent a violent crime. Criminal homicide occurs when a person purposely, knowingly, recklessly or negligently causes the death of another. Murder and manslaughter are both examples of criminal homicide [1, 2].

Murder is the unlawful killing of another human person with malice aforethought as defined in common law countries.(Common law refers to law and the corresponding legal system developed through decisions of courts rather than through legislative statutes. The common law is created and refined by judges: a decision in the case currently pending depends on decisions in previous cases and affects the law to be applied in future cases. When there is no authoritative statement of the law, judges have the authority and duty to make law by creating precedent. The body of precedent is called "common law" and it binds future decisions. In future cases if a similar dispute has been resolved in the past, the court is bound to follow the reasoning used in the prior decision -this principle is known as stare decisis. If however the current dispute is fundamentally distinct from all previous cases, the court will decide it as a matter of first impression and thereafter the new decision becomes precedent, and will bind future courts) [3].Common law murder is defined as the unlawful killing of another human person with a state of mind known as "malice aforethought." The following states of mind are recognized as "malice aforethought":(i) Intent to kill; (ii) Intent to inflict serious bodily harm short of death; (iii) Reckless indifference to an unjustifiably high risk to human life; or (iv) Intent to commit a dangerous felony.

In India the laws regarding homicide are derived from the Indian Penal Code (IPC), 1860.

The IPC was drafted by Lord Macualy in 1833 which became law in 1860 and the same is being followed since then with various amendments from time to time.

Section 299 IPC [4] defines *culpable homicide*: whoever causes death by doing an act with the intention of causing death, or with the intention of causing such bodily injury as is likely to cause death, or with the knowledge, that he is likely by such act to cause death, commits the offence of culpable homicide.

Section 300 IPC [4] defines *murder:* except in the cases hereinafter excepted, culpable homicide is murder, if the act by which the death is caused is done with the intention of causing death, or

If it is done with the intention of causing such bodily injury as the offender knows to be likely to cause the death of the person to whom the harm is caused, or

If it is done with the intention of causing bodily injury to any person and the bodily injury intended to be inflicted is sufficient in the ordinary course of nature to cause death, or

If the person committing the act knows that it is so imminently dangerous that it must, in all probability, cause death or such bodily injury as is likely to cause death, and commits such act without any excuse for incurring the risk of causing death, or such injury as aforesaid.

Exceptions—Culpable homicide is *not* murder:

1. If the offender, whilst deprived of the power of self-control by grave and sudden provocation, causes the death of the person who gave the provocation or causes the death of any other person by mistake or accident. The provocation should not be sought or voluntarily provoked by the offender as an excuse for killing or doing harm to any person. Secondly the provocation is not given by anything done in obedience to the law, or by a public servant in the lawful exercise of the powers of such public servant. Thirdly the provocation is not given by anything done in the lawful exercise of the right of private defense.
2. If the offender, in the exercise in good faith of the right of private defense of person or property, exceeds the power given to him by law and causes the death of the person against whom he is exercising such right of defense.
3. If the offender, being a public servant or aiding a public servant acting for the advancement of public justice, exceeds the powers given to him by law, and causes death by doing an act which he, in good faith, believes to be lawful and necessary for the due discharge of his duty.
4. If it is committed without premeditation in a sudden fight in the heat of passion upon a sudden quarrel. It is immaterial in such cases which party offers the provocation or commits the first assault.
5. When the person whose death is caused, being above the age of eighteen years, suffers death or takes the risk of death with his own consent.

The punishments for culpable homicide not amounting to murder and murder are different and are given under Sections 304 and 302 of the IPC respectively.

The global homicide rate was 7.6 homicides per 100,000 populations for 2004, the last year for which comprehensive data is available. Murder rates in Japan, Ireland and Iceland are among the lowest in the world, around 0.5; the rate for the United States is among the highest of developed countries, around 5.6.

Delhi, the capital of India, currently has a population of about fourteen million (2001 census). It is considered the crime capital of the country having a crime rate of 357.2 against the national average of 167.7.The murder crime rate for Delhi in1991 was 5.1(for India it was 4.6) and in 2006 was 2.9(for India it was 2.9).The culpable homicide not amounting to murder crime rate for Delhi in 1991 was 0.65(for India it was 0.5) and in 2006 was 0.45(for India it was 0.3).Delhi's share of murder cases amongst the top five metro cities in India was 42%(more than that of Kolkatta, Chennai and Mumbai taken together) [5].

Population is one of the important factors influencing incidence of crime. A positive correlation between the growth in incidence of crime and the population of the country has been observed. Other factors influencing crime rate besides population are growing urbanization leading to migration of population from neighboring places, unemployment, economic inequality etc. The population of Delhi increased at the rate of 3.6% per annum during the ten year period 1991-2001 and occupies the second place amongst all the metros.

Delhi tops the list of migrant population – 32% in 2001 (percentage share of migrant population to total population).The per capita income of Delhi is the third highest in the country and twice the national average. The Annual Compound Growth Rate of Per Capita Income is 4.45 at constant prices and 11.6 at current prices. Percentage of unemployed persons to the total labor force was 5.67% in 1992 and 4.63% in 2003.

In view of all this, aim of this study firstly, was to assess the pattern of homicides in Delhi and secondly, to look for any changes in the homicide pattern in Delhi over a period of time.

Material and Methods

Guru Teg Bahadur Hospital is a tertiary care teaching hospital catering to North-east district of Delhi and currently serving a population of about 1.8 million people. Pattern of homicides in Delhi, India was studied here over a two year period from November 1991 to October 1993. After fifteen years the study was repeated over a two year period from January 2006 to December 2007.

During the period November 1991 to October 1993,134 homicidal deaths were autopsied out of 1045 total autopsies performed in the Department of Forensic Medicine, University College of Medical Sciences and associated Guru Teg Bahadur Hospital, Delhi. During the period January 2006 to December 2007, 183 homicidal deaths were autopsied out of 2895 total autopsies performed. In the two year period of 1991-1993 homicides constituted 12.82% of the total cases brought for autopsy whereas in the two year period 2006-2007 they constituted 6.32% of the total cases brought for autopsy.

The cases were analyzed for evaluation of various parameters like age and sex of the victim, survival time after the incident, types of fatal injuries and the body organs involved.

Standard autopsy techniques were used for the autopsies.

Results

The age distribution of the victims is given in Table 1. In the 1991-1993 study, the maximum number of victims were in the age group of 21-30 years constituting 45.5% of the total cases in this study, whereas in the 2006-2007 study, the number of victims in this age group constituted 35% of the cases. There was a decline in the number of victims in the most socially active age group of 21-30 years in the later study. However there was an increase in the number of victims in the age group of 41-50 years with 11.5% of the cases in the later study making up this group as compared to 5.2% in the earlier study. There was not any significant comparative change in the remaining age groups.

Males were the predominant victims in both the studies. They constituted 107 cases (79.9%) in the 1991-1993 study and 153 cases (83.6%) in the 2006-2007 study.

Spot deaths were those occurring at the scene of the crime/incident whereas victims brought dead to hospital were those who showed signs of life when help reached them but died on the way to hospital.

Spot deaths and victims brought dead to hospital constituted 81 cases (60.4%) in 1991-1993. Spot deaths and victims brought dead to hospital constituted 109 cases (59.6%) in 2006-2007 (Table 2). When comparing both the studies, there was a decline in the spot deaths in the later study. Spot deaths made up 25.1% of the total deaths in the later study as compared to 44% in the earlier study. However in 2006-2007, victims brought dead constituted 63 cases (34.4%) as compared to 22 cases (16.4%) in 1991-1993.

About 89% of the victims died within one day of the incident/crime in the earlier study and about 73% of the victims died within one day in the later study.

Table 1. Age distribution of victims

Age group (years)	Number of victims (Nov 91 to Oct 93)	Number of victims (Jan 06 to Dec 07)
0-10	06	07
11-20	19	34
21-30	61	64
31-40	28	39
41-50	07	21
51-60	07	10
60+	06	08
Grand Total	134	183

Table 2. Survival time of the victims

Duration of survival	1991-1993		2006-2007	
	Number of cases	Percentage	Number of cases	Percentage
Spot deaths	59	44.03	46	25.14
Brought dead to hospital	22	16.42	63	34.42
Less than 12 hours	27	20.15	16	8.74
Half day to 1 day	11	8.21	09	4.92
One day to 2 days	05	3.73	12	6.56
Two days to 3 days	01	0.75	07	3.83
Three days to 1 week	04	2.99	16	8.74
One week to 1 month	03	2.23	12	6.56
> 1 month	02	1.49	02	1.09
Grand Total	134		183	

The types of fatal injuries received by the victims are outlined in Table 3. In 1991-1993 stabs (41%), blunt force injuries (15.7%), ligature strangulation (10.5%) and bullet injuries (7.5%) were the commonest fatal injuries received by the victims, accounting for about 75% of the deaths. In 2006-2007 blunt force injuries (28.4%), stabs (24%), bullet injuries (23.5%) and ligature strangulation (6.6%) were the commonest fatal injuries received by the victims, accounting for about 83% of the deaths. In comparison to the earlier study, in the later study there was a significant fall in cases of stab injuries and a significant rise in cases of blunt force injuries and firearm injuries.

Throttling (manual strangulation) and poisoning as causes of death were rare in both the studies. Surprisingly, cut throat as a cause of death was uncommon in both the studies.

Table 3. Type of fatal injuries seen

	1991-1993	**2006-2007**
Type of injury	**Number of cases (%)**	**Number of cases (%)**
Stabs	55 (41.05%)	44 (24.04%)
Blunt force	21 (15.67%)	52 (28.42%)
Blunt force and stab	5 (3.73%)	0
Firearm (bullet)	10 (7.46%)	43 (23.5%)
Firearm (pellet)	4 (2.99%)	1 (0.55%)
Strangulation (ligature)	14 (10.45%)	12 (6.55%)
Strangulation (manual)	3 (2.24%)	5 (2.73%)
Manual and ligature strangulation	2 (1.49%)	1 (0.55%)
Suffocation	2 (1.49%)	7 (3.82%)
Cut throat	7 (5.22%)	5 (2.73%)
Heavy cutting weapon	0	3 (1.64%)
Decapitation and stab	2 (1.49%)	1 (0.55%)
Burns (flame)	4 (2.99%)	7 (3.82%)
Burns (acid)	3 (2.24%)	1 (0.55%)
Poisoning	2 (1.49%)	1 (0.55%)
Grand Total	134	183

There was hardly any change between the two studies with regard to the incidence of deaths due to manual strangulation, manual and ligature strangulation, suffocation, decapitation and stab, acid burns, flame burns and poisoning.

Involvement of the main body organs is shown in Table 4. Lungs, brain and the major blood vessels were the organs most commonly involved in the 1991-1993 study when involved alone and also when involved in combination with other organs. In the 2006-2007 study lungs and brain were the organs most commonly involved. Major blood vessels and other organs like stomach, intestines and pancreas also were involved in a large number of cases in the later study. Spleen and kidneys were rarely involved in both the studies. Skin along with internal organs was involved in cases which received acid/flame burn injuries.

There was not any significant change in the motives for the homicides in both the studies. The major motives in order of occurrence in both the studies were personal vendetta (12%-18%), property disputes (14%-15%), financial gain (7%-8%), love affairs/sexual causes (6%-10%). Dowry as a motive (6%) was present in only the 1991-1993 study. In about 30% to 40% of the cases in both the studies, the motives could not be ascertained.

Table 4. Involvement of body organs

Organs	1991-1993		2006-2007	
	Number of cases in which involved		Number of cases in which involved	
	Alone	In combination with others	Alone	In combination with others
Brain	19	22	62	2
Heart	6	13	4	6
Lungs	12	34	8	24
Liver	5	15	4	21
Spleen	1	3	0	0
Kidneys	0	4	1	0
Major blood vessels	12	30	11	8
Skin	0	7	0	8
Intestine, stomach etc	0	5	12	11

[Dowry is an Indian custom in which the bride brings property or money to her husband on marriage. Homicidal cases occur when the husband and/or his family feel that the bride has not brought sufficient money or has not brought the amount of money promised before the marriage. Greed or feelings of being insulted/family dishonour are behind the deaths.]

Discussion

The murder crime rate for Delhi in 1991 was 5.1 and in 2006 was 2.9.The culpable homicide not amounting to murder crime rate for Delhi in 1991 was 0.65 and in 2006 was 0.45. In Guru Teg Bahadur Hospital, Delhi during the two year period of 1991-1993 homicides constituted 12.82% of the total cases brought for autopsy whereas in the two year period of 2006-2007 they constituted 6.32% of the total cases brought for autopsy. Both these yardsticks tell us that the homicide crime rate in Delhi over a period of fifteen years has nearly halved (a drastic reduction).

Population is one of the important factors influencing incidence of crime. A positive correlation between the growth in incidence of crime and the population of the country has been observed. Other factors influencing crime rate besides population are growing urbanization leading to migration of population from neighboring places, unemployment, economic inequality etc. Massner felt that economic discrimination should have an appreciable effect on homicide rate [6].

The population of Delhi increased at the rate of 3.6% per annum during the ten year period 1991-2001 and occupies the second place amongst all the metros. Delhi tops the list of migrant population, 32% in 2001 (percentage share of migrant population to total population).Both these factors could have lead to an increase in the incidence of the crime and thus also the homicide rate. However two other factors, decrease in unemployment and economic progress, have offset any increase in the crime rate due to an increase in population and an increase in migrant population. The Annual Compound Growth Rate of Per Capita

Income in Delhi is 4.45 at constant prices and 11.6 at current prices. The per capita income of Delhi currently, is the third highest in the country and twice the national average. The percentage of unemployed persons to the total labor force was 5.67% in 1992 and 4.63% in 2003 indicating an increase in the number of people getting employment. Thus economic progress and better employment opportunities have greatly contributed to a drop in the homicide rate in Delhi. A modernized and effective police force installing fear of the law may have also made a contribution in this regard.

The maximum number of victims were in the age group of 21-30 years in both the studies. (There was however a decline of about 10% in the number of victims in the most socially active age group of 21-30 years in the later study, though it still constituted the largest group). This is the most socially active age group and thus is more prone to be involved both as victims and as aggressors. The youth in this age group no longer function under parental guidance. Their youthful exuberance, impulsiveness and lack of restraint all lead to a higher involvement as compared to other age groups. It is said that wisdom increases with age. The elderly act with restraint. The head of a family becomes more responsible as he is supposed to upkeep family honor and traditions. It is his role to settle family quarrels. Hence older persons get less involved in disputes, both as victims as well as aggressors. There is a long standing observation that there is a greater propensity for teenagers and young adults to commit more crimes than individuals of other ages [7]. A second perspective articulated is that teenagers and young adults not only commit crimes more frequently than those of the other age group but also are more likely to be victims [8].

Males were the predominant victims in both the studies (79.9% and 83.6% of the victims respectively). Males are affected more than females as they are more aggressive in nature and thus more prone to violence. Secondly, the male member of the family is expected to preserve the moral prestige and honor of the family and any threat to it could lead to violence thus affecting males more, both as aggressors as well as victims. Thirdly, males are more likely to be involved in brawling incidents leading to killings. Fourthly, males are generally working outside the house in greater numbers as compared to females who tend to remain indoors. They are thus more exposed to stress, frustration and rage in day to day activity and violence can ensue, making them victims.

Spot deaths and victims brought dead to hospital constituted the majority of cases in both the studies (60.4% in 1991-1993 and 59.6% in 2006-2007).Thus about 60% of the victims died before medical aid could be given to them. This was due to the involvement of vital organs like brain, lungs and major blood vessels in the majority of cases. It was also because of the psyche of the aggressor who inflicted the injuries in such an extensive and severe manner so as to ensure that the victim definitely died and thus the injuries led to an immediate or early death of the victim.

When comparing both the studies, there was a decline in the spot deaths in the later study (Figure 1).

Spot deaths made up 25.1% of the total deaths in the later study as compared to 44% in the earlier study. This decline was due to faster reach of help to the victims and immediate transportation of the victims to the hospital. This was brought about by the greater awareness amongst the public in this regard and the increased number and availability of patrolling police vans (as compared to the earlier period) who rushed the victims to hospital.

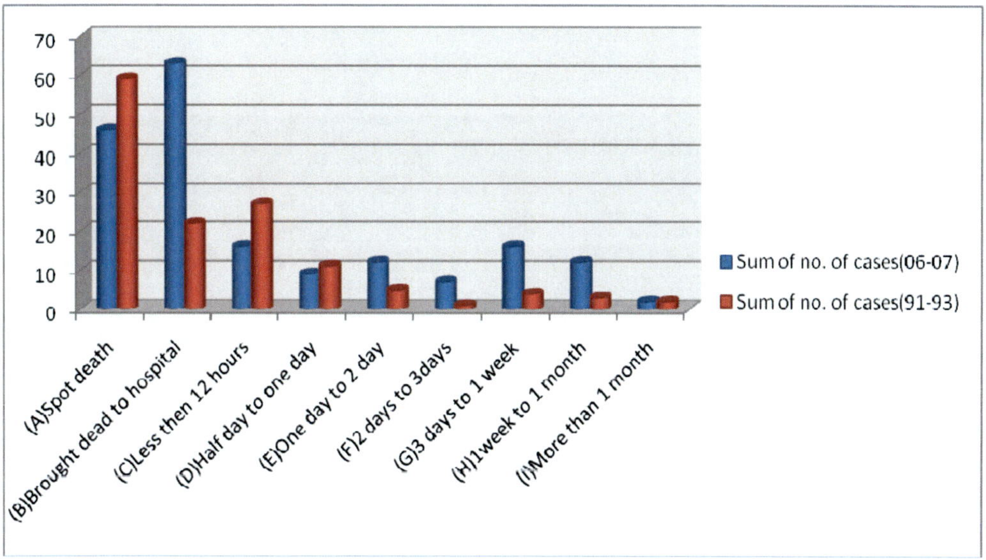

Figure 1. Duration of survival.

In spite of all this victims brought dead in 2006-2007 constituted 63 cases (34.4%) as compared to 22 cases (16.4%) in 1991-1993.This meant that though there was faster presence of help at the scene of crime, there was an increase in the number of victims dying during transportation due to absence of medical care during this period. This could be reduced by having ambulances having trained medical personnel transporting the victims so that medical care could be started during transportation itself. The need is to have ambulances transporting the injured instead of the prevalent practice of having patrolling police control room vans (PCR's as they are commonly called here) transport them.

About 89% of the victims died within one day of the incident/crime in the earlier study and about 73% of the victims died within one day in the later study. This decline was brought about by better medical care being available now which led to an increase in the survival time of the victims.

In comparison to the earlier study, in the later study there was a significant fall in cases of stab injuries and a significant rise in cases of firearm and blunt force injuries (Figure 2). One possible explanation for this is the low economic status of the people living in this part of Delhi which has however improved in comparison with the position fifteen years ago. Acquisition of firearms is costly in comparison to knives. Knives being cheaper could easily be disposed off after the crime, something not possible with the more expensive firearms. So there was the involvement of knives in a large number of homicides fifteen years ago. Since 1991-1993 the economic status of the people has improved and this has also got reflected in crime with an increase in use of firearms in the later study in comparison to the earlier one. There was also an increase in rage crimes in the later study which lead to the assailants attacking the victims with whatever they could lay their hands on thus leading to an increase in blunt force injuries.

The assailants' intention was to kill the victim and in a large number of cases firearms and knives were used. Thus the head and chest region were attacked with these weapons. Therefore in both the studies the lungs and brain were the organs most commonly involved.

Spleen and kidneys were rarely involved in both the studies because of their location which protected them.

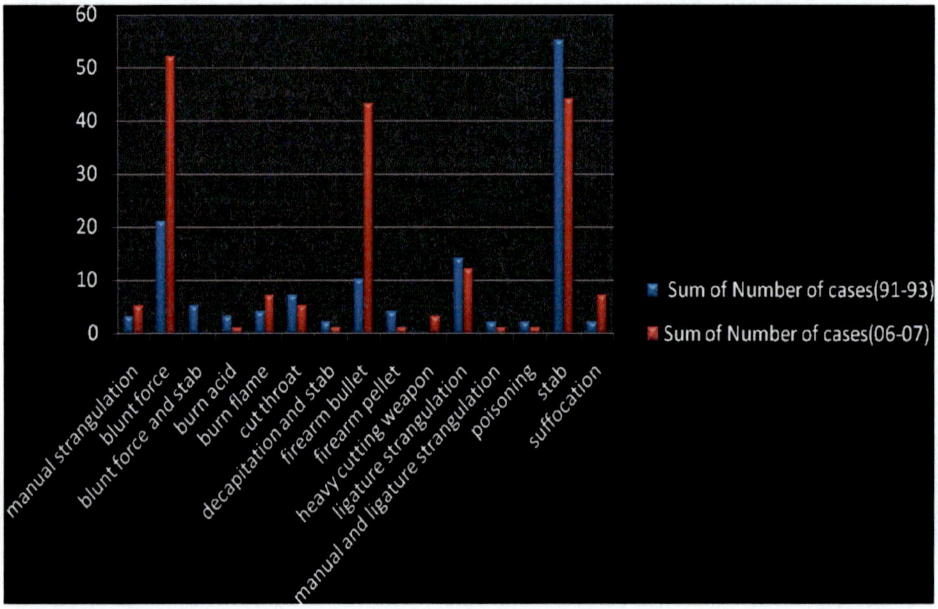

Figure 2. Types of injuries.

The homicidal death pattern in Delhi is compared with the homicidal death patterns of other cities of India (Figure 3). In Delhi homicidal deaths constituted 6.3% of the total cases brought for autopsy (2006-2007 study). Amritsar (12%) [9], Rohtak (8.7%) [10] and Allahabad (7.5%) [11] saw a larger percentage of autopsies of homicidal victims as compared to Delhi. Jamnagar (4%) [12, 13] and Surat (5.6%, 4.1%) [14, 15] saw a smaller percentage of autopsies of homicidal victims as compared to Delhi.

Males were the predominant victims in all the studies. Cities having more than 80% male victims were Guwahati (89%) [16], Delhi (84%), Amritsar (83%) [9], Surat (82%) [14] and Allahabad (82%) [11].

Stab injuries by sharp weapons were the commonest fatal injuries in Nagpur (54%) [17], Surat (48%) [14] and Manipal (38%) [18] .Blunt force injuries were the commonest fatal injuries in Amritsar (51%) [19], Rohtak (48%) [10], Surat (42%) [15], Jamnagar (32%) [12, 13] and Delhi (28%). Firearm injuries were the commonest fatal injuries in Varanasi (42%) [20] and Allahabad (35%) [11]. (Table 5).

Strangulation deaths had similar percentage distribution amongst all the cities with Delhi having the highest percentage of deaths due to strangulation as compared to the other cities.Burn deaths had more or less similar percentage distribution amongst all the cities except Nagpur [17] and Manipal [18]. Compared with other cities Nagpur [17] and Manipal [18] had a larger percentage of homicides caused by burns making up as much as 12% and 16% of the cases respectively.

Table 5. Types of common injuries seen in some Indian cities

	Stab	Blunt	Firearm	Burn	Strangulation
Allahabad	19%	24%	35%	3%	2%
Amritsar	21%	51%	13%	-	-
Jamnagar	26%	32%	0.6%	1%	4%
Manipal	38%	30%	5%	16%	5%
Nagpur	54%	22%	2%	12%	5%
Rohtak	13%	48%	11%	5%	7%
Surat[14]	48%	38%	5%	2%	6%
Surat[15]	34%	42%	3%	6%	5%
Varanasi	10%	14%	42%	-	8%
Delhi	24%	28%	24%	4%	9%

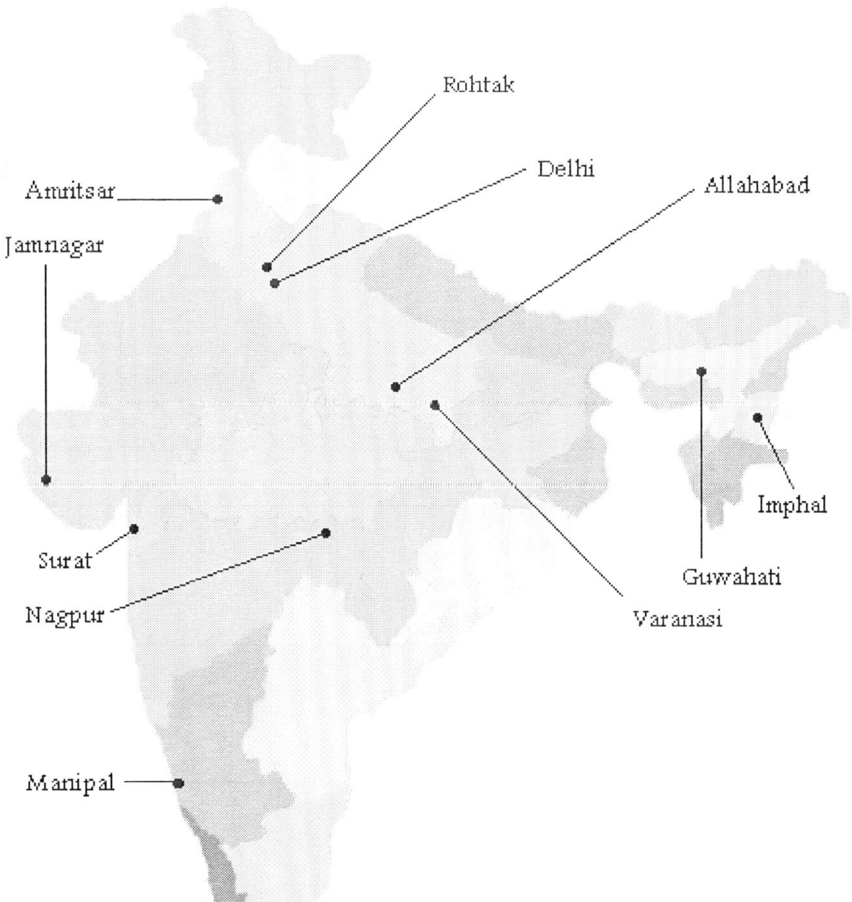

Figure 3. Cities in India where homicidal deaths were studied.

The homicides occurring in Imphal [21] need to be discussed separately. Imphal is the capital of Manipur state situated in the northeastern part of India. For the past many years it has been beset by violence due to insurgency and killings by underground militant organizations. Hence the crime in this region is influenced not only by socio-economic factors but also by the political situation present. Male victims were predominant (95.7%). Homicidal deaths constituted 42.5% of the total cases brought for autopsy. But if only civilian perpetrators are taken into consideration then homicidal deaths constituted 3.1% of the total cases brought for autopsy (about 75% of the homicidal victims autopsied in Imphal were killed by members/suspected members of underground militant organizations). Firearm injuries were the commonest fatal injuries(68%), followed by blunt force injury (13%), stab injuries by sharp weapons (12%), strangulation(1%) and burns(0.5%).If homicides by only civilian perpetrators are taken into consideration then the commonest fatal injuries were stab injuries by sharp weapons (73%), followed by blunt force injuries(25%) and burns(2%).

CONCLUSION

The homicide crime rate in Delhi over a period of fifteen years has nearly halved. Males were the predominant victims and the maximum number of victims were in the age group of 21-30 years. Spot deaths and victims brought dead to hospital constituted the majority of cases (about 60%). However in 2006-2007 spot deaths made up 25% of the total deaths as compared to 44% in the 1991-1993 study. However victims brought dead to hospital in 2006-2007 constituted 34% of the total cases as compared to 16% in 1991-1993. In 1991-1993 stab injuries were the commonest type of fatal injuries seen whereas in 2006-2007 blunt force injuries were the commonest fatal injuries seen. There was a significant rise in cases of firearm injuries and blunt force injuries in 2006-2007 as compared to the earlier study. Throttling and poisoning as causes of death were rare. Lungs and brain were the organs most commonly involved.

The trends of homicide in other cities of India also showed a preponderance of male victims with maximum number of victims belonging to the 21-30 years age group. The incidence of homicide varied from place to place depending on the local socio-economic factors and political situations present. Stab by sharp weapons and blunt force injuries were more or less equal in distribution amongst the various cities as the commonest type of fatal injuries seen. Firearm injuries as the commonest type of fatal injuries were seen in a few cities only.

Economic progress, better employment opportunities and a better equipped and effective police force could be some of the factors contributing to the drop in homicide crime rate. Though better public awareness, better patrolling and increased availability of police vans has led to faster transportation of the victims to hospitals, the lack or absence of medical care during transportation has led to a large number of fatalities occurring during transportation. This underlines the need to have well equipped and properly staffed ambulances transporting the victims to hospital instead of the police vans presently doing the bulk of the transportation.

References

[1] Homicide-Wikipedia, the free encyclopedia [homepage on the Internet]. United States: Wikimedia Foundation, Inc. [cited 2008 Nov 5]. Available from: http://en.wikipedia.org/wiki/ Homicide.

[2] Nolo's Legal Glossary [homepage on the Internet]. Berkeley, California: Nolo [cited 2008 Nov 5]. Available from: http://www.nolo.com/definition.cfm/Term/51AB22D3-86AB-4B55-8648BC28B45909C0/alpha/H/.

[3] Common law -Wikipedia, the free encyclopedia [homepage on the Internet]. United States: Wikimedia Foundation, Inc. [cited 2008 Nov 5]. Available from: http://en.wikipedia.org/wiki/Common_law.

[4] Universal Law Publishing Company. Universal's criminal manual. Delhi: Universal Law Publishing Company Pvt Ltd; 1996.

[5] National Crime Records Bureau [homepage on the Internet]. New Delhi: Ministry of Home Affairs [cited 2008 Nov 5]. Available from: http://nrcb.nic.in/cii2006/home.htm.

[6] Massner SF. Economic discrimination and societal homicide rates: further evidence on cost of inequality. *Am. Sociol. Rev.*1989; 54: 597-611.

[7] Travis H, Gottfredson MG. Age and explanation of crime. *Am. J. Sociol.*1983; 18:55-84.

[8] Cohan LE, Land KC. Age structure and crime: symmetry vs asymmetry and the projection of the crime rates through the 1990. *Am. Sociol. Rev.*1987; 52:170-83.

[9] Mittal S, Garg S, Mittal MS, Chanana A, Rai H. Homicides by sharp weapons. *J. Ind Acad. Forensic Med.* 2007; 29(2): 61-3.

[10] Pal V, Paliwal PK, Yadav DR. Profile of regional injuries and weapons used in homicidal victims in Haryana. *J. Forensic Med. Toxicol.*1994; 11(1-2):42-4.

[11] Sinha US, Kapoor AK, Pandey SK. Pattern of homicidal deaths in SRN Hospital's mortuary at Allahabad. *J. Forensic Med. Toxicol.*2003; 20(2): 33-6.

[12] Gupta BD, Singh OG. Trends of homicides in and around Jamnagar region of Gujarat, India-a retrospective study of 5 years. *J. Forensic Med. Toxicol.*2007; 24(2):6-11.

[13] Singh OG, Gupta BD. Evaluation of mechanical injuries in homicidal deaths (A retrospective study of 5 years). *J. Ind. Acad. Forensic. Med.* 2007; 29(3): 18-22.

[14] Sheikh MI, Subrahmanium BV. Study of homicide in Surat with special reference to changing trends. *J. Forensic Med. Toxicol.*1995; 12(1-2): 8-15.

[15] Gupta S, Prajapati P, Kumar S. Victimology of homicide: a Surat (South Gujarat) based study. *J. Ind Acad Forensic Med.* 2007; 29(3): 29-33.

[16] Patowary AJ. Study of pattern of injuries in homicidal firearm injury cases. *J. Ind. Acad Forensic Med.* 2007; 27(2): 92-5.

[17] Ghangale AL, Dhawane SG, Mukherjee AA. Study of homicidal deaths at Indira Gandhi Medical College, Nagpur. *J. Forensic Med. Toxicol.* 2003; 20(1): 47-51.

[18] Mohanty MK, Kumar TS, Mohanram A, Palimar V. Victims of homicidal deaths-an analysis of variables. *J. Clin. Forensic Med.*2005; 12(6): 302-4.

[19] Mittal S., Channa A., Hakumat R. Dalal JS. Medicolegal study of mechanical injuries in culpable homicides (excluding deaths due to rash and negligent act). *J. Ind. Acad. Forensic Med.* 2005; 27(4): 226-30.

[20] Upadhyay P, Tripathi CB. Homicidal deaths in Varanasi region. Ind Internet J Forensic Med Toxicol [serial on the Internet] 2004 Jun [cited 2008 Nov 5]; 2(2): [about 6 p.]. Available from: http://www.icfmt.org/vol2no2/varanasi.htm

[21] Memchoubi PH, Momonchand A, Fimate L. Homicides in and around Imphal. *J. Ind. Acad. Forensic Med.* 2003; 25(1): 13-5.

In: Homicide: Trends, Causes and Prevention
Editor: Randal B. Toliver and Ulrich R. Coyne
ISBN 978-1-60741-625-8

Chapter 7

HOMICIDE AS A SOURCE OF MATERNAL MORTALITY IN THE UNITED STATES

Christopher T. Lang* and Jeffrey C. King
Department of Obstetrics and Gynecology
The Ohio State University College of Medicine
Columbus, OH USA

ABBREVIATIONS

CDC	Centers for Disease Control and Prevention
ACOG	American College of Obstetricians and Gynecologists
IPV	Intimate partner violence
PMSS	Pregnancy-Related Mortality Surveillance System
MMWR	Maternal Mortality Weekly Report

ABSTRACT

Homicide is an especially tragic and very real source of maternal mortality in the United States. An appreciation for this issue was gathered only after so-called "pregnancy-associated" deaths were reported to the Centers for Disease Control and Prevention (CDC) or following an organized review of deaths which were incidental to pregnancy but not directly pregnancy-related. In addition, increasing the time limit up to one year between the conclusion of pregnancy and death also allowed for this source of mortality to be better recognized. Recent literature has highlighted the significant proportion of injury-related deaths which are violent and intentional, in addition to racial and age discrepancies, along with the fact that pregnancy represents a risk factor in and of itself for a woman to fall victim to a violent death. Perhaps the most important related topic is the issue of intimate partner violence (IPV), because of both the potential downstream association with homicide and the opportunity to screen for domestic/sexual

* Columbus, OH 43210; (614) 746-8663 (phone); (614) 293-5712 (fax); CTLMED1@AOL.com

abuse and to intervene on behalf of the mother to reduce the risk of maternal mortality. As opposed to pregnancy-related mortality secondary to embolism or pre-eclampsia, for example, prevention of violent acts against pregnant or recently pregnant women requires a unique approach from the physician and staff, including a thorough understanding of the mother's home life and social circumstances within the context of the stress imposed by pregnancy and the nurturing of a newborn child.

Introduction

Whenever retrospective data is examined to describe vital statistics, investigators must determine strict definitions for the outcome of interest. In addition, such research is only as good as the sources of data from which it is derived, and may underestimate the magnitude of the problem. An especially poignant example of this is the study of maternal mortality. Understandably, early literature focused upon causes related to pregnancy (*ie* if the woman had not been pregnant, she would not have died), but fortunately also considered "other" or "nonmaternal" causes as well. As a result, causes of death not directly related to pregnancy, such as homicide, appear in one of the first studies presenting nationwide maternal mortality statistics by Kaunitz *et al* – of 314 maternal deaths secondary to "other" causes, eight resulted from homicide. [1] It has become increasingly clear that a reliance solely upon death certificates is an unreliable means of portraying "real life" statistics in this regard, and amassing data from a variety of sources including data linkages and medical examiner records is required. Increasing the temporal restriction from six weeks to one year following the conclusion of pregnancy has properly contextualized this timeframe as a continuation of pregnancy when violence against women may be especially noticeable. Similar to pregnancy-related mortality, nonwhite race is overrepresented among cases of homicide in pregnancy and the postpartum period. An especially disheartening finding is the increased risk for homicide shouldered by adolescent mothers. In a significant proportion of cases, the stressors imposed by pregnancy and following delivery establish an environment in which previously abusive intimate partners may become especially violent. Reducing homicide as a cause of death in pregnancy and during the postpartum period is a seemingly daunting effort as it pushes physicians and the entire healthcare system beyond medicine and into the less comfortable realm of patient education and mentoring, a sensitivity to nonverbal cues, an ability to ask the right questions, a willingness to intervene, and most importantly, demands a legal system willing and able to respond promptly when asked.

Recent Data, Ascertainment, and Limitations

The Pregnancy-Related Mortality Surveillance System (PMSS) was introduced in 1987 by the CDC along with the American College of Obstetricians and Gynecologists (ACOG) and defines a "pregnancy-related" death as the "death of a woman while pregnant or within one year of the termination of pregnancy, regardless of duration and site of pregnancy, from any cause related to or aggravated by her pregnancy or its management." [2] Also defined is a "pregnancy-associated" death, or that which is secondary to any cause during the same timeframe. [2] It is within this category that homicide is included, although one could argue that a homicide may, in some cases, be pregnancy-related since pregnancy is itself a risk factor for a violent death, as will be discussed in more detail later. Since the initial publication of Kaunitz *et al.* published in 1985, maternal mortality data has been presented as a ratio rather than a rate, with 100,000 live births as the denominator. [1] Along with the specific definitions of maternal mortality used for the numerator, linkages between maternal deaths and fetal death or birth certificates became feasible, yielding an overall pregnancy-related mortality ratio of 11.8 deaths per 100,000 live births when analyzed by Chang *et al.* in a Maternal Mortality Weekly Report (MMWR) of US data from 1991-1999. [3]

These investigators turned their attention specifically to homicide as a source of pregnancy-associated mortality utilizing the same MMWR data. [4] There were a total of 1,993 pregnancy-associated deaths involving injury, 617 (31%) resulting from homicide (second only to motor vehicle accidents), yielding a pregnancy-associated homicide ratio of 1.7 deaths per 100,000 live births. In a retrospective, cross-sectional analysis of multiple sources in Maryland from 1993-1998, homicide was found to be the leading cause of pregnancy-associated death, accounting for 20% of cases. [5] Similarly, Harper and Parsons identified homicide as the most common cause of injury-related death in North Carolina from 1992-1994, accounting for 35.5% of cases. [6] In New York City from 1987-1991, Dannenberg *et al.* identified 115 injury-related deaths, of which an astonishing 63% were due to homicide,[7] while Fildes *et al.* attributed 57% of all traumatic maternal deaths to homicide following a review of the Cook County, Illinois Medical Examiner records from January, 1986 to December, 1989 [8]. In a recent and thorough systematic review of the world literature on homicide in pregnancy and the postpartum period, Shadigian and Bauer concluded that homicide is clearly a leading cause of pregnancy-associated death. [9]

On a more general level, homicide remains a leading cause of death among reproductive age women regardless of whether or not they are pregnant. This is especially true for African-American women and those aged 15-24 years; the most common means of homicide among such women is firearms. [4, 10] Furthermore, and particularly relevant to this topic, is the fact that 32.1% of such homicides were at the hands of a husband, ex-husband, or boyfriend. [4, 11]

As alluded to earlier, an underestimation of maternal mortality was the norm particularly prior to the establishment of the PMSS. Since that time, utilizing multiple data sources and performing linkages has increased detection of not only pregnancy-related mortality but also pregnancy-associated mortality, and has uncovered the significance of homicide-related mortality. Somewhat unique in this circumstance, however, is the utmost importance of medical examiner records.

Table 1 is adapted from the study of Horon and Cheng, and depicts the relative contributions of death certificates, record linkages, medical examiner records, and a combination of these sources in the collection of these cases. [5] Of note, reviewing death certificates alone failed to identify a single case within a total of 50 homicides, and record linkages, although extremely helpful in the detection of pregnancy-related mortality, failed to identify any homicides which occurred during pregnancy. These lessons learned have led to the development of the National Violent Death Reporting System by the CDC, which serves as an all-inclusive source of data taken from not only the aforementioned sources, but also from law enforcement records and crime laboratories. [12]

Table 1. Number of pregnancy-associated homicide deaths by source of data and time of death (Maryland, 1993-1998), adapted from [5] with permission

Source	Total homicides	Homicides during pregnancy	Homicides ≤ 42 days PP or after term	Homicides 43-365 days PP or after term
All	50	23	3	24
Death certificates	0	0	0	0
Record linkages	27	0	3	24
Medical examiner records	25	23	1	1

PP = postpartum.
Term = termination.

Although utilizing multiple resources to the fullest extent possible clearly improves detection of cases, it may also lead to the potential for "enhanced ascertainment" [4] in the postpartum period when record linkages are performed, since the fetal/neonatal record is only available once the pregnancy has reached a conclusion. This leads to the dilemma as to whether or not this suggests pregnancy as being protective, or simply reduced ascertainment if a woman falls victim to homicide while she is still pregnant or less than 20 weeks' gestation. In addition, as also alluded to by Chang *et al.*, there is enhanced ascertainment secondary to the use of "pregnancy check-boxes" on some states' death certificates. [4, 13] Horon and Cheng point out another potential source of enhanced ascertainment – as all homicide victims undergo a complete autopsy, a pregnancy is more likely to be discovered, as opposed to other cases of pregnancy-associated mortality such as a motor vehicle accident where autopsy may not be "indicated" or is declined by the surviving family. [5] Even in cases in which an autopsy is performed, pregnancy is not routinely considered, [9] and at least according to the data of Dannenberg *et al.*, it is common for pregnancies at less than 10 weeks' gestation to go undetected. [7] In a recent review, Lang and King make mention of the inherent limitations of death certificates with respect to confusing terminology and difficulties completing them, especially for non-obstetricians. [14] In light of this, it is not surprising that Krulewitch *et al.* identified 43.3% of pregnant women who fell victim to homicide were not reported to the District of Columbia State Center for Health Statistics for the years 1988-1996. [15] Lastly, and quite unfortunately, the PMSS does not record any relationship which may exist between the victim and perpetrator, forcing reliance upon other sources of information, such as addresses of residence, to make a link with a domestic partner. [15]

Associations

Race

There clearly remains a racial discrepancy in this country with respect to maternal mortality. Between 1987 and 1996, the African-American-to-Caucasian mortality ratio varied from 2.6 to 6.3 across the US, according to the June 18, 1999 MMWR. [16] Unfortunately, this trend appears to continue with homicide-related mortality, as well, with Chang *et al.*

reporting a seven-fold increased risk as compared to Caucasian women. [4] On a more general level, of a total of 62 injury-related deaths occurring in North Carolina from 1992-1996, 22 were homicides, 14 of which involved nonwhite victims. [6] Similarly, of the aforementioned 63% of injury-related deaths secondary to homicide in New York City from 1987-1991, 77% involved African-American and Hispanic women [7].

There is no clear explanation for this racial discrepancy. The socioeconomic disadvantages shouldered by minorities may play a role as discussed in the aforementioned review by Lang and King [14] with the potential downstream consequence of less prenatal care which is itself a risk factor for pregnancy-associated homicide. [4] While previous literature has also reported increased risks of nonfatal abuse among nonwhite women as the most significant and consistent risk factor associated with homicide, [17-20] others report increased risk for Caucasian women [21].

Age

An additional discrepancy, and perhaps even more disheartening, is the greater likelihood of homicide-related mortality among adolescents. Chang *et al.* found age less than 20 years to be a risk factor, [4] while Dannenberg *et al.* determined that 43% of the 115 women who succumbed to an injury-related death (including homicide) in New York City from 1987-1991 were aged 15 to 24 years. [7] Table 2 depicts data as adapted from Krulewitch *et al.* for the District of Columbia, 1988-1996. [15] Krulewitch *et al.* also focused on adolescent pregnancy and homicide using data from the Maryland Office of the Chief Medical Examiner from 1994-1998 and found that adolescent homicide victims were 3.7 times more likely to be pregnant as compared to adult homicide victims. [22] The obvious caveat here is that women under the age of 35 also account for the majority of pregnancies as compared to older women.

Table 2. Age distribution for victims of homicide (District of Columbia, 1988 1996), adapted from [15] with permission

Homicides by age group	Evidence of pregnancy *n* (column %)	Not pregnant *n* (column %)	Total *n* (column %)
All	13 (100)	201 (100)	214 (100)
15-19 yrs	2 (15.4)	28 (13.9)	30 (14)
20-34 yrs	11 (84.6)	116 (57.7)	127 (59.3)
35-50 yrs	0 (0)	57 (28.4)[1]	57 (26.6)

[1] Only pregnancy status comparison which is statistically significant.

Adolescent mothers may delay seeking prenatal care or avoid care altogether either because of denial or in an effort to keep the pregnancy secret from their parents and/or peers, with an ensuing increased risk for pregnancy-associated homicide as mentioned above. Furthermore, Krulewitch *et al.* refer to the "volatility of adolescence" in which the strain of pregnancy and impending parenthood may pave the way for worsening IPV leading to a homicide, especially if the father is significantly older. [22] Also, associating with older partners may facilitate higher-risk codependent behaviors such as drug use, which fosters an environment of instability and violence. [22]

Pregnancy

At the crux of this issue is whether or not by virtue of being pregnant, a woman is at greater risk of homicide-related mortality. Cheng *et al.* [4] reference three studies which shed light on this issue:

- Krulewitch *et al.* – 11% more homicides occurred among women with evidence of pregnancy as compared to non-pregnant woman in the District of Columbia from 1988-1996 (not statistically significant, see Table 1). [15]
- Horon and Cheng – Homicide was more common among pregnant and postpartum women (20.2%) than among women who had not been pregnant in the year preceding death (11.2%, adjusted) in Maryland from 1993-1998 (statistically significant). [5]
- Dietz *et al.* – Postpartum women aged 15 to 19 years were 2.6-fold more likely to be victims of homicide as compared with nonpregnant, nonpostpartum women in the same age group in Georgia from 1990-1992 (statistically significant). [23]

An obvious association in this light is IPV. The emotional and financial stress associated with impending or current parenthood, especially in the context of a strained relationship, can lead to IPV and a resulting homicide. The literature does in fact bear out an increased risk for IPV among pregnant and postpartum women, [7, 24, 25] especially in cases when pregnancy was unintended or mistimed. [19] Based upon the previously referenced works of Krulewitch *et al.*, there is a trend towards homicide occurring at less than 20 weeks' gestation, at least among teen victims, [22] and more than three out of four women with evidence of pregnancy who are victims of homicide are in the first 20 weeks of pregnancy. [15] The implication of these findings is a possible protective effect of advanced pregnancy, as a perpetrator may be less inclined to violently assault an overtly pregnant woman.

Means

Multiple sources identify firearms as the leading mechanism of homicide-associated mortality. [4, 6-8, 15, 17] However, in cases in which homicide is clearly at the hands of a partner, the most common mechanisms are unclear. Krulewitch *et al.* found that many of the accused perpetrators in their study shared a common address with the victim, and gunshot trauma was a leading mechanism as compared to non-pregnant women. [15] In the aforementioned review by Shoffner, mechanisms associated with homicide-associated mortality following IPV are not forwarded, which likely reflects the limited data available to the PMSS with respect to any relationship between the perpetrator and victim.

Intimate Partner Violence

As alluded to earlier in this review, IPV represents a significant risk factor for pregnancy-associated homicide. There is an abundance of literature examining IPV but, for the purposes of this discussion, categories for consideration include:

- Scope and associations
- Data limitations
- Temporal aspects
- Means of evaluation

Scope and Associations

In 1992, the American Medical Association recorded an overall 14% prevalence of abusive relationships among women evaluated in ambulatory care internal medicine clinics and found that 28% had a history of abuse. [15, 26] Literature as referenced by Chang *et al.* [4] supports a 4-8% prevalence of abuse during pregnancy especially by intimate partners. [27, 28] In a recent review by Shoffner, [19] however, the prevalence may be as high as 7.4%-20.1% depending upon how many times during pregnancy a woman is screened for IPV. [28-30] In the previously referenced work by Parsons and Harper and by Dannenberg *et al.*, 21 of 41 women (51.2%) succumbing to an injury-related maternal death were known to have or suspected of having been abused, and of 72 pregnancy-associated homicides at least 12 involved a husband or boyfriend, respectively. [17, 7] Martin *et al.* noted in a recent literature review that intimate partners perpetrate one- to two-thirds of pregnancy-associated homicides in the US. [31] In a ten-city case-control study, McFarlane *et al.* found that an abused woman during pregnancy was at a three-fold higher risk of becoming an attempted or actual homicide victim even after controlling for a multitude of confounding variables. [32] Among all of the domestic violence cases in the previously referenced work by Krulewitch *et al.*, all led to a homicide. [22] Not surprisingly, there are a multitude of associations which have been linked to IPV including crowded living conditions, late prenatal care, tobacco use as well as polysubstance abuse among the abused women and their perpetrators, prior abuse, younger age, unmarried and less-educated status, underlying medical and/or obstetrical complications, reduced inter-pregnancy interval, government-sponsored insurance, [19, 33] as well as depression and anxiety in addition to a reliance upon non-familial support systems. [33] An additional association concerning abuse among pregnant adolescents is with sexual and physical abuse at the hands of a family member or trusted friend of the family. [34]

Limitations

Just as there are limitations concerning pregnancy-associated homicide literature as described earlier, the same holds true for IPV in pregnancy. In the previously referenced review by Shoffner, limitations include a lack of a consistent definition for "abuse" and failing to distinguish between current and past abuse, different populations and settings, and especially different means of screening – person-to-person interview or written questionnaire – with an ensuing impact on the number of IPV cases actually captured. [19]

Temporal Aspects

As mentioned earlier, the postpartum period may represent an especially dangerous situation with the stress that comes with parenthood. Not surprisingly, Parsons and Harper found that six of eight women killed by an intimate partner were postpartum. [17] Shoffner [19] makes reference to the fact that women with a history of abuse as a child or IPV during pregnancy are at increased risk for further abuse during the postpartum period, [35] and that teen mothers are especially at risk for abuse during the postpartum period. Furthermore, they are not likely to report it. [36]

Means of Evaluation

There are several different means by which the healthcare team may screen for IPV and further evaluate those in whom it is suspected. A full discussion of these is beyond the scope of this review, but clinically useful tools include:

- Woman's Abuse Screening Tool [19]
- Hurt, Insult, Threat, Scream Screen [19]
- Abuse Assessment Screen [19, 37]
- Conflict Tactics Scale [37]
- Index of Spouse Abuse [37]
- Danger Assessment Scale [37]

None of these methods has been clearly proven superior. More importantly, as highlighted in Shoffner's review, regardless of how screening and evaluation are accomplished, a sensitive and skillful approach on the part of the healthcare professional is required. [19] Interestingly, it is controversial as to whether or not person-to-person interviews or written questionnaires yield the most true-to-life statistics – in studies supporting the former as being more effective, [19, 28, 38] one may logically conclude that a well-conducted interview involving "asking the right questions" and adapting to the verbal and non-verbal cues of the patient is the preferred approach. Also important is clear and thorough documentation of such interviews, as well as photographic documentation of the findings during the physical exam, when appropriate.

The team's concern should always be raised when the male partner answers all of the questions, when he is never separated from the patient, or when the patient's answers are kept short in his presence. Providing a time for individual private conversation with the patient may allow her to divulge IPV and ask for help.

PREVENTION OF PREGNANCY-ASSOCIATED HOMICIDE

Obviously, the only viable means of "treating" this problem is by preventing it, either in a primary and/or secondary fashion. Several of the references utilized for this review include at least some insight into how pregnancy-associated homicides may be prevented, whether it is by patient education and frequent screening for IPV and non-domestic violence [4, 6, 15] or by better recognition of the scope of the problem through improved ascertainment and record-keeping such that common associations and means for intervention can be identified. [5, 7] Ultimately, data is lacking to support primary and secondary prevention strategies in reducing pregnancy-associated homicide. One may argue that primary prevention lands squarely on the shoulders of the parents and/or guardians of the adolescent or young adult woman, hopefully yielding an individual with stronger self-esteem and sound moral character as well as an awareness of the potentially life-altering consequences of risky behavior such as promiscuous sexual activity, drug use, and associating with dangerous crowds. Of course, in this day and age accomplishing effective primary prevention is a daunting task, given the growing number of single-parent households, the sexual attitudes among young women fostered by their peers and the media, and a significant teenage pregnancy rate "locking" her into a relationship with a potentially dangerous partner. Once the opportunity for the parents is lost, expecting teachers, mentors, and/or physicians to convince young women of how to properly conduct themselves seems unrealistic, but certainly no less worthy of the attempt.

From a clinical perspective, one may argue that efforts are best devoted towards identifying women who are clearly at risk for homicide during their pregnancy and intervening *to actually remove her from a violent environment.* In the aforementioned review by Shoffner, concrete means of intervening in this regard and assisting women experiencing IPV are reviewed, including anticipating violent behavior from a partner, having contact information and escape plans readily available, and an understanding of options with respect to legal action. [19] In cases of non-domestic violence, similar interventions serve to keep the woman away from dangerous individuals or to keep her protected should she encounter them (*eg* by always having a cell phone or not being alone in such circumstances). In essence, a team of healthcare professionals becomes ready to respond to a woman disclosing a history of violent injury just as a "stroke" team is prepared to promptly assist a patient following a cerebrovascular accident.

Alarmingly, screening for these risks for homicide during pregnancy is uncomfortable enough for many physicians such that they routinely avoid asking. [9, 39] According to Parsons and Harper, IPV and depression were often unrecognized by the provider in cases eventually involving an injury-related maternal death, and in some cases, in retrospect the provider admitted to knowing or having a suspicion for these issues. [6] Following a review of data from a previous multicity study looking at risk factors for homicide, Sharps *et al.* discovered that two-fifths of women killed by an intimate partner had sought medical care in the year prior to their death, especially for psychiatric illness or substance abuse disorders; this held true for the perpetrators, as well (Table 3). [40] Since most patients who are pregnant will not be denied an "emergency visit" by their partners, those who make frequent visits to the triage area may be trying to communicate their exposure to IPV and in fact are seeking help.

Table 3. Health care, criminal justice, and support service use by victims and perpetrators of femicide during the year prior to femicide (n=311, 11 US cities, 1994-1999), [40] with permission

Resource use	Femicide victims		Femicide perpetrators	
	n	%	n	%
Health care use related to fair or poor health status[a]				
Visits for physical health problems (65, 70)	46	70.8%	37	52.9%
Visits for mental health problems (95, 146)	24	25.3%	22	15.1%
Health care use related to abuse				
Medical care for injuries (311)	44	14.1%		
Mental health provider for abuse (311)	31	10%		
Alcohol treatment[b] (43, 130)	9	20.9%	7	5.4%
Drug treatment[b] (55, 140)	9	16.4%	8	5.7%

[a] Numbers in parentheses are of those who were reported to have fair or poor health among victims and perpetrators, respectively.
[b] Numbers in parentheses are of those who were reported to have alcohol or drug use problems among victims and perpetrators, respectively.

Even with identification of risk factors and supportive services in place, prevention of pregnancy-associated homicide requires an intervention. In the setting of a busy office or postpartum rounds, intervening can be especially difficult given time constraints and the responsibility it entails. It is perhaps simpler for the physician to defer to a social worker or to ignore it entirely. Shoffner's review ends with an anecdotal case highlighting the role played by healthcare professionals in addition to physicians – in this case, a nurse who was willing to speak with the patient in private, gained an understanding of her fears, and allowed for placement in a shelter to protect her from an abusive partner. Obviously, such intervention on behalf of a pregnant or recently postpartum woman has the potential to spare not only a maternal mortality, but also fetal or neonatal mortality, as well.

Conclusions

Injury-associated deaths in pregnancy are a significant source of maternal mortality, and among these are homicides. Pregnancy and the postpartum period appear to be risk factors for homicide in and of themselves. Similar to maternal mortality as a whole, there is racial disparity, but specific to pregnancy-associated homicide is an age discrepancy revealing that adolescents and young women are at increased risk. For every woman who falls victim to a homicide, there are likely many more who face IPV on a regular basis. Prevention requires a reliable means of identifying risk factors and signs of trauma and/or abuse and, more importantly, a willingness to intervene in order to physically protect a pregnant or postpartum woman as well as her unborn child or infant.

References

[1] Kaunitz AM; Hughes JM; *et al.* Causes of maternal mortality in the United States. *Obstet. Gynecol*, 1985, 65, 605-12.

[2] Atrash HK; Rowley D; *et al.* Maternal and perinatal mortality. *Curr. Opin. Obstet Gynecol,* 1992, 4, 61-71.

[3] Chang J; Elam-Evans LD; *et al.* Pregnancy-related mortality surveillance – United States, 1991-1999. MMWR Surveill Summ, 2003, 52, 1-8.

[4] Chang J; Berg CJ; *et al.* Homicide: A leading cause of injury deaths among pregnant and postpartum women in the United States, 1991-1999. *Am. J. Pub Health*, 2005, 95, 471-7.

[5] Horon IL and Cheng D. Enhanced surveillance for pregnancy-associated mortality – Mryland, 1993-1998. *JAMA,* 2001, 285, 1455-9.

[6] Harper M and Parsons L. Maternal deaths due to homicide and other injuries in North Carolina: 1992-1994. *Obstet. Gynecol*, 1997, 90, 920-3.

[7] Dannenberg AL; Carter DM; *et al.* Obstetrics: Homicide and other injuries as causes of maternal death in New York City, 1987 through 1991. *Am. J. Obstet Gynecol*, 1995, 172, 1557-64.

[8] Fildes J; Reed L; *et al.* Trauma: The leading cause of maternal death. *J. Trauma*, 1992, 32, 643-5.

[9] Shadigian EM and Bauer ST. Pregnancy-associated death: A qualitative systematic review of homicide and suicide. *Obstet. Gynecol. Surv.*, 2005, 60, 183-90.

[10] Moracco KE and Runyan CW. Femicide in North Carolina, 1991-1993. Homicide Stud, 1998, 2, 422-47.

[11] Crime in the United States 2002: Uniform crime reports. Washington, DC: US Department of Justice, 2003.

[12] Paulozzi LJ; Mercy J; *et al.* CDC's National Violent Death Reporting System: background and methodology *Inj. Prev*, 2004, 10: 47 52.

[13] MacKay AP; Rochat R; *et al.* The check box determining pregnancy status to improve maternal mortality surveillance. *Am. J. Prev. Med.*, 2000, 19, 35-9.

[14] Lang CT and King JC. Maternal mortality in the United States. *Best Pract. Res. Clin. Obstet. Gynaecol.*, 2008, 22, 517-31.

[15] Krulewitch CJ; Pierre-Louis ML; *et al.* Hidden from view: Violent deaths among pregnant women in the District of Columbia, 1988-1996. *J. Midwif. Wom. Health*, 2001, 46, 4-10.

[16] CDC. State-specific maternal mortality among black and white women – United States, 1987-1996. MMWR Morb Mortal Wkly Rep, 1999, 48, 492-6.

[17] Parsons LH and Harper MA. Violent maternal deaths in North Carolina. *Obstet Gynecol.,* 1999, 94, 990-3.

[18] Wilbanks CR. Lifetime and annual incidence of intimate partner violence and resulting injuries – Georgia, 1995. *MMWR Morb. Mortal Wkly Rep*, 1998, 47, 849-53.

[19] Shoffner DH. We don't like to think about it: intimate partner violence during pregnancy and postpartum. *J. Perinat. Neonat. Nurs*, 2008, 22, 39-48.

[20] Silverman JG; Decker MR; *et al.* Intimate partner victimization prior to and during pregnancy among women residing in 26 US states: associations with maternal and neonatal death. *Am. J. Obstet Gynecol*, 2006, 195, 140-8.

[21] O'Campo P; Gielen AC; *et al.* Violence by male partners against women during the childbearing years: a contextual analysis. *Am. J. Pub. Health*, 1995, 85, 1092-7.

[22] Krulewitch CJ; Roberts DW; *et al.* Adolescent pregnancy and homicide: findings from the Maryland Office of the Chief Medical Examiner, 1994-1998. *Child Maltreat*, 2003, 8, 122-8.

[23] Dietz PM; Rochat R; *et al.* Differences in the risk of homicide and other fatal injuries between postpartum women and other women of childbearing age: implications for prevention. *Am. J. Pub Health*, 1998, 88, 641-3.

[24] Helton AS; McFarlane J; *et al.* Battered and pregnant: a prevalence study. *Am. J. Pub* Health, 1987, 77, 1337-9.

[25] VandeCastle M; Danna J; *et al.* Physical violence during the 12 months preceding childbirth – Alaska, Maine, Oklahoma, and West Virginia, 1990-1991. MMWR Morb Mortal Wkly Rep, 1994, 43, 132-7.

[26] American Medical Association (AMA). Diagnostic and treatment guidelines on domestic violence. Chicago, 1992.

[27] Saltzman LE; Johnson CH; *et al.* Physical abuse around the time of pregnancy: an examination of prevalence and risk factors in 16 states. *Matern. Child Health J.*, 2003, 7, 31-43.

[28] Gazmarian JA; Lazorick S; *et al.* Prevalence of violence against pregnant women. *JAMA*, 1996, 275, 1915-19.

[29] Murphy CC; Schei B; *et al.* Abuse: A risk factor for low birth weight? A systematic review and meta-analysis. *Can. Med. Assoc. J.*, 2001, 164, 1567-72.

[30] Covington DL; Dalton VK; *et al.* Improving detection of violence among pregnant adolescents. *J. Adolesc. Health*, 1997, 21, 18-24.

[31] Martin SL; Macy RJ; *et al.* Pregnancy-associated violent deaths: the role of Intimate Partner Violence. *Trauma Viol. Abuse*, 2007, 8, 135-48.

[32] McFarlane J; Campbell JC; *et al.* Abuse during pregnancy and femicide: urgent implications for women's health. *Obstet. Gynecol.*, 2002, 100, 27-36.

[33] Espinosa L and Osborne K. Domestic violence during pregnancy: implications for practice. *J. Midwif. Wom. Health*, 2002, 47, 305-17.

[34] Boyer D and Fine D. Sexual abuse as a factor in adolescent pregnancy and child maltreatment. *Fam. Planning Perspect*, 1992, 24, 4-11.

[35] Kendall-Tackett KA. Depression in New Mothers: Causes, Consequences, and Treatment Options. New York, Haworth, 1992.

[36] Harrykossoon SD; Rickert VI; *et al.* Prevalence and patterns of intimate partner violence among adolescent mothers during the post-partum period. *Arch. Pediatr Adolesc. Med.*, 2002, 156, 325-30.

[37] McFarlane J; Parker B; *et al.* Abuse during pregnancy: frequency, severity, perpetrator, and risk factors of homicide. *Pub. Health Nurs*, 1995, 12, 284-9.

[38] McFarlane J; Christoffel K; *et al.* Assessing for abuse: self-report versus nurse interview. *Pub. Health Nurse*, 1991, 8, 245-50.

[39] Rodriguez MA; Bauer HM; *et al.* Screening and intervention for intimate partner abuse: practices and attitudes of primary care physicians. *JAMA,* 1999, 282, 468-74.

[40] Sharps PW; Koziol-McLain J; *et al.* Health care providers' missed opportunities for preventing femicide. *Prev. Med.,* 2001, 33, 373-80.

In: Homicide: Trends, Causes and Prevention
Editor: Randal B. Toliver and Ulrich R. Coyne

ISBN 978-1-60741-625-8

Chapter 8

THE EFFECT OF MARITAL STATUS ON MALE HOMICIDE VICTIMIZATION: A RACE SPECIFIC ANALYSIS

Steven Stack*

Wayne State University, Detroit, Michigan, USA

ABSTRACT

The nature of the relationship between marital status and homicide risk has been clouded by the use of aggregated data. Further, precise measures of marital status in individual level research are largely unavailable. The present paper tests a multivariate model of the relationship between marital status and homicide victimization among males. It uses individual level data on 826,178 deaths including 7,112 African American and 6,683 Caucasian American male homicide victims. Bivariate analysis demonstrates that single black men are at 7.65 times and single white men are at 8.57 times greater risk of homicide than their married counterparts. However, the results of a multivariate analysis determined that these risks fall to 1.15 and -0.30 once controls are included for the covariates of marital status. Marriage offers only slight protection for black men and aggravates the odds of homicide for white men. The findings are interpreted in light of a subcultural theory of violence.

INTRODUCTION

Research on family factors and homicide has followed two traditions. First there have been studies based on highly aggregated data such as that corresponding to large ecological units as cities, SMSA's, and states. This work has typically found strong relationships between the incidence of family disruption indicators such as divorce rates and homicide rates (e.g. Almgren et al., 1998; Blau and Blau, 1982; Gillis, 1996; Kowalski and Stack, 1992; Land et al., 1990; Lester, 1986; 2001; Lester and Krysinska, 2004; Parker, 1998; Sampson,

* Email: aa1051@wayne.edu

1986; Simpson, 1985; Williams and Flewelling, 1988). This work is marked by the potential problem of the ecological fallacy (Robinson 1950). We cannot be certain from the assessment of highly aggregated data to what extent nonmarried persons account for the relationship between indicators of family disruption and homicide.

Second, there has been work at the individual level, which has often been restricted to homicide within the family unit (e.g. Browne, et al., 1999; Gelles, 1987; Goetting, 1995; Mann, 1992; Puzone, et al., 2000; Saltzman et al., 1990). This work contains estimates of the incidence of homicide among spouses, acquaintances, strangers, as well as cases where the offender is unknown; however, national data on the odds of dying in a homicide for each major marital status per se, both inside and outside the family unit, are apparently not available. For example, a study of homicide in Detroit found that only 11.2% of all closed homicides in that city were spousal homicides (Goetting 1995:62). Nationally, the rate of family based homicide is 1.4/100,000 and accounts for less than one fifth of homicides (Saltzman et al., 1990:4). Homicide between spouses and former spouses account for approximately 10% of all homicides (Browne et al., 1999). Further, much of the existing work on homicide at the individual level of analysis is based on case histories, percentages, and simple bivariate analyses of separate risk factors (e.g. Wolfgang 1958; Goetting 1995; Cazenave and Zahn 1992; Mann 1992; Curtis 1975). It is not clear if various risk factors related to homicide at the bivariate level would be found to be spurious if subjected to multivariate analysis. Finally, previous work has neglected race-specific analyses (see Browne et al, 1999, and Lester 2001 for reviews). Given long standing, substantial differences in the distribution of marital status by race (U.S. Bureau of the census 2006), with the proportion of single parent families among African Americans more than double that of Caucasians, marital status may have different effects on homicide between racial groups.

The present study contributes to the literature in several ways. First, individual level data are employed to minimize the problem of the ecological fallacy. Unlike most of the previous research that is done on samples at the local level, the present study employs national data on over 13,000 homicides. In this fashion, it will be able to provide generalizations for the nation as a whole that may be masked by results from small, local samples. This investigation apparently constitutes the first analysis of such national data as they refer to marital status. Second, multivariate analysis techniques are used in order to test for spuriousness in any zero order relationship. Age, for example, is correlated with marital status and may render any association between marital status and homicide spurious. Third, separate analyses are performed for African Americans and Caucasian Americans. Given differences in the meanings of marital status between the races, patterns between marital status and homicide may vary between the races.

The focus of the present study is on men. Homicide among men is significant due to men's disproportionate involvement in the behavior. Men account for the large majority of homicide victims. For example, the percentage of homicides with male victims in selected cities ranges from a low of 74% in Atlanta to a high of 91% in Pittsburgh (Rose and Deskin, 1992:84). Nationally, men account for 90% of the offenders in homicides (Browne et al., 1999).

Previous Research

Ecological Level Research

Research on marital status, marital disruption, and homicide has often been done using aggregated data (e.g. Almgren et al., 1998; Blau and Blau, 1982; Gillis, 1996; Kowalski and Stack, 1992; Lester, 1986; 2001; Lester and Krysinska, 2004; Parker, 1998; Sampson, 1986; Simpson, 1985; Williams and Flewelling, 1988). Land et al (1990) reviewed 21 major studies containing many findings from over 40 statistical models. All studies reviewed were based on aggregated, cross sectional data. In these investigations, the homicide rates of cities, metropolitan areas, and states were correlated with various socio-demographic variables. While only a small minority of the models incorporated family-oriented variables, these variables exhibited the most consistent findings. Eight of eight models including a term for the percentage of children not living with both parents found that term to be significant and often substantially related to homicide rates. Further, 6/7 models containing divorce rate reported significant results for the relationship between divorce and homicide rates. In contrast, the relative number of significant findings for the relationship between homicide rates and the other socio-demographic variables were as follows: unemployment rate 0/9, income inequality 7/27, percent poor 22/32, median income 1/5, Southern subculture of violence 13/33, percent 15-29 3/34, percent black 38/43, and population density 2/23.

In this work the association between family disruption/ malintegration and homicide is often explained in relation to theories of social control and social disorganization (e.g. Hirschi, 1969; Shaw and McKay, 1942; Sampson, 1987). Factors such as the percent of single parent families and the divorce rate are taken as indicators of a low level of parental supervision of youth, lessened guardianship, and weakened community control. These factors can influence the development of delinquent and violent subcultures which can affect both the short and long term incidence of homicide.

A key limitation of ecological research has been the problem of the ecological fallacy. It is not clear, for example, to what extent an association between the divorce rate and the homicide rate in cities is due to divorced people acting as homicide offenders and/or becoming the victims in homicides. The association may be more due to conditions that are associated with divorce such as a general weakness in the vitality of family life, a high proportion of dysfunctional families, an elevated incidence of violence within the family, and so forth. Indeed, it is possible that divorced people may not be responsible for the association if the association is due mainly to violence in dysfunctional families that exist before legal divorces take place. That is, homicides may take place in lieu of divorces in the many violence-oriented families that exist in a city with a high divorce rate. If so, divorced people themselves may not be at risk of homicide. Research using individual level data is needed as a check on ecological-based research in order to address this question.

Individual Level Research

The previous research on homicide and marital status tends to obscure marital status of the victims by focusing instead on more general victim-offender relationships. For example, between 1976 and 1984 13.2% of black males and 12.0% of white male victims were family members with their assailants. It is often not clear, however, if they were brothers, spouses, or the children of their assailants. Similarly, other frequently used categories of victim-offender relationships contain victims of all marital statues. These include the category "acquaintances" and a category "unknown relationship." The latter group typically contains one third of all homicides, thereby constituting a problem of measurement error (e.g. O'Carroll and Mercy, 1986; Humphrey and Palmer, 1992; Mercy et al., 1986; Wilbanks, 1992). Further, unsolved homicides cloud the picture of the marital status of offenders and victims. Unsolved homicides are often omitted from analyses. While data are sometimes available on the marital status of persons whose killers were never found, these data on marital status are typically not reported in the research to date.

Wilbanks (1992) reports that in the U.S. in 1980, 306 black husbands and 280 black wives were murdered by their spouses out of a total of 8,380 black homicide victims. No data are available, however, on the overall risk of homicide among married African Americans. That is, from these official data there is no systematic information on the number of homicide victims who are married and who are not killed by their spouses. The relative risk of being murdered at home vs. being murdered on the street is unclear. The same is true for Caucasian Americans. However, Curtis (1975:49-60) suggests that homicide victimization for black males is more common on the street than in intimate relationships. Generally speaking, there is little or no information on the number of homicide victims who are single, divorced, separated and widowed (e.g. Block 1985; Browne et al., 1999; Centers for Disease Control, 1985; Centerwall, 1995; Curtis, 1975; F.B.I., 1990; Humphrey and Palmer, 1986; Mann, 1992; O'Carroll and Mercy, 1986).

The past research also has the disadvantage of being based on bivariate models. While it is often assumed that persons who are in nonmarried marital statuses tend to be at risk of homicide (e.g. Curtis 1975), it is not clear if this presumed relationship will hold up under controls for the covariates of marital status. For example, it is not clear if any high incidence of homicide among single men is due to their being single or to their being young. Single people tend to be younger than nonsingle people. After a control is incorporated for age, the relationship between singleness and homicide risk may weaken or even become insignificant.

This is not to say that married men are not at risk of homicide. According to the national official data, while wives are more apt than men to be killed by their spouses (n=10,529 wives were killed by husbands between 1976-1985), a substantial number of men are killed by their wives (n=7,888 between 1976-1985). Possible racial differences were not reported (McCue, 1995:94).

Routine Activities and Homicide Victimization

The present paper focuses on homicide victims, not homicide offenders. The link between marital status and homicide at the individual level can be interpreted from the standpoint of a routine activities theory of victimization (e.g. Cohen and Felson, 1979; Meithe et al., 1991). This perspective argues that several conditions must coexist in order to maximize the probability that crime will occur: (1) a motivated offender (2) an unguarded victim (3) a suitable target (4) proximity to a motivated offender. Generally speaking, this theory has been mostly applied to property offenses (e.g. Cohen and Felson 1979; Rice and

Smith, 2002). Therein, it has been assumed that time spent away from home increases victim's exposure to crime given that time spent away from home decreases the distance between potential victims and motivated offenders, and separates the potential victim from the guardians who can offer protection while at home.

It is contended that male homicide risk is reduced for married men relative to divorced, single, and widowed men. Married men have various domestic responsibilities and follow various life styles or routines that minimize homicide risk. They are, for example, less likely than single or divorced men to put themselves into situations where the risk of being the victim of a homicide is increased. These dangerous situations can include heavy drinking, displays of disorderly conduct, public drunkenness, maintaining late night hours on the street, and frequenting dangerous places such as bars and pool halls (e.g. Curtis, 1975; Kposowa, Singh and Breault, 1994). It is assumed that they are less likely to venture outside of the home than their nonmarried counterparts to places where men are typically killed. Spending more time at home decreases homicide risk for men. To the extent that men stay at home they should be at less risk of homicide. To the extent that married men stay at home more than nonmarried men, this should reduce their homicide risk.

There may be, however, collinearity between age and marital status. As men get older, they are probably less likely to leave home even if they are not married. Careers, home ownership, home repair, hobbies, and other relatively safe routine activities associated with increasing age may reduce any association between marital status and homicide risk. Widowers, for example, although not married tend to be at an advanced age. These men, it is contended, would probably be more mature than younger men and not be as apt to frequent dangerous placed such as bars and other nightspots.

It is assumed that divorced men would also be more likely than married men to frequent dangerous places and to engage in behaviors such as drinking which contribute to homicide risk. Drinking has often been closely associated with nonmarried marital statuses (e.g. Lester 1995; Stack and Bankowski, 1994). Homicide risk among the divorced can also be increased from attacks by ex spouses. For example, in Atlanta 22% of homicide victims were killed by former spouses or partners (Saltzman, Mercy, Rosenberg et al., 1990).

Race, Marital Status, and Homicide

Racial differences in the meanings of marital statuses may result in differences in the marital status- homicide linkage. A majority of African Americans are born outside of marriage and raised in single parent families (U. S. Bureau of the Census 1992; 2006). In contrast, this is true for less than a quarter of Caucasian Americans. Hence, the status of "single male" has a somewhat different meaning for each race. A single white male is considerably less likely to be a father than a single black male. This life style difference may be indicative of a much broader range in routine life style differences noted by writers such as Curtis (1975) and Stack (1974).

The familial lifestyle differences between blacks and whites are typically attributed to major differences in economic opportunities. That is, family structure is responsive to labor market conditions such as unemployment rates and income levels (e.g., Almgren et al., 1998; Sampson, 1987). Black males have fewer economic opportunities than whites. An adequate economic base improves the probability of stable families. The routines of black family life are marked by much higher rates of disruption and illegitimacy than those found among Caucasians (e.g. Almgren et al., 1998; Curtis 1975; Sampson 1987; U.S. Bureau of the Census; 2006).

A hallmark of the black subculture of violence is sexual prowess and exploitation (Curtis 1975). The economic marginality of black street corner men contributes to their having quick changing and ill defined relationships with women. As a corollary, there is often considerable disagreement and distrust about sexual faithfulness. This jealousy can be quickly turned against male competitors. It is an important risk factor in precipitating homicides (Almgren et al., 1998; Curtis 1975).

Other key life style difference between street corner black and white males may lie in the areas of differential weapons possession and substance abuse. Both of these factors are considered important risk factors in homicide (e.g. Curtis, 1975; Gelles, 1987:111; Killias et al., 2001; Lester, 1995; Singh, 2004; Wolfgang, 1958). For example, to the extent that African American unmarried males are more likely than whites to carry weapons, and to be involved with persons who are likely to carry weapons themselves, they would be expected to be at greater risk than whites for homicide. Weapons provide more opportunities for assaults to turn into lethal violence (McDowell, 1991; Singh, 2004).

The notion that African American single men are more likely than white single men to be around people with firearms is tested with data from the General Social Survey (Davis, 1995) in table 1. The one available measure of this phenomenon is the lifetime prevalence of ever having been threatened with a gun or shot at. Since this is directly related to veteran status, veterans were omitted from the analysis. The data in table 1 indicate that 42.8% of African American single men reported having either been threatened or shot at compared to 25.8% of their white counterparts. Black single men are nearly twice as likely to have been in a dangerous situation with someone wielding a firearm than white single men. These results were not replicated, however, for widowed or divorced men. There was a slight tendency for black married men to have been so threatened with a gun or shot at more than white married men. These data are consistent with the thesis that single black men have greater exposure to risky life styles compared to single white men.

Some additional attention is called to the economic differences in the life styles of Caucasian and African American men. African Americans are still twice as likely to be unemployed than their Caucasian counterparts (U.S. Bureau of the census 2006). While differences in education level have narrowed, Caucasian American still higher than African American on a number of educational indexes such as graduation rates from professional schools (U.S. Bureau of the Census 1992; 2006).

Table 1. Responses to the Question: "Have you ever been threatened with a gun or shot at?" by Single African American and Single Caucasian American males, Non Veterans, General Social Surveys, 1972-1994

Response	Racial Group	
	African American	Caucasian American
Yes	42.8%	25.8%
No	57.2%	74.2%

Chi Square: 30.6, $p < 0.001$.

Singleness in the context of impoverishment would be expected to increase the odds of following a dangerous life style. For example, such persons might be more attracted to gangs, drug dealing, and various activities of a life risking nature where the risk of homicide and/or death is greater.

Given considerations such as black's having a greater likelihood to be around persons who carry firearms, and having fewer marital, educational and employment ties to conventional society than Caucasian Americans (e.g., Almgren et al., 1998; Sampson, 1987; U.S. Bureau of the Census, 2006), it is possible that the often reported association between singleness and homicide may be stronger for African Americans than Caucasian Americans. Indeed, once a control is introduced for age, the association between singleness and homicide risk may reverse or vanish for whites.

METHODOLOGY

Data on homicide are from the 1990 national mortality tapes (U.S. Public Health Service, 1994). The risk of homicide was measured as a binary variable, where 1 = death by homicide and 0 = death by all other causes. Complete data were available on 6,683 white male homicide victims and 7,112 African American male homicide victims. In addition, complete data were available on 725,267 Caucasian men and 87,116 African American men who died of other causes. In all, complete data were available on the deaths of 826,178 men. Because the dependent variable was a dichotomy, logistic regression techniques were appropriate (Menard, 1995; Pampel, 2002).

Marital status is measured in terms of a series of binary variables. Following rules for coding nominal variables with n categories, one category needs to be used as a baseline category and coded as zero (Kuter et al., 2005). Marital status is thus coded as divorced (0,1), widowed (0,1), single (0,1) and married serves as the baseline or comparison category.

Race was measured as a binary variable, where 1 = African American, and 0 = Caucasian American. Controls are introduced for standard demographic variables found in the literature on homicide (e.g., Land et al., 1990; Messner and Rosenfeld, 1999). Age is coded in years. Education level, an index of social status, is coded in years of school completed. A distinction is drawn between persons residing in urban areas (1), defined as counties with a population of 1,000,000 or more persons, vs. nonurban areas (0). Finally a series of binary variables are introduced to control for the variation in homicide among regions of the nation. The regional variables are West (0,1), South (0,1), Midwest (0,1), and the Northeast region serves as the comparison category. The latter region tends to have the lowest rate of homicide. However, there are some racial differences in this bivariate relationship (O'Carroll and Mercy, 1986:35).

ANALYSIS

Table 2 provides the results for the two bivariate regressions. Panel A gives the coefficients for the marital status terms for African Americans. From the odds ratios, divorced African Americans are 1.54 time more likely to be homicide victims than their married counterparts. Single African Americans are 7.65 times more likely to die of homicide than married African Americans.

Table 2. The Effect of Marital Status on the Odds of Dying from Homicide vs. Other Causes in 1990, By Race. (N=94,228 African American Deaths, and 731,950 Caucasian American Deaths)

Variable	Beta	Standard Error	Wald Chi Square	Standardized Estimate	odds Ratio
Panel A: African Americans:					
Intercept	-3.35*	0.03	16085.3		0.04
Marital Status:					
Divorced	0.43*	0.05	75.7	0.078	1.54
Widowed	-1.69*	0.10	264.3	-0.345	0.19
Single	2.03*	0.03	4336.4	0.483	7.65
Contingency C:	0.770				
Panel B: Caucasian American:					
Intercept	-5.36*	0.02	61221.9		0.005
Marital Status:					
Divorced	1.31*	0.04	1258.1	0.206	3.72
Widowed	-1.48*	0.09	271.6	-0.295	0.24
Single	2.15*	0.03	5863.1	0.378	8.57
Contingency C:	0.760				

* $p < 0.05$.

Widowers are, however, less likely to die of homicide than married persons. From the standardized estimate, the variable most predictive of homicide is singleness, (standardized coefficient = 0.483). The degree of fit between the predicted and the actual cause of death is good as indicated by the contingency C correlation statistic of 0.770.

The results for Caucasian Americans are provided in table 2, panel B. These follow much the same pattern as those for African Americans. Both divorced and single Caucasians are at greater risk of homicide than their married counterparts. The odds ratios are higher, however, than those for African Americans (3.72 and 8.57 respectively). Like African Americans, widowed Caucasians are less likely to be homicide victims (odds ratio = 0.24, 1-.24 = 0.76 times less likely). The fit between the observed and expected cause of death is good as indicated by the Contingency C coefficient of 0.762.

Table 3 presents the results of the full logistic regression model with the terms representing demographic and regional controls entered into the equation. Panel A provides the results for African Americans. Controlling for age and the other predictor variables, divorced African Americans are 1.15 times at greater risk of dying from homicide than their married counterparts. Single African American males are 1.13 times more at risk of dying from homicide than their married counterparts. In results not reported here, where the variables were entered into the analysis one at a time, the variable that greatly reduced the impact of marital status on homicide risk was age. Even with age controlled, however, being a widow reduces homicide risk by 0.38 times.

Table 3. The Effect of Marital Status, and Controls on the Odds of Dying from Homicide vs. Other Causes in 1990, By Race. (N=94,228 African American Deaths, and 731,950 Caucasian American Deaths)

Variable	Beta	Standard Error	Wald Chi Square	Standardized Estimate	odds Ratio
Panel A: African Americans:					
Intercept	0.65*	0.08	74.60		1.91
Marital Status:					
Divorced	0.14*	0.05	7.55	0.025	1.15
Widowed	-0.48*	0.11	19.90	-0.10	0.62
Single	0.12*	0.04	9.24	0.028	1.13
Demographic Controls:					
Age	-0.08*	0.001	5520.1	-0.91	0.93
College	-0.61*	0.08	54.5	-0.07	0.54
Urban	0.45*	0.03	196.18	0.11	1.57
Region:					
West	0.35*	0.06	33.02	0.06	1.43
South	0.29*	0.05	31.20	0.08	1.34
Midwest	0.38*	0.05	47.36	0.09	1.46
Contingency C between predicted and observed values: C=0.906.					
Panel B. Caucasian Americans.					
Intercept	-1.27*	0.07	357.1		0.28
Marital Status:					
Divorced	0.52*	0.04	190.3	0.08	1.69
Widowed	-0.18*	0.09	4.10	-0.04	0.84
Single	-0.36*	0.04	88.4	-0.06	0.70
Demographic Controls:					
Age	-0.08*	0.0009	8236.8	-0.760	0.92
College	-0.61*	0.05	125.6	-0.11	0.54
Urban	0.82*	0.03	832.1	0.17	2.27
Region:					
West	0.84*	0.05	253.4	0.19	2.32
South	0.84*	0.05	259.5	0.22	2.31
Midwest	0.14*	0.06	6.43	0.04	1.15
Contingency C between predicted and observed values: C=0.920.					

*p<.05.

The variable most closely tied to the risk of homicide is age (standardized coefficient= -0.91). A one unit increase in age lowers the odds of homicide by 0.07 times or 7%. As anticipated, education lowers homicide risk. A year of education decreases the odds of homicide by 46%. Residence in an urban area increases homicide risk 1.57 times.

Homicide risk also varies by region with the West increasing the risk by 1.43 times, the South 1.34 times, and the Midwest 1.46 times compared to the Northeast. The degree of fit between the observed and expected values is given by the Contingency C coefficient and is 0.906.

The results for Caucasian Americans are given in table 3, panel B. As in the case of African Americans, divorced whites have a higher risk of homicide than married whites. Controlling for the other variables in the equation, the risk to divorced white men of death through homicide is 1.69 times greater than that for married white men. Widowed white men have a 16% lower risk of death by homicide than married white men.

In contrast to single African American males, single Caucasian American males have a lower risk of death by homicide than their married counterparts. Their risk is 30% lower than that of married white males.

The variable most closely associated with death from homicide is age (standardized coefficient= -0.760). Each year of age lowers homicide risk 0.08 times or 8%. As anticipated, education lowers homicide risk; the amount is 46% lower risk for each year of educational attainment. Living in an urban area increases homicide risk 2.32 times over that in nonurban areas. Controlling for the other variables, region is also related to homicide risk. Homicide risk is elevated 2.32 times in the West, 2.31 times in the South, and 1.15 times in the Midwest compared to the Northeast.

The contingency C coefficient for the association between the predicted and the actual values of the dependent variable is 0.920. That indicates that the model provides a relatively good fit to the data at hand (Menard, 1995; Pampel, 2002).

Conclusion

Previous research on marital status and homicide has generally used ecological data (e.g. see reviews in Browne et al., 1999; Land et al., 1990; Lester, 2001). Its results need to be taken with caution due to the hazards of the ecological fallacy. Individual level analyses have generally not provided analytic national data on homicide risk by marital status. Further, past research has tended to fail to use race specific data on homicide (e.g., Browne et al., 1999). The present study corrects for these problems by using individual-based, national, race-specific data. Controlling for age, region and other covariates of marital status, there is mixed evidence for a relationship between marital status and the odds of death by homicide.

First, divorced persons, a group removed from the institution of marriage, have a higher risk of death from homicide than married persons. This is true for both races. While the strength of the bivariate relationship was reduced after controlling for the covariates of divorce, this was especially true for white men. The risk was reduced for white men from an odds ratio of 3.72 to 1.69.

At the bivariate level, single men of both races have a substantially greater risk of homicide than their married counterparts. This risk level is eight times that of married men. At the multivariate level of analysis, however, the strength of the relationship is greatly reduced. Single African Americans still have a higher risk of death from homicide than married African Americans, but the same is not true of single whites. Single white men are more protected against homicide than married white men.

It is speculated that single black males may be at risk of homicide, independent of age effects, due to their differential involvement in dangerous lifestyles. It is beyond the scope of the present paper to test this thesis in any rigorous way. Data from the General Social Surveys indicated, however, that single black males were more apt than single white males to have been in dangerous situations involving being threatened with a gun or actually being shot at. This was largely not the case for other marital statuses.

The result that single white men are at lower risk of homicide than married white men would not be anticipated from a previous report which was also based on individual level data (Kposowa et al., 1994). However, that study was based on only 103 homicides. It also did not run separate analyses of homicide risk by race. The present study broadened the analysis to 13,795 homicide victims and did run separate analyses by race.

The reduction in the risk of homicide associated with being a divorced or single man once controls are included for age and the other covariates of these statuses, can be interpreted from a subcultural explanation of criminality. Curtis (1975) attributes violence to being socialized in a culture which values: thrill-seeking and change (2) physical prowess and toughness (3) sexual prowess and exploitation (4) shrewdness and manipulation. It is possible that these values are age related for various reasons. As men age they are less likely to be able to compete with younger men for realization of these values. Older men are not as strong, perhaps not as sexually desirable, and perhaps simply not as interested in thrill seeking and other values. The maturation process and market forces may contribute to the exit of many older men from the subculture of violence (e.g., Stack, 2002; Wolfgang, 1958). The present results suggest that this may be especially true for single men. Once a control for age is included in the analysis a powerful relationship between singleness and homicide victimization becomes minimal or reverses as in the case of Anglo men.

Widowed men have a lower risk of being homicide victims than married men, and this is true for both races. Controlling for the covariates of widowhood, this relationship still remains.

These individual level results have some implications for the interpretation of ecological based research on marital variables and homicide rates. With age controlled, marital status had relatively little impact on homicide risk. Indeed, for whites, being married increased homicide risk. This indicates that a macro-oriented association between the divorce and homicide rates is probably not restricted to homicides involving only divorced people. It may be picking up on violence in dysfunctional families including that which precedes or fails to result in divorce.

References

Almgren, G., Guest, A., Immerwahr, G., and Spittrl, M. (1998). Joblessness, family disruption, and violent death in Chicago, 1970-1990. *Social Forces,* 76, 1465-1493.

Blau, J. and Blau, P. (1982). The cost of inequality: metropolitan structure and violent crime. *American Sociological Review, 47,* 114-129.

Block, C. (1985). Race/Ethnicity and patterns of Chicago homicide 1965-1981. *Crime and Delinquency, 31,* 104-116.

Browne, A., Williams, K., and Dutton, D.G. (1999). Homicide between intimate partners: a 20-year review. In Smith, M.D. and Zahn, M. (Eds.) *Homicide: A sourcebook of social research* (pp. 149-164), Thousand Oaks, Ca., Sage.

Cazenave, N. and Zahn, M. (1992). Women, murder, and male domination: police reports of domestic violence in Chicago and Philadelphia. In Viano, E. (Ed.) *Intimate Violence*, Washington: Hemisphere Publishing.

Centers for Disease Control. (1985). Homicide among young black males- U.S., 1970-1982. *Morbidity and Mortality Weekly Report*, October 11, 34(41):629-633.

Centerwall, B. (1995). Race, socioeconomic status, and domestic homicide. *JAMA, 273,*1755-1758.

Cohen, L. and Felson,R. (1979). Social change and crime rate trends:A routine activities approach. *American Sociological Review, 44,*588-608.

Curtis, L. (1975). *Violence, Race, and Culture*. Lexington, MA: Lexington Books.

Davis, J. (1995). *Codebook: General Social Surveys*, Storrs, Ct:

Roper Center. Federal Bureau of Investigation. (1990). Uniform Crime Report 1989. Washington: Government Printing Office.

Gelles, R. (1987). *The Violent Home*. Beverly Hills, CA: Sage. Gillis, A.R. (1996). So long as they both shall live: marital dissolution and the decline of domestic homicide in France, 1852-1909. *American Journal of Sociology*, *101*, 1275-1305.

Goetting, A. (1995). *Homicide in Families*. New York: Springer.

Hirschi, T. (1969). *The Causes of Delinquency*, Berkeley: University of California Press.

Humphrey, J. and Palmer, S. (1986). Race, sex, and criminal homicide. In Hawkins, D. (Ed.) *Homicide Among Black Americans*, (pp. 57-68). New York: University Press of America.

Killias, M., van Kesteren, J. and Rindlisbacher, M. (2001). Guns, violent crime, and suicide in 21 countries. *Canadian Journal of criminology, 43*, 429-448.

Kowalski, G.S. and Stack, S. (1992). The effect of divorce on homicide. *Journal of Divorce and Remarriage*, *18*, 215-218.

Kposowa, A.J., Singh, G.K., and Breault, K.D. (1994). The effects of marital status and social isolation on adult male homicides in the United States. *Journal of Quantitative Criminology, 10,* 277-289.

Kuter, M.H., Nachtsheim, C.J., Neter, J., and Li, W. (2005). *Applied Linear Statistical Models.* Boston: McGraw Hill.

Land, K., McCall, P., and Cohen. L. (1990). Structural covariates of homicide rates: Are there any invariances across time and social space? *American Journal of Sociology, 95*, 922-963.

Lester, D. (1986). The interaction of divorce, suicide, and homicide. Journal of Divorce, 9, 103-109.

Lester, D. (1995). The association between alcohol consumption and suicide and homicide rates. *Alcohol and Alcoholism, 30*, 465-468.

Lester, D. (2001). Regional studies of homicide: a meta analysis. *Death Studies, 25*, 705-708.

Lester, D. and Krysinska, K. (2004). The regional variation of murder and suicide in Poland. *Omega: Journal of Death and Dying, 49,* 321-326.

Lewis-Beck, Michael. 1980. *Applied Regression Analysis*. Beverly Hills: Sage Publishers.

Mann, C. (1992). Female murderers and their motives: A tale of two cities: Women, murder, and male domination: police reports of domestic violence in Chicago and Philadelphia. In Viano, E. (Ed.) *Intimate Violence*, Washington: Hemisphere Publishing.

McCue, M.L. (1995). *Domestic Violence*. Denver, CO.: ABC-CLIO.

McDowell, D. (1991). Firearm availability and homicide rates in Detroit, 1951-1986. *Social Forces, 69,*1085-1101.

Meithe, T., Hughes, M., and McDowell, D. (1991). Social Change and crime rates. *Social Forces, 70,*165-185.

Menard, S. 1995. *Applied Logistic Regression Analysis*. Thousand Oaks, CA: Sage.

Mercy, J.A., Goodman, R., Rosenberg, M., Allen, N., Loya,F., Smith, J., and Vargas, L. (1986). Patterns of homicide victimization in the city of Los Angeles. *Bulletin of the New York Academy of Medicine, 62,* 427-445.

Messner, S.F. and Rosenfeld, R. (1999). Social structure and homicide. In Smith, M.D. and Zahn, M. (Eds.) *Homicide: A sourcebook of social research* (pp. 27-41), Thousand Oaks, Ca., Sage.

O'Carroll, P. and Mercy, J. (1986). Patterns and recent trends in black homicide. In Hawkins, D. (Ed.). *Homicide Among Black Americans* (pp. 29-42), New York: University Press of America.

Pampel, F. (2002). *Logistic Regression*. Thousand Oaks, Ca.: Sage.

Parker, K. (2001). A move towards specificity: examining urban disadvantage and race and relationship-specific homicide rates. *Journal of Quantitative Criminology, 17,* 89-110.

Parker, R.N. (1998). Alcohol, homicide, and cultural context: a cross-national analysis of gender specific homicide victimization. *Homicide Studies, 2*, 6-30.

Puzone, C.A., Saltzman, L.E., Kresnow, M., Thompson, M.P., and Mercy, J.A. (2000). National trends in intimate partner violence. *Violence Against Women, 6*, 409-426.

Rice, K.J. and Smith, W.R. (2002). Socio-ecological models of automobile theft: integrating routine activity and social disorganization approaches. *Journal of Research in Crime and Delinquency, 39*, 304-336.

Robinson, W.S. (1950). Ecological Correlations and the Behavior of Individuals. *American Sociological Review, 15,*351-357.

Rose, H. and Deskins, D. (1992). Handguns and homicide in urban black communities. In Hawkins, D. (Ed.), *Homicide Among Black Americans (pp.69-97)*, New York: University Press of America.

Saltzman, L., Mercy, J., Rosenberg, M., Elsea, W., Napper, G., Sikes, R.K., Waxweiler, R., and the Collaborate Working Group. (1990). Magnitude and patterns of family and intimate assault in Atlanta, Georgia, 1984. *Violence and Victims,5,*3-17.

Sampson, R. (1986). Crime in Cities: The Effects of Formal and Informal Social Control. In Reiss, A. and Tonry, M. (Eds.) *Communities and Crime (pp. 271-312)*, Chicago: University of Chicago Press.

Sampson, R. (1987). "Urban black violence: the effect of male joblessness and family disruption. *American Journal of Sociology, 93,* 348-382.

Shaw, C. and McKay, H. (1942). *Juvenile Delinquency and Urban Areas*, Chicago: University of Chicago Press.

Simpson, M. (1985). Violent crime, income inequality, and regional culture: Another look. *Sociological Focus, 18,* 199-208.

Singh, P. (2004). *Weaponry, age and violence: exploring the link between youth violence and firearms*. Unpublished PhD Dissertation. Pittsburgh: Carnegie Mellon University.

Stack, C. (1974). *All Our Kin*. Berkeley: University of California Press.

Stack, S. (2002). Southern migration and homicide risk. *American Journal of Criminal Justice*, 26, 165-179.

Stack, S. and Bankowski, E. (1994). Divorce and Drinking. *Journal of Marriage and the Family, 56*,805-812.

U.S. Bureau of the Census (1992). *Statistical Abstract of the U.S.* Washington, D.C.: Government Printing Office.

U.S. Bureau of the Census (2006). *Statistical Abstract of the U.S.* Washington, D.C.: Government Printing Office.

U. S. Public Health Service (1994). *Mortality detail files, 1968- 1991: Volume IX. 1990 data.* Ann Arbor, MI: Inter-university Consortium for Political and Social Research.

Wilbanks, W. (1986). Criminal homicide offenders in the U.S. In Hawkins, D. (Ed.) *Homicide Among Black Americans (pp. 43-55)*, New York: University Press of America.

Williams, K. and Flewelling, R. (1988). The Social production of criminal homicide. *American Sociological Review, 53*,421-431.

Wolfgang, M. (1958). *Patterns in criminal homicide*. Philadelphia: University of Pennsylvania Press.

In: Homicide: Trends, Causes and Prevention
Editor: Randal B. Toliver and Ulrich R. Coyne
ISBN 978-1-60741-625-8

Chapter 9

HOMICIDAL CASES BY SHARP FORCE INJURIES

***Klára Törő*[*1], *Szilvia Fehér*[1], *István Kristóf*[1], *Sándor Kosztya*[2] and *György Dunay*[1]**

[1]Semmelweis University Department of Forensic and Insurance Medicine, Hungary
[2]Budapest Police Headquarter Crime Scene Investigation Department, Hungary

ABSTRACT

Introduction: Fatal sharp injuries need careful post mortem scene investigation and forensic autopsy. Characterization of manner of death and the cause of death in lethal sharp injuries represent an investment in deterring circumstances. Sharp wound are frequently chosen methods of homicides and of suicides as well, however, the final confirmation of suicide or homicide expects a careful and systematic medico-legal investigation. In this chapter the purpose of our examination was to examine the characteristics of homicidal sharp injuries in a 10 year-long period in capital Budapest. Copies of death certificates relating to homicidal sharp damages were obtained. The results of scene investigations were also presented.

Material and methods: Cases with sharp injuries were collected from 1998 to 2007 using the database of the Department of Forensic and Insurance Medicine at Semmelweis University in Budapest. Autopsy reports were analyzed to determine the proportion of fatal sharp injuries. Gender differences, types and location of injuries, survival period, and blood alcohol concentrations were evaluated in different age groups.

Results: A total of 148 (100 males, 48 females) homicidal cases due to sharp force injuries (cut and/or stab wounds) were investigated. 125 (84%) victims were between the age of 20 and 60 years. Data of the scene investigation, detailed forensic autopsy, anamnestic data have important role in the differentiation of fatal homicidal sharp injuries.

Conclusion: Sharp injuries play an important role in homicidal mortality. Our results underline the importance of the careful medico-legal evaluation and the collaboration between the representatives of several sciences, including forensic medicine in every homicidal case.

---

[*] Tel: 3612157300, Fax: 3612162676, E-mail: torok@igaz.sote.hu

Keywords: sharp injuries, homicide, scene investigation, medico-legal evaluation.

INTRODUCTION

Fatalities from sharp force are mainly homicides, however, suicides and accidents can also occur. The main common denominator of the injury-inflicting objects in sharp trauma is that they can pierce and slice the human body and thus cause internal damage [1]. Assault involving knives and sharp instruments is a recognized and common problem [2-4]. In order to examine the relative risks of death after assault with a knife and to investigate why some patients die whilst others survive, it is necessary to study a complete population [3].

Sharp force injuries may be classified by forensic pathologists according to the relative length of the wound compared with its depth. Incisions are wounds caused by sharp instruments that clearly separate tissue structures with well defined margins. Where the length is greater than the depth, the determination slashed wound can be used. Stab wounds occur when a relatively sharp object penetrates the body. Compared to an incision, a stab wound is typically much deeper than it is wide and is much more dangerous to the internal structure. In the assessment of sharp trauma, issues such as the wound morphology, which may help to determine the type of weapon involved, the number and location of the injuries, the wound channel, the injuries inflicted to the soft tissues and the skeleton, as well as the cause of death should always be addressed in order to evaluate a possible third party involvement and to undertake an incident reconstruction [1].

Data such as the psychiatric history of the victim, the multiplicity and site of wounds, the implement used, the presence of hesitation, and defense wounds were studied to elucidate the manner of death, and the suicidal nature of the event was established after police investigation [5]. There are single and multiple stab wounds in murder cases. Death due to this harming of the body's integrity is manifold; exsanguinations by injury of blood vessels is the most frequently encountered form; however, death due to air embolism, haemopericardium, pneumothorax, etc. are also encountered regularly [1].

The goal of the study is to investigate the characteristics of the victims of homicides autopsied at Semmelweis University Department of Forensic and Insurance Medicine.

MATERIAL AND METHODS

Cases with sharp injuries were collected from 1998 to 2007 using the database of the Department of Forensic and Insurance Medicine at Semmelweis University in Budapest. Autopsy reports were analyzed to determine the proportion of fatal sharp injuries. In every case scene investigation was performed by the police. Gender differences, types and location of injuries, survival period, cause of death and blood alcohol concentrations were evaluated in different age groups. Data include deaths in each year, using the 10th revisions of the International Classification of Diseases (ICD) 10th (assault by sharp object, X99). Homicidal cases in the investigated period in Budapest are presented in Table 1.

Records of scene investigations of the Budapest Police Headquarter Crime Scene Investigation Department were collected, and the types of sharp weapons were detected.

Table 1. All homicide cases and fatal sharp injuries in Budapest in different time periods (1960-2007)

Time periods	Average number of cases		
	Male homicides (fatal sharp wounds)	Female homicides (fatal sharp wounds)	All homicides (fatal sharp wounds)
1960 - 1969	17.9 (4.3)	16.2 (3.5)	34.1 (7.8)
1970 - 1979	19.0 (3.6)	15.8 (2.2)	34.8 (5.8)
1980 - 1989	27.5 (7.5)	18.8 (2.8)	46.3 (10.3)
1990 - 1999	57.9 (19.9)	32.5 (6.9)	90.4 (26.8)
2000 - 2007	32.3 (9.0)	20.0 (4.8)	52.3 (13.8)

The rate of the levels of alcohol intoxication was recorded. The blood alcohol concentrations (BACs) were used only, if death occurred on the same day as the injury. Influence of alcohol was categorized as slight degree (BAC: 51-80 mg/100ml), mild degree (BAC: 81-150 mg/100ml), moderate (BAC: 151-250 mg/100 ml), severe (BAC: 251-350 mg/100ml) and very severe (BAC: above 351 mg/100ml). Alcohol-involved deaths were defined as those with detectable BAC of more than 500 mg/100ml. In all cases full toxicology was done.

Results

A total of 148 (100 males, 48 females) homicidal cases due to sharp force injuries (cut and/or stab wounds) were investigated (Table 2). All together there were 520 (334 males, 186 females) homicide cases in the investigated period. Deaths by sharp force injuries represented 28.5%. Age distribution is demonstrated in Figure 1. Most of the 125 (84%) victims were between the age of 20 and 60 years. There was no seasonal distribution among homicidal cases by sharp force.

Table 2. Homicide cases due to sharp force injuries

Year	Male	Female	All
1998	14	5	19
1999	14	5	19
2000	8	6	14
2001	16	6	22
2002	15	10	25
2003	10	2	12
2004	5	7	12
2005	6	1	7
2006	7	4	11
2007	5	2	7
All	100	48	148

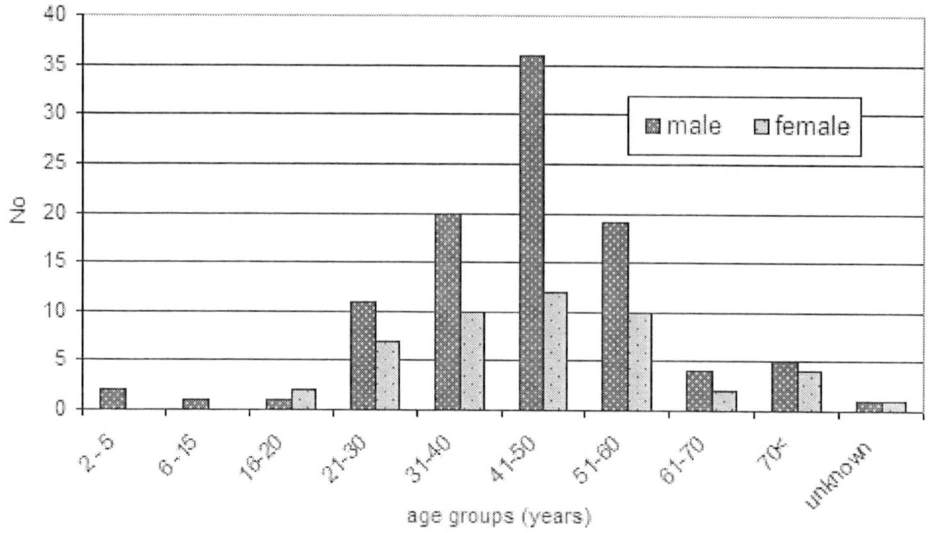

Figure 1. Age distribution of homicide victims with sharp injuries (1998-2007).

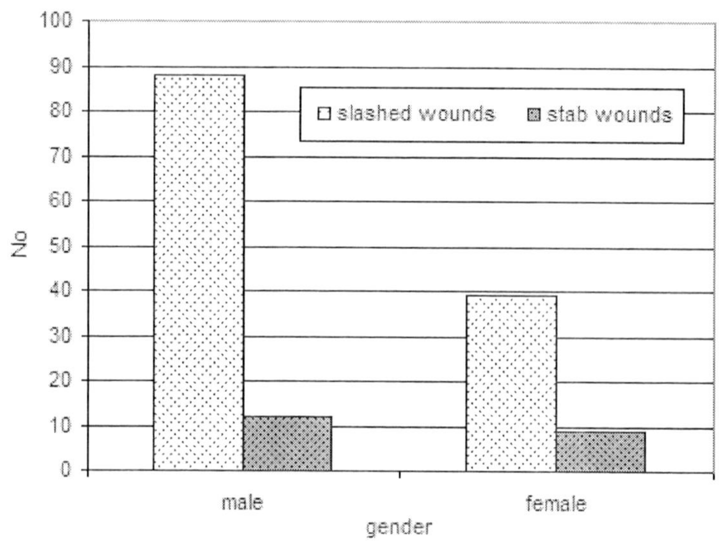

Figure 2. Fatal stab wounds and slashed wounds in male and female victims.

Fatal stab wound caused death among 88 males and 39 females, and lethal slashed wounds were the cause of death in 12 males and 9 females (Figure 2).

Most frequently the places of death (Figure 3) were the victim's home (Figure 4), and public places (Figure 5). Most common sharp injuries were knives (Figure 6), snare, crank or scissors. Table 3 demonstrates the BAC levels of the victims. Alcohol was found in the blood of 66% of the homicide victims, while 8 had illicit drugs.

Of 102 (69%) cases with fatal cut or stab wounds localized on the back or chest (Figure 7, Figure 8) in 34 (23%) cases, in 34 (23%) cases sharp injuries were found on the neck (Figure 9).

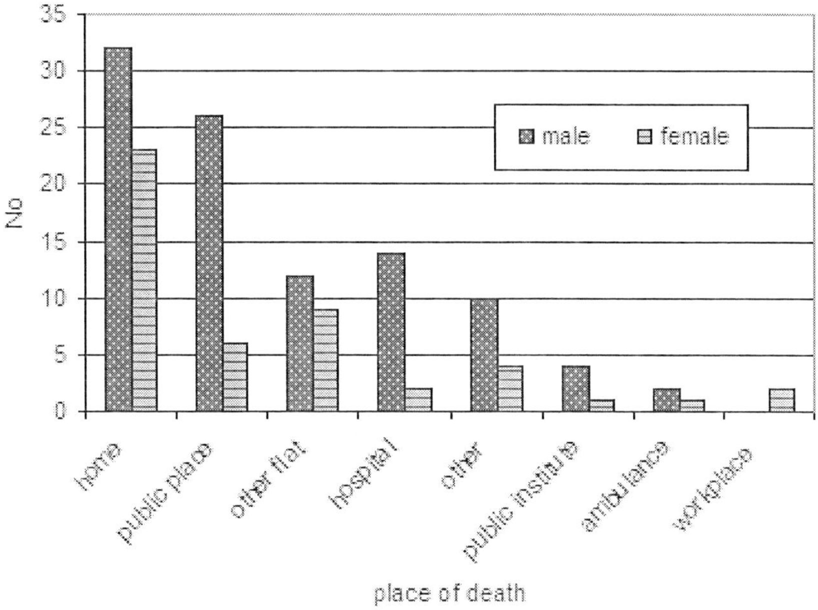

Figure 3. Most common places of homicides.

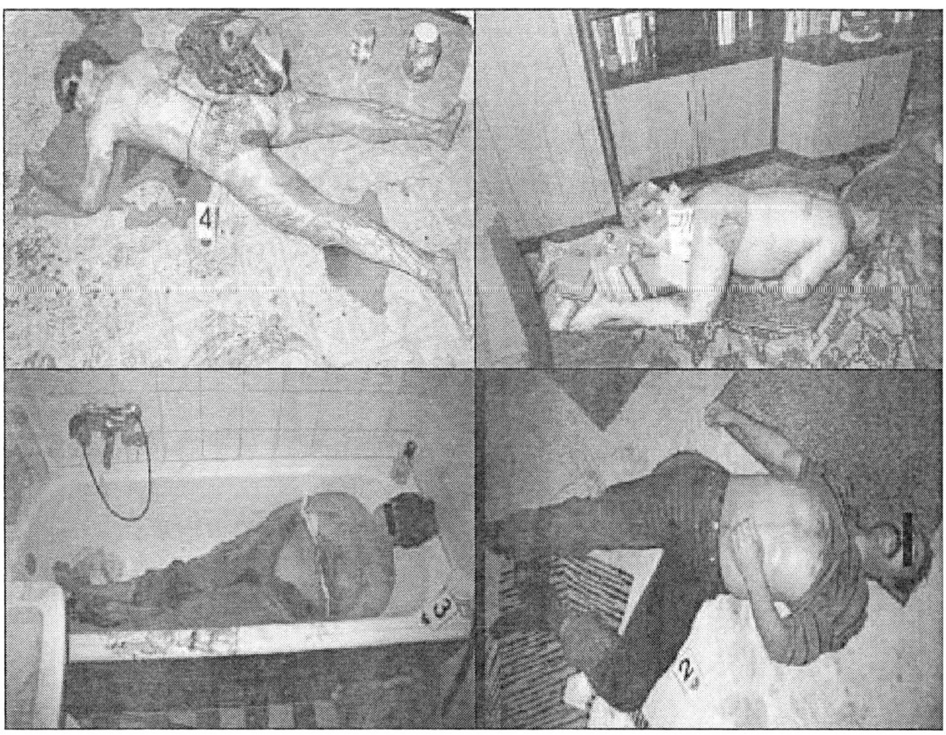

Figure 4. Homicide victims found in their home (documentation of scene investigation).

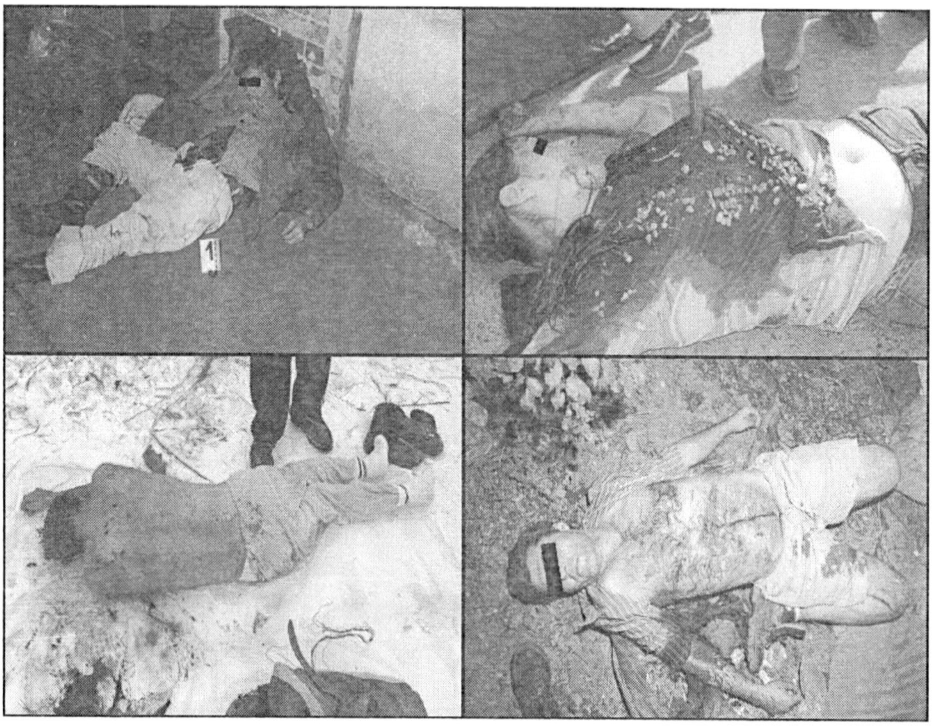

Figure 5. Homicide victims found at public places (documentation of scene investigation).

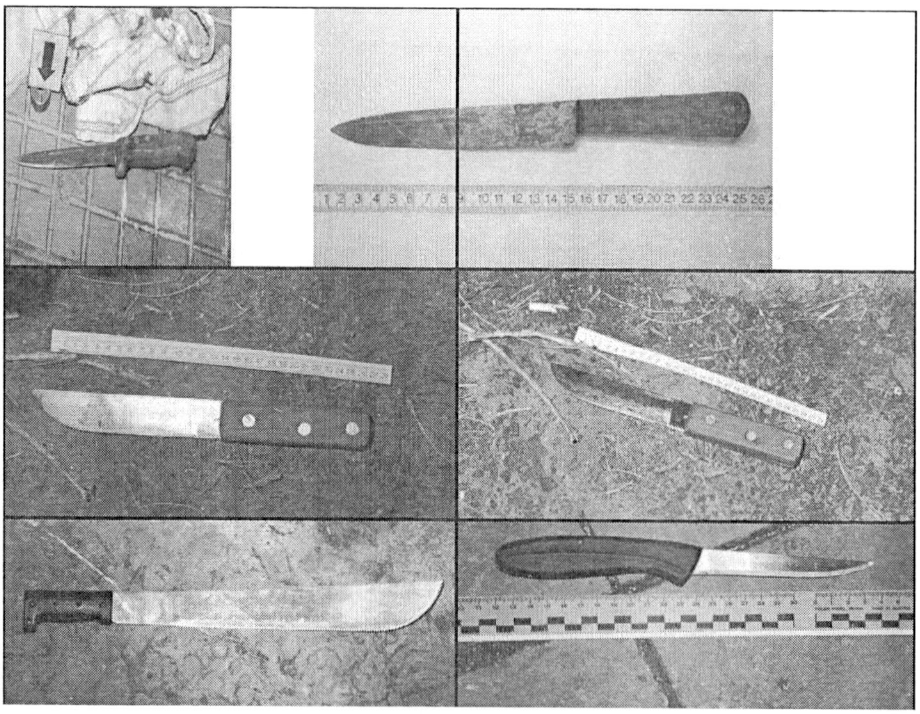

Figure 6. Collection of knives used by the perpetrators.

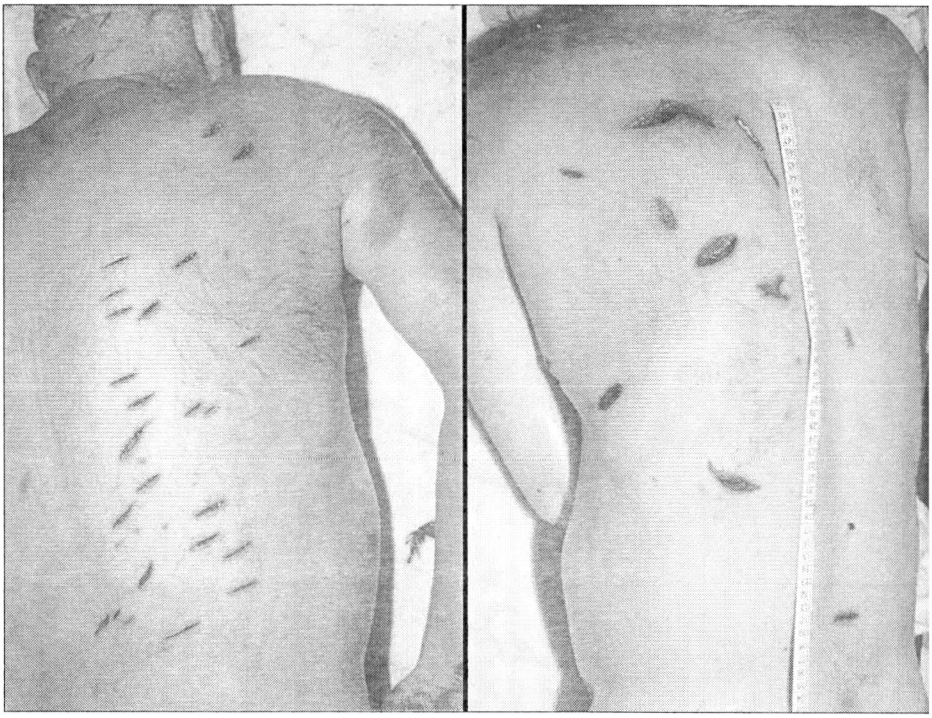

Figure 7. Stab wounds on the back.

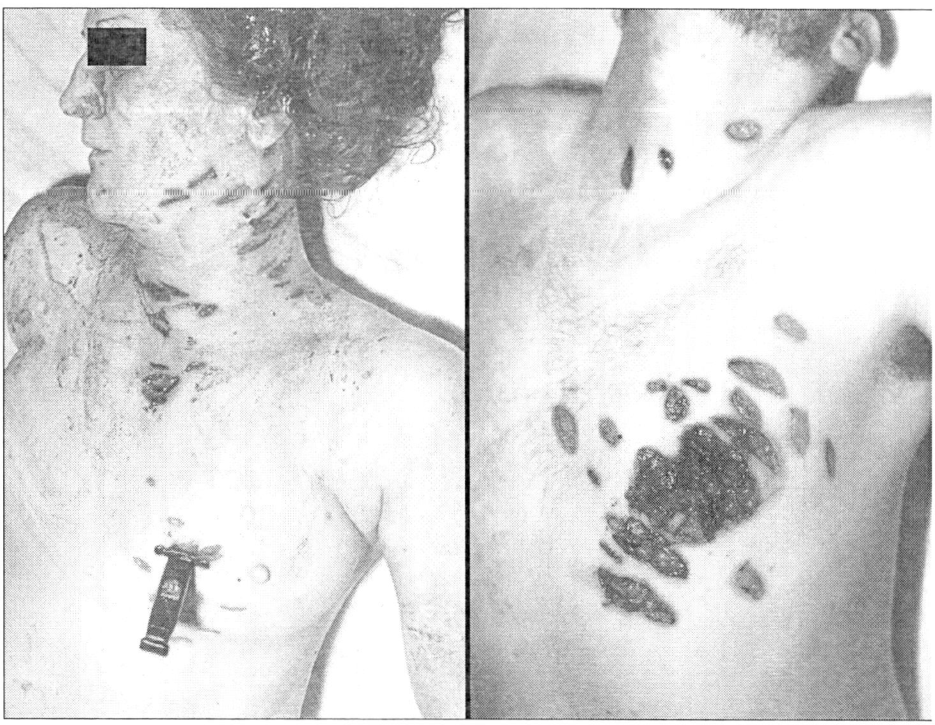

Figure 8. Stab wounds on the chest with severe heart damage.

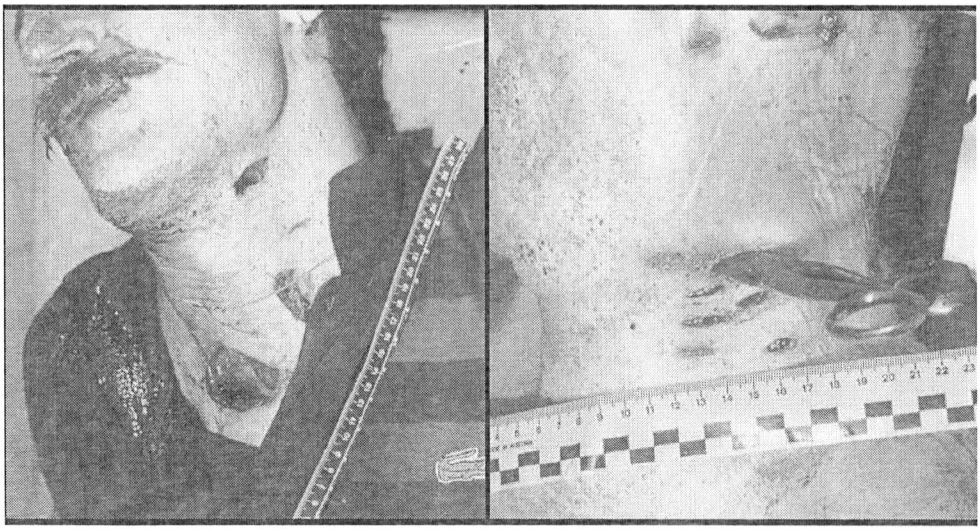

Figure 9. Stab wounds on the neck.

Table 3. BAC levels of homicide victims with sharp injuries

BAC (mg/100 ml)	Male	Female	All
negative	38	12	50
51-80	17	22	39
81-150	1	1	2
151-250	8	2	10
251-350	18	4	22
351 <	18	7	25
All	100	48	148

In 19 (13%) cases stub wounds caused heart wounds with hemopericardium. Abdominal in 20 (14%) cases and head injuries in 37 (25%) caused fatal outcome with much less frequency. The number of stab wounds counted between the number of 1 and 65. In 36% of cases sharp injuries were detected in two or more regions. Defense injuries were found on the arm, forearm and wrist in 26% of cases. The perpetrators were father, son, husband, wife, companion, homeless and strange persons.

Discussion

Violence is a significant public health problem. Thus, so as to prevent this problem, homicide, the severest form of violence depriving a human being of his right to live, deserves a detailed examination [6]. Sharp force injuries represent a big amount among homicidal cases [7,8], in our material the rate of fatal sharp injuries was 28.5%. We confirmed study results that most of the victims were males [9,10]. In our material the rate of child victims was 2%, however other study reported that the homicides were stab wounds in 18% among child victims [11]. Physical abuse/inflicted trauma is generally considered the most extreme form of elder mistreatment and includes sharp trauma [12].

Rygol K [13] has reviewed medico-legal opinions relating to 3690 autopsy cases of homicides. Forensic analysis of all these cases showed a gradual increase in the number of homicides, and great number of homicides with incised or stab wounds. Lemard G [14] reported that the majority of homicide victims were male (over 89%), and 15-44 years old (80%). The rate of homicide for males age 15-44 years was 121 per 100 000 compared with a rate of 12 per 100 000 for females in the same age group. It was reported that homicide rates have been increasing, and homicides involving knives are of particular concern the rapid increase in homicide involving knives is becoming a public health problem, and proposed changes to legislation are unlikely to halt this rise.

In fatal cases stab wounds most frequently hurt trunk and caused cardiac and lung injuries [15]. Males with stab wound accounted for 90% of hospital admissions [4], 49% of the men, and 41% of the women, had injuries to the head, neck or thorax.

Sharp Injuries

Meyer P [16] collected historical data of cardiac damages: Since antiquity, wounds of the heart had been considered immediately fatal, until Paré observed a delayed death after a stab to the heart in the 16th century. The physiology of cardiac tamponade was then elucidated by Richard Lower in 1669. However, it was only in the 19th century that the main clinical features of cardiac tamponade were described and the first treatments attempted. Kussmaul identified its most important clinical hallmark, pulses paradoxes, in 1873 and the term "tamponade of the heart" was coined for the first time by Rose in 1884. Romero and Larrey pioneered the open drainage of the pericardium early in the century, and Rehn performed the first successful surgical suture of a heart wound in 1896. Patients with blunt or penetrating cardiac injury usually present with cardiac tamponade and hemorrhagic shock upon hospital arrival. Many victims die before they reach hospital.

Altun G [15] reported hemopericardium-related fatalities: 12.5% of patients with cardiac activity reached the hospital, twenty individuals (50%) were victims of stabbings, which was the most common cause of death, the most commonly encountered manner of death was homicide (79%). 77.5% of victims died of hemorrhagic shock and 22.5% of cardiac tamponade. Entrance wounds were frequently located on the left chest. The perforated cardiac chambers were the left atrium, the left ventricle, the right atrium and the right ventricle, coronary artery perforation, and perforations on the intrapericardial part of the aorta.

Famous historical case: On September 10, 1898, Empress Elizabeth of Austria, known as Sissi, was stabbed with a stiletto knife in her chest by an Italian anarchist in Geneva, Switzerland, and died 1 hour later. The autopsy revealed a large clot in the pericardial sac due to a perforation of the left ventricular wall, and the report concluded, "Death was undoubtedly caused by a progressive and slow blood leak, sufficient to compress the heart and to suspend its functions." In conclusion, logistics aside, medical knowledge at the end of the 19th century would have been theoretically sufficient to save the empress from death [16].

Penetrating stab wounds of the brain are uncommonly seen in modern times and occur almost exclusively in homicides [5]. A fatal case of a homicidal penetrating head injury by retained blade of knife is reported by Bhootra BL [17]. The blade of knife penetrated the skull bone after breaking from a knife handle and remained lodged in the intracranial cavity for 5 days resulting in death from intracranial bleeding and brain edema. Atypical injuries as transcranial stab wounds require a careful forensic investigation, and medico-legal aspects of the differentiation between homicide and suicide [5].

Survival Period

Homicides with a survival of several days are not uncommon in forensic routine work. Reconstructions of these cases by autopsy alone are very difficult and may occasionally lead to unsatisfying results [5]. Maxwell R [4] investigated recent trends in in-patient admissions in England for assaults that involve a stabbing. The number of people admitted to hospital reportedly following an assault involving a sharp object rose by 30% and 0.5% died. The number of recorded hospital admissions from stabbing assaults increased. Further research is required to identify effective interventions to reduce the number of stabbings. Assault using a knife is a common problem in the United Kingdom [3]. Comparison of the survivors with non-survivors revealed both groups to have similar age and sex distributions, but those who died had significantly more severe injuries when scored according to the Abbreviated Injury Scale. The risk of death appears to depend mostly upon injuries sustained and also to a lesser extent upon other factors such as alcohol consumption and the presence of a bystander capable and willing to request emergency medical assistance.

Weapon

Stab wounds encountered in medico-legal autopsies are usually caused by sharp pointed weapons [18]. Peculiarities of the wound of entry in stab wounds, for example due to the hilt of the weapon, movement of the weapon and sometimes by the hand of the assailant holding the weapon is often described in literature. In cases of penetrating stab wounds by different knives it is highly relevant to prove which knife caused which injury, especially if one of the injuries was lethal. This is possible by immunocytochemical examination of cellular material remaining on the injuring blade because some organs have organ-specific antigen determinants such as alpha-l-fetoprotein in the liver cells or cardiac troponin I in the heart muscle cells, to which antibodies can bind. Even when penetrations occur through several layers of clothing, enough cells from the injured organ remain on the blade of a knife to allow immunohistochemical examination. These cells can be collected by means of adhesive film or wiping the blade and can be stained immunocytochemically. The organ specificity of the examined proteins allows proof of their origin [19].

Machetes are sharp, long knives with a broad blade having a slightly curved edge and a thick back. They are used for clearing paths in rough, densely wooded areas. Just like axes and swords they are suitable for causing not only soft tissue wounds, but also deep slashes in the underlying bone. In military conflicts they are often used as short-range weapons, whereas it is in the nature of things that they are rarely used in Europe. Nadjem H [20] reported that in 2 cases long chop injuries were inflicted on the head causing sharp-edged transections of the bony skullcap; in one case in which the victim survived a broken off part of the blade lodged in the right parietal bone, and in another 2 cases complete and subtotal decapitation respectively occurred in the victims. As the instrument can be used both for cutting and stabbing there were not only long cutting injuries, but also gaping stab wounds severing the skin over a length of several centimeters; due to the great length of the blade through-and-through wounds were also seen on the trunk. Massive blows with the thick back of the blade caused streak-like bruising.

Post Mortem Imaging Techniques

Modern cross-sectional imaging techniques are being increasingly implemented in forensic pathology. For the medico-legal reconstruction of cases with survival period, ante-mortem and post-mortem radiological imaging should always be included in the expertise [5]. In order to assess the practicability of such a method, namely post-mortem multislice computed tomography (MSCT) in cases of fatal cut and stab injuries, corpses may underwent such an examination prior to forensic autopsy [1]. Oesterhelweg [21] reported a case of fatal penetrating stab wounds to the skull in which a case reconstruction was only possible by combining the radiological ante- and post-mortem data with the autopsy findings. The questions regarding detection of foreign bodies, wound channels, skeletal and organ injuries, as well as the cause of death were addressed at MSCT and autopsy. The results of the two techniques revealed that post-mortem MSCT is a useful tool in the assessment of such injuries [1].

Differentiation between Homicide and Suicide

Differentiation between self-damage, suicidal stab and a homicidal act (assassination) represents a challenge for forensic pathologists [7-10,22]. In view of the appearance of cases of homicides by stabbing in which the killer claims that the victim committed suicide cases of homicides and suicides of this type have been compared. Contrary to the opinions appearing in the medico-legal issues stating that the commonly described features of the suicidal wounds such as tentative wounds, stabbing in the intercostals space, "removal" of clothes do not appear in some of the suicides, a few of these features do appear in each of the examined cases. Having considered the horizontal wound arrangement in the skin, which is a newly described feature, the differentiation between homicides and suicides are more categorical. In addition to that, the low level of alcohol in the blood is an extremely characteristic feature of the suicide by chest stabbing. On the contrary, typical features of suicidal death don't appear in cases of "aggressive self-destruction", self inflicted fatal wounds inflicted by a person with mental disorders [23].

Bloch-Bogusławska E [24] reported two cases of homicide-suicide (post-aggression suicide). In the first case, a young man had killed his wife and mother-in-law inflicting numerous stab wounds to the chest and neck of both victims, subsequently strangled his daughter with his bare hands and then committed suicide by cutting his veins. In the second instance, a woman had killed one of her sons and tried to murder another by giving both victims psychostimulants and medicines against worms, as well as stabbing them repeatedly. She then committed suicide by hanging.

The injury pattern on the hands of five perpetrators, who suffered accidental cuts during knife attacks, as seen by the authors during the clinical forensic examination, was presented [25]. The injuries were localized on the ulnar aspect of the thumb facing the index finger, the radial aspect of the index finger facing the thumb and variable sites on the flexor or extensor side of the middle and ring fingers. Especially in those cases in which the injuries of the victim (e.g. involvement of bony structures) and the dominant hand of the perpetrator are known, additional information for the reconstruction of the course of events may be derived from the cut wounds occurring during the knife attack as the hand slipped onto the blade.

Domestic Violence

Inoue H [26] retrospectively reviewed 35 autopsy cases where death had resulted from homicidal sharp force injuries and compared cases where the injuries had been inflicted by family members or relatives (relative group) with cases where the injuries had been inflicted by an unrelated person (stranger group). The following tendencies were detected: (a) a female victim was more frequently killed by a relative than by a stranger; (b) the percentage of cases receiving a single stab wound and the percentage of cases receiving more than ten stab wounds were both unexpectedly higher in the relative group than in the stranger group, and (c) in the stranger group, when there were no defense wounds, the victim had usually consumed alcohol, whereas when there were neither defense wounds nor alcohol intake, the case usually fell into the relative group.

Post Mortem Sharp Injuries

Di Nunno N [27] described 3 cases of dismemberment. Numerous methods of hiding a body and thus erasing proof of murder have been devised. Those most frequently described in the literature include: burial of the body in an unusual or impervious place such as a wood, grotto or mountain; charring the body by wrapping it in a tire, for example, to fuel the fire until all traces of the crime have been erased and identification of the victim is difficult; and dropping the weighted-down body in the open sea or in a well in the hope that it will never be found. Dismemberment is in reality a relatively rare method whereby, after killing the victim, the murderer uses a very sharp cutting weapon (a saw, axe, etc.) to sever the limbs and cut the body into small pieces. The operation is generally carried out immediately after the crime. Obviously the offender wanted to mislead the police in their investigations [28].

Summary

Data of the scene investigation, detailed forensic autopsy, anamnestic data have important role in the differentiation of fatal homicidal sharp injuries. The characterization of the injuries may help the final determination of violent death causes. In the future more effort should be directed to the effective prevention strategy of homicidal death cases.

REFERENCES

[1] Schnider J, Thali MJ, Ross S, Oesterhelweg L, Spendlove D, Bolliger SA. Injuries due to sharp trauma detected by post-mortem multislice computed tomography (MSCT): A feasibility study. *Leg. Med.* (Tokyo) 2008.

[2] Leyland AH. Homicides involving knives and other sharp objects in Scotland, 1981-2003. *J. Public Health* (Oxf). 2006;28:145-7.

[3] Webb E, Wyatt JP, Henry J, Busuttil A. A comparison of fatal with non-fatal knife injuries in Edinburgh. *Forensic Sci. Int.* 1999;99:179-187.

[4] Maxwell R, Trotter C, Verne J, Brown P, Gunnell D. Trends in admissions to hospital involving an assault using a knife or other sharp instrument, England, 1997-2005. *J. Public Health* (Oxf) 2007;29:186-190.

[5] Saint-Martin P, Prat S, Bouyssy M, Sarraj S, O'Byrne P. An unusual death by transcranial stab wound: homicide or suicide? *Am. J. Forensic Med. Pathol.* 2008;29:268-270.

[6] Hilal A, Cekin N, Gülmen MK, Ozdemir MH, Karanfil R. Homicide in Adana, Turkey: a 5-year review. *Am. J. Forensic Med. Pathol.* 2005;26:141-5.

[7] Morrison KA. A case of stalking in the workplace and subsequent sexual homicide. *J. Forensic Sci.* 2007;52:726-730.

[8] Mazzolo GM, Desinan L. Sharp force fatalities: suicide, homicide or accident? A series of 21 cases. *Forensic Sci Int.* 2005 17;147 Suppl:S33-5.

[9] Olze H, Hosse U, Rosenbaum F, Schmeling A, Schneider V. Homicide by stab to the neck with subsequent attempted suicide by cut to the neck. *Arch. Kriminol.* 2005;215:85-93.

[10] Fracasso T, Karger B. Two unusual stab injuries to the neck: homicide or self-infliction? *Int J Legal Med.* 2006;120:369-71.

[11] Meel BL. Unnatural deaths among children in the Transkei region of South Africa *Med. Sci. Law* 2008,48.232-236.

[12] Collins KA, Sellars K.Vertebral artery laceration mimicking elder abuse. *Am. J. Forensic* Med Pathol. 2005;26:150-4.

[13] Rygol K, Chowaniec C, Kobek M, Chowaniec M. Forensic analysis of homicides on the basis of cases examined in the Forensic Medicine Department, Medical University of Silesia, Katowice, in the years 1991-2002. *Forensic Sci. Int.* 2005 17;147 Suppl:S75-6.

[14] Lemard G, Hemenway D. Violence in Jamaica: an analysis of homicides 1998-2002. *Inj. Prev.* 2006;12:15-8.

[15] Altun G, Altun A, Yilmaz A. Hemopericardium-related fatalities: a 10-year medicolegal autopsy experience. *Cardiology.* 2005;104:133-7.

[16] Meyer P, Keller PF, Spodick DH. Empress Sissi and cardiac tamponade: an historical perspective. *Am. J. Cardiol.* 2008;102:1278-1280.

[17] Bhootra BL. Retained intra cranial blade - medicolegal perspectives. *J. Forensic Leg. Med.* 2007;14:31-34.

[18] Menon A, Kanchan T, Monteiro FN, Rao NG. Atypical wound of entry and unusual presentation in a fatal stab injury. *J. Forensic Leg. Med.* 2008;15:524-526.

[19] Wehner F, Stiegler A, Schulz MM, Heinz-Dieter W, Martin D. Immunocytochemical examination of biological traces on knife blades. *Arch. Kriminol.* 2007;219:180-190.

[20] Nadjem H, Bohnert M, Pollak S. Appearance of injuries caused by machetes and unusually large knives. *Arch. Kriminol.* 1999;204:163-174.

[21] Oesterhelweg L, Ross S, Spendlove D, Schoen CA, Christe A, Thali MJ, Bolliger SA. Virtopsy: fatal stab wounds to the skull--the relevance of ante-mortem and post-mortem radiological data in case reconstructions. *Leg. Med.* (Tokyo) 2007;9:314-317.

[22] Risse M, Bartsch C, Dreyer T, Weiler G. The death of Kaspar Hauser (17 Dec 1833)--assassination, suicide or self-inflicted injury? *Arch. Kriminol.* 2005;216:43-53.

[23] Konopka T, Bolechała F, Strona M. Chest stab wound comparison in suicidal and homicidal cases. *Arch. Med. Sadowej. Kryminol.* 2003;53:117-128

[24] Bloch-Bogusławska E, Wolska E, Engelgardt P, Pufal E. Cases of homicide-suicide (post-aggression suicide) in the material of the Chair and Department of Forensic Medicine in Bydgoszcz. *Arch. Med. Sadowej Kryminol.* 2006;56:169-72.

[25] Tsokos M, Braun C. Injury pattern on the hand after slipping onto the blade during a knife attack--a contribution to the differential diagnostic classification of sharp force injuries of the upper extremities. *Arch. Kriminol.* 2005;215:1-10.

[26] Inoue H, Ikeda N, Ito T, Tsuji A, Kudo K. Homicidal sharp force injuries inflicted by family members or relatives. *Med. Sci. Law.* 2006;46:135-40.

[27] Di Nunno N, Costantinides F, Vacca M, Di Nunno C. Dismemberment: a review of the literature and description of 3 cases. *Am. J. Forensic Med. Pathol.* 2006 ;27:307-12.

[28] Strauch H, Wirth I. Homicides with post mortal emasculation of the victim. *Arch. Kriminol.* 2005;215:140-50.

In: Homicide: Trends, Causes and Prevention
Editor: Randal B. Toliver and Ulrich R. Coyne

ISBN 978-1-60741-625-8

Chapter 10

CULPABLE HOMICIDE NOT AMOUNTING TO MURDER AS A CAUSE OF MORTALITY IN THE DISTRICT OF SOUTH CANARA- A SCENARIO FROM SOUTH INDIA

Ritesh G. Menezes [1], ***B. Suresh Kumar Shetty*** [1], ***Tanuj Kanchan*** [1], ***Anand Menon*** [1], ***Francis N. P. Monteiro*** [2], ***Deepa Salian*** [3] ***and Vinod C. Nayak*** [2]

[1] Department of Forensic Medicine and Toxicology, Kasturba Medical College, Mangalore- 575001, India

[2] Department of Forensic Medicine and Toxicology, Kasturba Medical College, Manipal- 576104, India

[3] S.D.M. College of Business Management, Mangalore- 575003, India

ABSTRACT

Homicide is the highest level of aggression found in all cultures worldwide. When preplanning or malice aforethought is not evident adequately, the term 'culpable homicide not amounting to murder' is used in India. As per the Indian Penal Code, culpable homicide does not amount to murder, if the offender commits the act whilst deprived of the power of self-control by grave and sudden provocation by the victim; if the act is committed by the offender in good faith of the right of private defense of person or property; if the act is committed by a public servant acting for the advancement of public justice; if the act is committed without premeditation in the heat of passion upon a sudden quarrel; and if the victim aged eighteen years and above takes the risk of death with his own consent. A seven-year retrospective review of files at the Crime Records Bureau, Mangalore, South Canara in South India was undertaken for cases of culpable homicide not amounting to murder occurring between July 2001 and July 2008. A total of five cases were identified in the coastal district of South Canara in the Southern Indian state of Karnataka. In our region, the rate of culpable homicide not amounting to murder was less than 0.10 per 100,000 population per year during the study period which was low when compared to the rate of murder that ranged from 1.27 to 1.84 per 100,000 population per year during the same period. The victims, three males and two females, were aged between three and sixty years (mean = 39 years) and the offenders, all males, were aged between 25 and 45 years (mean = 31.6 years). In all five cases weapons such as blunt objects ($N = 4$) and firearms ($N = 1$) were involved in battery. There were no sharp weapons involved in any of the cases. The head bore the fatal injury in four cases and the abdomen in one case. The circumstances leading to the act of culpable homicide not amounting to murder are discussed with a concise review of the Indian law on homicide.

INTRODUCTION

Life is often considered as the most precious gift of God. However, life that begins with birth as construed by many, though some would argue that life begins at conception or with the development of an embryo, has to meet its end with death. Even though defining the beginning and the end of human life is debatable in recent times, a substantial share of the literature in criminal offenses and related law is devoted to questions surrounding the beginning of life and its end. As generally scribed in literature, death may be natural or non-natural in manner. Non-natural deaths are usually further subdivided into three separate categories based on the manner of causation: accident, suicide, and homicide.

Regardless of ethnic and social disparity, homicide is considered the highest level of aggression against mankind found in all cultures worldwide. Homicide, unlike other crimes, is almost universally ranked by the civilized society as the most heinous of all criminal offenses [1]. The first ever homicide in the history of mankind was committed by Cain, a farmer, the first son of Adam and Eve. Cain killed his brother Abel out of jealousy because God was pleased with Abel and his offering, but rejected Cain and his offering. As a punishment to Cain, God made him a homeless wanderer on earth [2]. In the present world, the gravity of the crime of homicide demands the most serious of criminal punishments [3-5]. The seriousness of the issues and views of the public about homicide are reflected in criminal statutes and their determination that the most severe punishments- prolonged terms of rigorous imprisonment, compulsory life imprisonment without parole, and even the death penalty- should be handed down to the offender in the case of homicide [6].

Homicide being a complex heterogeneous criminal phenomenon is often categorized by penal codes based on the killer's mens rea or the criminal intent of the killer at the time of committing the offense [7]. Based on mens rea and actus reus, homicides are generally classified into three distinct subdivisions of seriousness: murder (intentional and planned homicide), manslaughter (intentional but undeliberated homicide), and negligent (unintentional and rash or reckless) homicide [6].

CRIMINAL STATUTES ON HOMICIDE IN INDIA

The literal meaning of homicide is killing of one person by another [8]. However, the legal description of homicide as an offense is different in different jurisdictions. In India, culpable homicide is the broader term used to describe the killing of one person by another under section 299 of the Indian Penal Code (IPC) [9,10]. Accordingly, "whoever causes death by doing an act with the intention of causing death, or with the intention of causing such bodily injury as is likely to cause death, or with the knowledge that he is likely by such act to cause death, commits the offense of culpable homicide" [9,10]. Section 300 of the IPC further subdivides culpable homicide as that amounting to murder and that not amounting to murder [9,10]. Thus, murder is a subset of culpable homicide. In other words, every case of murder is a case of culpable homicide but not vice versa.

When preplanning or malice aforethought is not evident adequately, the term culpable homicide not amounting to murder is used [11]. As per the IPC, culpable homicide does not amount to murder, if the offender commits the act whilst deprived of the power of self-control by grave and sudden provocation by the victim; if the act is committed by the offender in good faith of the right of private defense of person or property; if the act is committed by a public servant acting for the advancement of public justice; if the act is committed without premeditation in the heat of passion upon a sudden quarrel; and if the victim aged eighteen years and above takes the risk of death with his own consent. Culpable homicide under every other circumstance, though not satisfactorily defined, is termed murder [9,10]. Furthermore, causing death by a rash and negligent act not amounting to culpable homicide is described disjointedly under section 304A of the IPC [9,10].

Certain mitigating circumstances are described under section 300 of the IPC as mentioned above that allows the recognition of some intentional but undeliberated or unplanned culpable homicides to be treated as not amounting to murder. This distinction means that on conviction, unlike murder, which usually carries a mandatory death penalty or a compulsory sentence of rigorous imprisonment for life, the sentence is of a lesser gravity and at the discretion of the presiding judge. Sections 302 and 304 of the IPC describe the punishment for murder and culpable homicide not amounting to murder, respectively [9,10]. If a life convict, a person being under sentence of imprisonment for life, commits murder, he shall be punished with the only option of death as per section 303 of the IPC [9,10].

Authors' Present Study

The distinction of murder from culpable homicide not amounting to murder has its utmost implication in sentencing the convict or offender with the appropriate punishment. Homicide as a clustered entity discussing the victim profile, trends, causes and prevention has been studied over the years at various centers in India [12-23]. However, culpable homicide not amounting to murder as a subset is rarely touched upon by researchers in India. The purpose of the present study is to describe the demographic correlates and determine the incidence of culpable homicide not amounting to murder with an understanding of the underlying circumstances involved in South Canara (Dakshina Kannada) region in South India. This retrospective study includes all the cases of culpable homicide not amounting to murder from mid-2001 to mid-2008 in South Canara. In addition, a comparison of the rates of murder and culpable homicide not amounting to murder in the region is made.

South Canara is a district in the Southern Indian state of Karnataka along the West coast of India, about half way between Bombay (Mumbai) to the north and Cape Comorin (Kanyakumari) to the south, with both urban and rural areas. Mangalore is the chief city and headquarter of South Canara. There are 354 villages in the district housing nearly 62% of the total population. South Canara has an area of 4,866 square kilometers with 416 persons per square kilometer as its density of human population. As per the 2001 census, the district has a population of 1,897,730 with a sex ratio of 1000 males for every 1022 females. The literacy rate of the district is 83.4% [24,25].

A seven-year retrospective review of files at the Crime Records Bureau, Mangalore was undertaken for cases of culpable homicide not amounting to murder occurring between July 2001 and July 2008. The Crime Records Bureau at Mangalore maintains a record of all the crimes committed in the district of South Canara. A total of five cases of culpable homicide not amounting to murder were identified in South Canara district. *Case #1:* A three-year-old girl succumbed to head injuries sustained following head impact with the blunt housing wall when her paternal uncle, aged 28 years, pushed her toward the wall with formidable force. The incident occurred when the offender had a frenzied verbal argument with his elder brother, the victim's father, and in the heat of the moment he pushed his niece, who was silently standing by, against the wall. *Case #2:* A 35-year-old man succumbed to gun-shot abdominal injuries when he was shot by his younger brother aged 32 years. The incident occurred when the two brothers were on a hunt for wild hogs in the thick forest adjoining their village. During the hunt, the brothers went individually following two different tracks. Hours later, the elder brother fired in the direction of rumbling sound that he heard. He thought that the sound was in most reasonable probability made by a wild hog and mistakenly shot his younger brother instead. However, based of historical information regarding the strained relationship between the brothers in the recent past obtained by the police, the case was registered as culpable homicide not amounting to murder instead of rash and negligent homicide. *Case #3:* The victim aged 60 years was the chief of a typical rural Indian joint family. The victim and his wife lived in the same house with his son and daughter who were both married. Their respective spouses also lived in the same house. The victim had a grandson, his daughter's son aged 25 years, the offender in the present case. On the fateful day, the offender had a tussle with his uncle over a petty issue related to returning a belt. To avoid progression of the tussle, the victim intervened between his son and his grandson. In the process, the victim was wrestled to the ground by his grandson. The victim lost his consciousness when his head struck a stone on the ground and he died the following day while on treatment in the hospital. *Case #4:* A 52-year-old man succumbed to head injuries sustained when he was struck on the head with a wooden stick by his son aged 28 years. The victim, a drunkard, used to fist his wife in the face and drag her along by her hair almost every evening after returning home from work being under the influence of alcohol. The accused who understood his mother's grief had all the sympathy for her, a sufferer of wife battery. On the fateful evening, in a fit of anger, the accused struck his father on the head with a blunt weapon lying in the kitchen fire place when he witnessed his father battering his mother. The accused confessed that his intention was to put an end to the fight between his parents that evening. *Case #5:* A 45-year-old female was a victim of property dispute wherein she fell unconscious after being punched in the temporal region of the head by her neighbor, a male aged 45 years, following an argument regarding their disputed land boundary. The argument broke up as a consequence of shifting of the fence by the victim in her favor. The victim did not regain consciousness following the incident and died a couple of days later while on treatment in the hospital.

In our region, the rate of culpable homicide not amounting to murder was less than 0.10 per 100,000 population per year during the study period which was low when compared to the rate of murder that ranged from 1.27 to 1.84 per 100,000 population per year during the same period. Three cases occurred in rural areas and the other two cases occurred in urban areas of the district. The victims, three males and two females, were aged between three and sixty years (mean = 39 years) and the offenders, all males, were aged between 25 and 45 years (mean = 31.6 years). In all five cases weapons such as blunt objects ($N = 4$) and firearms ($N = 1$) were involved in battery either directly or indirectly. There were no sharp weapons involved in any of the cases. The head bore the fatal injury in four cases and the abdomen in one case. Domestic violence was the most common cause for culpable homicide not amounting to murder. All the victims were known to their respective offenders. There were no strangers involved in any of the cases. In one case the victim and the offender were not related but were neighbors. In the other four cases, the victim was related to the offender. The various victim-offender relationships that we encountered in our study were neice-uncle, elder brother-younger brother (siblings), grandfather-grandson, and father-son. In all the cases only a single offender was involved. Most of the victims were elder than their respective offenders. Two of the events were unwitnessed, while witnesses were present in three other events. Almost every offense scenario included provocative circumstances.

CONCLUSION

Homicide is an undesirable facet of social life. The nature and intensity of this undesirability is reflected in the criminal statutes laid down. The law focuses on criminal intent as a dimension affecting seriousness of homicide and the subsequent punishment to be awarded to the offender. In South Canara, because of the relatively small number of cases of culpable homicide not amounting to murder, a significant or insignificant year-to-year fluctuation is not noted. Nevertheless, it is evident that the rate of culpable homicide not amounting to murder has not increased as dramatically. Moreover, the proportionality of culpable homicide not amounting to murder as a cause of mortality is significantly less when compared to murder. Culpable homicide not amounting to murder in South Canara is largely a domestic affair. Most of the offense scenarios included an instantaneous and unthoughtful reaction to a particular provocation, in the frame of a sudden and temporary loss of temper or heat of passion.

REFERENCES

[1] Rossi P, Waite E, Bose C, Berk R. The seriousness of crimes: normative structure and individual differences. *American Sociological Review* 1974; 39: 224-237.

[2] Genesis 4: 1-12. Good News Bible. Catholic Edition. Calcutta: Swapna Printing Works (P) Ltd; 1979.

[3] Applegate B, Wright J, Dunaway R, Cullen F, Wooldredge J. Victim-offender race and support for capital punishment: a factorial design approach. *American Journal of Criminal Justice* 1993; 18: 95-115.

[4] Mitchell B. Public perceptions of homicide and criminal justice. *British Journal of Criminology* 1998; 38: 453-472.

[5] Jacoby J, Cullen F. The structure of punishment norms: applying the Rossi-Berk model. *Journal of Criminal Law and Criminology* 1999; 89: 245-307.
[6] Ashworth A. Principles of Criminal Law. Oxford: Oxford University Press; 1999.
[7] Herzog S. Public perceptions of the seriousness of victim-precipitated homicides: an empirical analysis of the consensus model of the law on homicide in Israel. *International Journal of the Sociology of Law* 2005; 33: 169-178.
[8] The Pocket Oxford Dictionary of Current English. 7th ed. Delhi: Oxford University Press; 1984.
[9] Chandrachud YV, Manohar VR, Singh A. Ratanlal and Dhirajlal's The Indian Penal Code. 28th ed. Nagpur: Wadhwa and Company Law Publishers; 1997.
[10] Misra SN, Misra RK. The Indian Penal Code. 8th ed. Allahabad: Central Law Publications; 1998.
[11] Mohanty MK. Variants of homicide: a review. *Journal of Clinical Forensic Medicine* 2004; 11: 214-218.
[12] Dikshit PC, Dogra TD, Chandra J. Comprehensive study of homicides in South Delhi, 1969-79. *Medicine Science and the Law* 1986; 26: 230-234.
[13] Dikshit PC, Kumar A. Study of homicidal deaths in Central Delhi. *Journal of Forensic Medicine and Toxicology* 1997; 14: 44-46.
[14] Ghangale AL, Dhawane SG, Mukherjee AA. Study of homicidal deaths at Indira Gandhi Medical College, Napgur. *Journal of Forensic Medicine and Toxicology* 2003; 20: 47-51.
[15] Sinha US, Kapoor AK, Pandey SK. Pattern of homicidal deaths in S.R.N Hospital's mortuary at Allahabad. *Journal of Forensic Medicine and Toxicology* 2003; 20: 33-36.
[16] Mohanty MK, Mohanty S, Acharya S. Defense wounds in homicidal deaths. *Journal of Forensic Medicine and Toxicology* 2004; 21: 34-36.
[17] Mohanty MK, Pannigrahi MK, Mohanty S, Das SK. Victimiologic study of female homicide. *Legal Medicine (Tokyo)* 2004; 6: 151-156.
[18] Kumar V, Tripathi CB. Burnt wives: a study of homicides. *Medicine Science and the Law* 2004; 44: 55-60.
[19] Gupta A, Rani M, Mittal AK, Dikshit PC. A study of homicidal deaths in Delhi. *Medicine Science and the Law* 2004; 44: 127-132.
[20] Mohanty MK, Mohanty S, Acharya S. Circumstances of crime in homicidal deaths. *Medicine Science and the Law* 2004; 44: 160-164.
[21] Mohanty S, Mohanty MK, Panigrahi MK, Das SK. Fatal head injury in homicidal victims. *Medicine Science and the Law* 2005; 45: 244-248.
[22] Mohanty MK, Kumar TSM, Mohanram A, Palimar V. Victims of homicidal deaths- an analysis of variables. *Journal of Clinical Forensic Medicine* 2005; 12: 302-304.
[23] Mohanty MK, Panigrahi MK, Mohanty S, Dash JK, Dash SK. Self-defense injuries in homicidal deaths. *Journal of Forensic and Legal Medicine* 2007; 14: 213-215.
[24] Available from URL: www.wikipedia.org (accessed on 24 October 2008).
[25] Available from URL: www.kar.nic.in (accessed on 24 October 2008).

INDEX

B

C

D

E

H

I

O

P

Q

R

S

T